ATLAS OF
TWENTIETH
CENTURY
WORLD HISTORY

ATLAS OF
TWENTIETH
CENTURY
WORLD HISTORY

Michael Dockrill

HarperPerennial

A Division of HarperCollinsPublishers

THE ATLAS OF TWENTIETH
CENTURY WORLD HISTORY.
Copyright © 1991 Ilex Publishers
Limited.

FIRST U.S. EDITION

An Ilex Book

Created and produced by Ilex
Publishers Limited
29–31 George Street, Oxford
OX1 2AJ, England.

Project editor Nicholas Harris
Text editors Elizabeth Miles,
Simon Adams
Map editors Nicholas Harris,
Zoë Goodwin, Alan Mais
Design Wolfgang Mezger,
Phil Jacobs
Picture research Linda Proud
Index Peter Barber

Maps produced by Lovell Johns
Ltd., Alan Mais
Typesetting by Opus, Oxford and
Getset, Oxford
Printed by Eurograph s.p.a. - Milano - Italy
ISBN 0 06 096385 9

Photograph Credits

KEY: AP – Associated Press, London; EQ – Equinox Archive,
Oxford; FRL – French Railways Limited; FSP – Frank Spooner
Pictures, London; H-DC – Hulton-Deutsch, London; M –
Magnum, London; P – Popperfoto, London; PNL – Pictorial
Nostalgia Library, West Wickham, Kent; RA – Retrograph
Archive Collection, London; VM – Vintage Magazine Company,
London. b bottom; bc bottom centre; bl bottom left; br bottom
right; cr centre right; t top; tl top left; tr top right.

Front Cover tl AP; bl FSP; br FSP; cr P; tr P.
Page 2–3 H-DC; p7 FSP; p8 H-DC; p9 tr H-DC; b VM; p10 tl EQ;
p10–11 H-DC; p11 t EQ; p22 EQ; p23 P; p36 P; p37 H-DC; p38 bl
RA; br H-DC; p39 EQ; p42 H-DC; p44 H-DC; p45 VM; p52 H-DC;
p54 H-DC; p55 tl PNL; tr H-DC; p57 H-DC; p70 H-DC; p71 tr H-
DC; cr EQ; p77 EQ; p92 H-DC; p93 tl H-DC; tr P; p96 bl P; bc H-
DC; p102 H-DC; p103 t AP; b FSP; p107 H-DC; p117 FSP; p118 FSP;
p119 FSP; p127 P; p138 FRL; p139 tl M, Ferdinando Scianna; tr FSP;
p140 M, Stuart Franklin; p141 tr P; b FSP.

Ilex and the author wish to acknowledge the assistance of Anna
Bramwell in the preparation of this book.

Other acknowledgments: Nicola Barber, Andras Bereznay, Malcolm
Day, Designers and Partners (Oxford), Saki Dockrill, Asad Ismi, Latha
Menon, Richard Rowan.

Contents

Preface

Since the beginning of the twentieth century the world has been transformed from the Eurocentric one in which Britain, France, Germany and Russia held economic and political dominance, to that of 1991 in which the United States of America, despite its increasing economic problems, polices the globe. It is a period which has seen the rise, spread and fragmentation of communism; the decline of European colonial empires and the growth of non-European nationalism; the economic dominance of the Western powers and the debt burden and economic hardships of developing countries; the growth of religious fundamentalism and fanaticism; and the threat of international terrorism. Over the same period, there have been spectacular developments in transport, communications, medicine, military technology and space exploration, along with changes in attitude to social welfare and the exploitation of the planet.

In providing a graphic illustration of these political, social and technological changes by means of maps, the **Atlas of Twentieth Century World History** provides an accessible introduction to this complex period. The 94 maps, employing a wide range of cartographic techniques, cover both global and local themes. On the one hand they chart global shifts in territorial control and political power and on the other they scrutinize a particular region, revealing for example how wars were won or lost or how the patchwork of ethnic distribution has been − or may prove to be − a major cause of historical change.

The events of 1989 and 1990 in Eastern Europe show just how quickly these changes can occur. The reunification of Germany, unthinkable at the start of 1989, has become a reality, while other countries in Eastern Europe are beginning to experience the problems of adapting to democracy. Meanwhile, the Soviet Union, against whom the United States and Western Europe allied and rearmed after 1949, has ceased to be a major threat as it grapples with a wide range of internal problems. The Atlas contains up-to-date maps to illustrate the changes in Eastern Europe and the USSR.

Such changes, with their opportunities and difficulties, are by no means peculiar to the present but have been magnified by the complexity of events in recent years and by the rapidity with which modern technology allows them to take place. Moreover as the threat of nuclear war recedes we are now faced with the potential consequences of environmental pollution, itself a product of the technology that has contributed to human betterment. Although environmental problems, and diseases such as AIDS, threaten life today as much as any military weapon, the close of the Cold War has still created a mood of optimism in the West. But progress is not predictable and in the twenty-first century human ingenuity will continue to be tested as efforts are made to share out resources and to contain war, poverty, disease and world-wide pollution.

THE CRACKS IN THE EDIFICE

Commercial, industrial, imperial and military competition created a potentially unstable Europe.

The early 20th century marked the zenith of European dominance throughout the world. Western Europe controlled, directly or indirectly, most of the world's surface and the bulk of its trade and investment. It shared with the United States a virtual monopoly in technological innovation. As colonial powers, the European nations justified their control of foreign lands by claiming that they were engaged upon a 'civilizing mission', bringing to backward peoples the benefits of Western civilization – Christianity, justice, efficient government, modern transport, education, sanitation and medicine.

Yet cracks were beginning to appear in the edifice of Western power. Given the smaller population of the West, which had to rule huge numbers of people in Africa and Asia, European dominance depended to a large degree on a mixture of self-confidence and bluff, although superior military and naval technology could always be brought to bear if these failed to convince. The West was also beginning to experience the first manifestations of nationalism in India, Indo-China, China, Turkey, Persia and Ireland. Countries such as Britain and France, which prided themselves on their constitutional freedoms, were faced with a dilemma when they continued to deny these blessings to the peoples of India or Indo-China, especially when the growing middle class in these possessions, most of whom had received a Western education, was able to turn such principles against its rulers. Nor was socialism, whose growth in the West after 1900 so alarmed the propertied classes, entirely sympathetic to empires that appeared to exploit their overseas subjects as ruthlessly as they did their working classes at home.

The country that most felt these pressures was Britain. The death of Queen Victoria in 1901, and the elaborate ceremonial surrounding her funeral, which was attended by all the crowned heads of Europe, were seen by many contemporaries as marking the end of more than 60 years of unfettered British industrial and imperial progress. Other nations were now challenging Britain's industrial pre-eminence. In particular, the rapid industrialization and increased urbanization of Germany had created a formidable economic rival, which had overtaken Britain in many of the indicators of national power, especially in iron and steel production, the basis of military strength. Not only did Germany possess the strongest army on the continent, but also after 1898 it began to construct a large ocean-going battle fleet. At the same time, the United States, while not so immediately threatening to Britain, was becoming an even more formidable

◀ **Wilhelm II (1859–1941) became German Emperor in 1888. He was ambitious and vain, personifying the spirit of Imperial Germany. After Germany's defeat in 1918 he went into exile.**

▶ **The British in India enjoyed a privileged life style. British men monopolized the major administrative and military posts, while their wives led a pampered existence.**

Where the Money Was

At the turn of the century, standards of living were highest in the industrialized nations and in those areas of European settlement where raw materials and land were abundant. Statistics for this period are, however, unreliable. For example, in poor economies there is always a large non-cash element owing to factors such as self-sufficiency, barter and a reluctance to disclose information to revenue officials. Furthermore, figures for standards of living and national income are averages and do not clearly indicate the sharp differences between rich and poor. On the whole, however, while this difference was relatively large in the industrialized West, it was smaller in the United States and Canada.

During the first decade of the 20th century, world trade in primary and manufactured goods almost doubled, but by 1910 Europe's share of industrial production began to decline, as that of the US, Japan and Russia rose. Russia's industrial expansion relied on foreign capital, particularly from France, which alone held one third of Russia's total debt. This debt was serviced by high taxes on the peasantry, which led to increasing resentment against foreign capitalists.

Capital for industrial expansion was still provided mainly by West European investors. Joint-stock companies were formed to build railways in Egypt and tramways in Warsaw. Most of the utilities in South America were constructed through money raised from British shareholders.

To start with, there was little fear of expropriation. When Venezuela threatened to default on her debt repayments in 1902, British and German warships blockaded her ports. In reality however, investment in areas not under the political control of the investing nations was vulnerable to political change, and much European capital invested in Russia, Latin America, China and elsewhere was expropriated or lost as a result of internal upheaval in the years during and following the First World War.

World Development

In 1900 the world was shrinking: continents were now linked internally and externally by metalled roads, railways, steamships and the telegraph. The Trans-Siberian railway was all but completed in 1904 and the Andes were crossed by a railway in 1910. Over 600,000 miles of railways had been built by that year, mostly by British, French and North American engineers. The steam locomotive allowed an expansion of markets for industrial goods. Oil-fired instead of steam-propelled ships were making their first appearance. Important technological developments were also taking place during this period, notably in the United States: the first powered flight occurred in 1903, while the first mass production motor car – the Model T Ford – rolled off the production line in Detroit in 1907. These developments were all helping to increase the pace of industrialization throughout the world.

Britain, formerly the 'workshop of the world', was slipping behind her major competitors, notably Germany and the United States, which were not only overtaking it in coal, iron and steel production but were also developing newer industries and techniques, such as electrical engineering and chemicals. Japan too was advancing industrially in this period. Most countries in Western Europe, however, remained dependent on Third World countries (then mostly colonial or semi-colonial societies) for their raw materials, such as cotton, oil or rubber, which they turned into manufactured goods. Most also had to import large quantities of food, as France was the only country self-sufficient in agriculture.

industrial power than Germany. France, Austria–Hungary and Russia had also made considerable economic strides during the 1890s and by the 1900s, when France had recovered from the effects of the scandalous Dreyfus Affair, the country became increasingly confident that it could defeat Germany in a war. Commercial, industrial, imperial and military competition were all therefore helping to create a potentially unstable continent.

This was not how the situation was viewed in Europe. The Western bourgeoisie believed that the rapid advances since the mid-19th century in technology, communications, medicine, sanitation and in wealth-creation of all forms would continue unabated in the future, spreading the benefits of progress and prosperity throughout the world. That these benefits were restricted to the well-to-do was ignored. Indeed the new rich, whose wealth was based on profits from industrial, commercial and banking enterprises, enjoyed a most opulent lifestyle, while throughout Europe the old landed aristocracy lived a life of extraordinary elegance and formality.

In the political sphere, although the imperial governments of Germany and Austria–Hungary remained autocratic, constitutions had been granted and were based on universal manhood suffrage. Even in Russia, the most politically backward nation, a limited constitution based on a severely restricted

▲ The Krupp factory in Essen, showing Germany's industrial strength early in the twentieth century. Steel is being prepared for tanks.

franchise was granted by the Tsar in 1905. However the parliaments in these imperial governments were little more than debating chambers, and carried no real powers.

There were also some improvements in the social conditions of the working classes, at least in the West. Germany had introduced a system of unemployment insurance and old age pensions in the 1880s, and Britain and France began to follow suit in the 1900s. Liberal middle-class consciences had been pricked by the appalling conditions that existed in the urban areas, a legacy of the Industrial Revolution. In the United States, the Progressive Movement, and in Western Europe, numerous municipal reformers, began to work towards improving housing, sanitation and medical facilities and providing better recreational and educational facilities for working class families. Yet in the years leading up to 1914, working-class dissatisfaction with wages and conditions manifested itself in numerous strikes and demonstrations, particularly in Britain and France, while St Petersburg was gripped by a General Strike on the very eve of the Great War. Social forces were at work across the continent that would eventually bring the entire edifice tumbling down around its rulers' ears.

◄ Anti-imperialism in China led to a siege of European embassies in Beijing in 1900 by the nationalist group, the Boxers. The embassies were eventually relieved by a six-nation force but the harsh means used to subdue the rising only served to exacerbate nationalist feeling. The picture shows a public execution in front of European troops.

The Imperial Powers

SPITSBERGEN
(Norway)

GREENLAND
(Denmark)

ICELAND
(Denmark)

FAEROES
(Denmark)

CANADA

LABRADOR

NEWFOUNDLAND

ST. PIERRE & MIQUELON

UNITED
KINGDOM   DENMARK

NETHERLANDS
BELGIUM   GERMANY

FRANCE   AUSTRIA -
HUNGARY

ITALY

PORTUGAL   SPAIN

AZORES

SPANISH   Gibraltar (Br)
MOROCCO

MALTA

CYPRL

UNITED STATES

BERMUDA

MADEIRA   MOROCCO

CANARY IS.   ALGERIA   LIBYA

RIO DE ORO   EGYP

BAHAMAS

TURKS & CAICOS IS.

BRITISH
HONDURAS   CAYMAN
IS.

JAMAICA

PUERTO
RICO

TRINIDAD AND
TOBAGO

C. VERDE IS.

FRENCH WEST AFRICA

FRENCH
EQUATORIAL
AFRICA

ANGLO
EGYPTI
SUDA

GAMBIA
PORT.
GUINEA
SIERRA
LEONE

TOGO

GOLD
COAST

NIGERIA

CAMEROON

RIO
MUNI

UGAN

FERNANDO PO

SÃO TOME & PRINCIPE

ANNOBON

BELGIAN
CONGO

GERM.
AFRIC

Caribbean Is.

ARUBA
CURAÇAO
BONAIRE
BR. VIRGIN IS.
DANISH VIRGIN IS.
ANGUILLA
S. MARTIN
S. BARTHOLOMEW
ST. EUSTATIUS & SABA
ST. KITTS-NEVIS
BARBUDA
ANTIGUA
MONSERRAT
GUADELOUPE
DOMINICA
MARTINIQUE
ST. LUCIA
ST. VINCENT
BARBADOS
GRENADINES
GRE...

Panama
Canal

GUIANA

ASCENSION

ST. HELENA

ANGOLA   N. RHO

S.
RHOI

GERMAN
SOUTH-WEST
AFRICA

BECHUANA-
LAND

SWAZILAND
BASUTO

UNION OF
SOUTH AFRICA

MARQUESAS
IS.

TUAMOTU ARCHIPELAGO

PITCAIRN I.

TRISTAN DA CUNHA

FALKLAND IS.

SOUTH GEORGIA

Of the major colonial powers, Britain in 1914 possessed the largest overseas empire, occupying about 11 million square miles of territory on every continent and ruling over some 400 million people. The older settlements of Canada, Australia and New Zealand had achieved self-governing status by 1907, but remained united to the motherland by close cultural, defence and economic ties. In addition, Britain controlled an 'informal empire' of protectorates and defensive alliances over the Sudan, Egypt (including the Suez Canal), southern Persia and the Persian Gulf; investments in, and trade with, China and South America gave Britain considerable influence in those countries as well.

France possessed the second largest overseas empire, with extensive territories in Africa, Indo-China, the Caribbean and the Pacific. Although it was an important source of manpower and raw materials, France had acquired most of its empire after 1870 in order to strengthen its prestige as a European great power. After 1900 France sought to take over Morocco, the last remaining independent state in North Africa, an ambition finally achieved in 1911.

Germany had arrived late in the scramble for overseas colonies. By 1914 it had acquired territories in South-West and East Africa, Togoland and Cameroon in West Africa, several islands in the Pacific, and had seized Jiaozhou from China. Germany was not satisfied with these gains, believing that as a leading industrial and military power it was entitled to a much greater share of the world's resources. In the late 1890s, it began to construct a large battle fleet with the intention of forcing Britain to share some of its colonial holdings with Germany. The ensuing naval race poisoned Anglo–German relations down to the outbreak of war in 1914.

In contrast the United States acquired its colonies during the 1890s almost by accident. Victory in a war with Spain in 1898 over Cuba enabled it to annex Puerto Rico, Guam and the Philippines. Hawaii and the eastern Samoan Islands also fell to the United States in 1898, followed by other Pacific islands.

Colonial powers and their possessions, including protectorates

British		Italian	
French		German	
Dutch		Belgian	
Portuguese		United States	
Spanish		Japanese	

The Doomed Empires

**Legend (upper map):**
- —— Maximum extent of Ottoman Empire, 1683
- Losses 1683–1878
- Losses 1879–1914
- Ottoman Empire, 1914
- 1878 Date of independence
- International boundary, 1914

RUSSIAN EMPIRE
Kiev
GERMAN EMPIRE
Vienna
Budapest
Odessa
AUSTRO-HUNGARIAN EMPIRE
KHANATE OF CRIMEA Tributary state
1774
Crimea
Sevastopol
CASPIAN SEA
ROMANIA 1878
Belgrade
1878
Bucharest
BLACK SEA
Tiflis
Rome
ITALY
MONTENEGRO
SERBIA
Sofia
BULGARIA
1908
Baku
ALBANIA
1913
MACEDONIA
Constantinople
Erzurum
Ankara
ADRIATIC SEA
GREECE
Smyrna
Berlin-Baghdad Railway
Tributary states
PERSIA
Tehran
Algiers
Tunis
Athens
1830
Aleppo
ALGERIA Tributary states
1710
TUNISIA French protectorate. 1881
Malta (Br.)
MEDITERRANEAN SEA
Crete
Dodecanese Italian, 1912
Cyprus Br prot.,1878
SYRIA
Damascus
MESOPOTAMIA
Baghdad
Tripoli
Benghazi
Alexandria
PALESTINE
Jerusalem
Basra
KUWAIT Br prot.,1899
TRIPOLI Italian, 1912
CYRENAICA Italian, 1912
Cairo
Arabia
FEZZAN Italian, 1912
EGYPT British occupation, 1882
HEJAZ
Medina
RED SEA
Mecca

0 km 750
0 mls 500

Legend (lower map):
- —— Boundary of Russia, 1914
- Acquisitions, 1855–1914
- Under Russian occupation or protectorship
- Russian sphere of influence

to Alaska,1867
Anadyr
Murmansk
FINLAND
Helsingfors
Arkhangelsk
YAKUTSK
KAMCHATKA
Turukhansk
Yakutsk
Okhotsk
Petropavlovsk
Riga
St. Petersburg
YENISEYSK
Warsaw
POLAND
Moscow
TOBOLSK
Kiev
Kazan
Tobolsk
Tomsk
IRKUTSK
Nikolayevsk
Sakhalin
Odessa
UKRAINE
TOMSK
Irkutsk
TRANS-BAYKAL
Chita
AMUR REGION
Turgai
Semipalatinsk
TANNU TUVA Russian prot. 1912–21
MANCHURIA Russian occupation, 1900–05
USSURI
OTTOMAN EMPIRE
Tiflis
Baku
Russian protectorate. 1873
Khiva
SYR DARYA
Tashkent
1871–81
MONGOLIA
Mukden
KOREA
TRANSCASPIAN REGION
Bukhara
Samarkand
Port Arthur 1898–1905
Tehran
PERSIA
Kabul
Russian protectorate,1868
AFGHANISTAN
Beijing
CHINA

0 km 1500
0 mls 1000

14

The Ottoman (or Turkish) Empire was in continuous decline from the end of the 18th century. The inefficiency of the Sultan's government in Constantinople resulted in the loss of a large part of its Balkan lands; Serbia, Greece and Romania had all emerged as independent nations by 1878. By 1900 the Ottoman Empire was struggling to retain a hold over its remaining European possessions in Macedonia, where rival Serbian–, Greek– and Bulgarian–backed guerrillas fought to overthrow Turkish rule. Its weakening power was made worse by the rivalry between Austria–Hungary and Russia for predominance in the Balkans, which had nearly resulted in conflict between them several times during the 19th century. War had, however, been prevented by the intervention of other European powers, anxious to avoid involvement in a major struggle if the Ottoman Empire collapsed. Their attempts to persuade the Turks to ameliorate the situation in Macedonia by introducing reforms were all frustrated by Turkish opposition. In the Middle East, Germany, Britain, France and Italy competed to wrest economic concessions from the Turks. By 1900 German influence was supreme: it had secured the

right to build a railway from Berlin to Baghdad and was equipping the Turkish army.

Austria–Hungary was also facing increasing unrest in its multi-national empire fanned by Serbia and Romania, which hoped to secure a share of the spoils if the empire collapsed. The emperor, Francis Joseph, ruled over a state that included Germans, Hungarians, Poles, Czechs, Italians and Romanians. In 1867 the empire had been divided between the Austrians and Hungarians, by which time other nationalities also demanded autonomy.

Unlike Austria–Hungary and the Ottoman Empire, the Russian Empire did not appear to be in a state of decline. A country of enormous economic and military potential, Russia had made considerable industrial strides in the 1890s. Moreover, having consolidated its earlier gains in Central Asia, Russia was extending its influence into Persia and Afghanistan, and was also advancing into Manchuria and northern China. However, seemingly the strongest of the three eastern empires, Russia was the first to suffer defeat in war (against Japan) and the outbreak of revolution, both in 1905.

Ethno-linguistic divisions

Boundary of Austro-Hungarian empire, 1914

German	Polish	Serbian
Italian	Czech	Croatian
Rhaeto-Romance	Slovak	Slovene
Romanian	Ruthenian	Hungarian

0 km 200
0 mls 150

15

World Population 1900

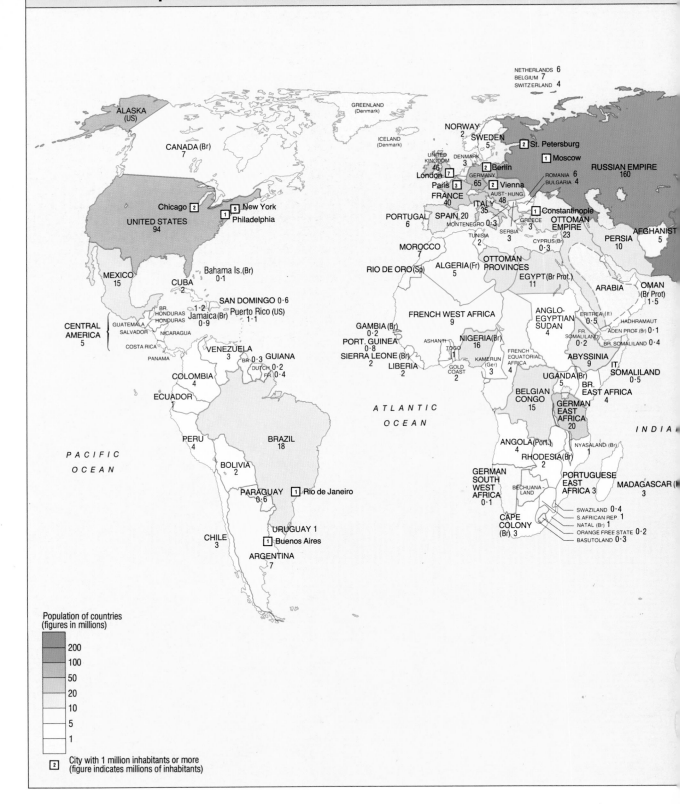

NETHERLANDS 6
BELGIUM 7
SWITZERLAND 4

GREENLAND
(Denmark)

ALASKA
(US)

CANADA (Br)
7

NORWAY
2
SWEDEN
5

ICELAND
(Denmark)

St. Petersburg 1

Moscow 1

RUSSIAN EMPIRE
160

UNITED
KINGDOM
46

DENMARK
3

Berlin 2

London 7

GERMANY
65

ROMANIA 6
BULGARIA 4

Paris 3

Vienna 2

FRANCE
40

AUST.-HUNG.
48

ITALY
35

Constantinople 1

AFGHANIST
5

Chicago 2

New York 5

UNITED STATES
94

Philadelphia 1

PORTUGAL
6

SPAIN 20

MONTENEGRO 0·3

GREECE
3

SERBIA
3

OTTOMAN
EMPIRE
23

PERSIA
10

MOROCCO
7

TUNISIA
2

CYPRUS (Br)
0·3

MEXICO
15

CUBA
2

Bahama Is.(Br)
0·1

RIO DE ORO (Sp)

ALGERIA (Fr)
5

OTTOMAN
PROVINCES

EGYPT (Br Prot.)
11

ARABIA

OMAN
(Br Prot)
1·5

SAN DOMINGO 0·6

BR.
HONDURAS
HONDURAS

Jamaica (Br)
0·9

1·2

Puerto Rico (US)
1·1

CENTRAL
AMERICA
5

GUATEMALA
SALVADOR

NICARAGUA

COSTA RICA

PANAMA

VENEZUELA
3

BR. 0·3 GUIANA

DUTCH 0·2

FR. 0·4

FRENCH WEST AFRICA
9

ANGLO-
EGYPTIAN
SUDAN
4

ERITREA (It)
0·5

HADHRAMAUT

ADEN PROT. (Br) 0·1

GAMBIA (Br)
0·2

PORT. GUINEA
0·8

SIERRA LEONE (Br)
2

ASHANTI

TOGO
1

NIGERIA (Br)
16

KAMERUN
(Ger)

FRENCH
EQUATORIAL
AFRICA

FR.
SOMALILAND
0·2

BR. SOMALILAND 0·4

COLOMBIA
4

LIBERIA
2

GOLD
COAST
2

3

ABYSSINIA
9

IT.
SOMALILAND
0·5

ECUADOR
1

UGANDA (Br)
5

BR.
EAST AFRICA
4

ATLANTIC

OCEAN

BELGIAN
CONGO
15

GERMAN
EAST
AFRICA
20

INDIA

PERU
4

BRAZIL
18

ANGOLA (Port.)
4

NYASALAND (Br)
1

PACIFIC

OCEAN

BOLIVIA
2

RHODESIA (Br)
2

PARAGUAY
0·6

Rio de Janeiro 1

GERMAN
SOUTH
WEST
AFRICA
0·1

BECHUANA-
LAND

PORTUGUESE
EAST
AFRICA 3

MADAGASCAR
3

URUGUAY 1

CHILE
3

Buenos Aires 1

ARGENTINA
7

CAPE
COLONY
(Br) 3

SWAZILAND 0·4

S. AFRICAN REP 1

NATAL (Br) 1

ORANGE FREE STATE 0·2

BASUTOLAND 0·3

**Population of countries
(figures in millions)**

200
100
50
20
10
5
1

2 City with 1 million inhabitants or more
(figure indicates millions of inhabitants)

There are two striking features about the population of the world between 1900 and 1913. The first is that while Europe was densely populated, most of what we now describe as the Third World, together with the United States, was sparsely populated. Europe had a population of about 325 million, Africa only 13.5 million; Canada, Australia and most of Asia, except India and China, similarly had low population densities. The second feature is that while the populations of China, Japan, Russia, the United States and South America increased rapidly, that of Western Europe barely changed. Indeed France suffered from a falling birth rate, which weakened it economically *vis à vis* Germany, whose population had soared in the last two decades of the 19th century.

Across the world, the rise in population was largely due to improved medicine and hygiene. However, much of the increase in the American population was the result of immigration. During the 19th century millions of Europeans had emigrated to North and South America. As death rates fell in Europe, the growing populations of countries as diverse as Norway, Italy and Germany could not be absorbed into new industries or agriculture, and people left to find better wages, land and space in the New World. In addition, many emigrants sought the political and religious freedoms denied to them in their own countries, especially after the failure of the 1848 revolutions in Europe. The same was true of emigrants from Russia and Central and Eastern Europe in the early 20th century.

During the first decade of the 20th century, emigration to the United States continued at a high level both from southern European countries, such as Portugal and Italy, and Eastern Europe, all of which were still dependent on agriculture. On the other hand, greater prosperity in Western Europe after 1900 resulted in a decline in emigration to the New World. Thus in Germany, economic growth meant a higher demand for labour, and workers began to pour in from Poland and Italy. Moreover, German workers benefited from state pensions and insurance schemes introduced during the 1880s. As a result, German emigration decreased dramatically between 1910 and 1914.

In Russia, too, the situation changed in the years before the First World War. Five out of every fourteen emigrants who had left Russia in the previous 30 years had returned by 1914. This process was encouraged by the progress of Russia's industrialization before 1914, which led to the growth of an urban middle class which hoped that the limited constitution granted in 1905 would be followed by more comprehensive political reforms.

Chronology 1900–1914

EUROPE	AMERICAS

1900

	EUROPE		AMERICAS
Feb	• British Labour Representation Committee founded (Labour Party)		
Sept	• Founding of Socialist Revolutionary Party of Russia		

1901

	EUROPE		AMERICAS
Jan	• Death of Queen Victoria and accession of Edward VII in Britain	Mar	• William McKinley becomes US President for second term
		Sept	• President McKinley is assassinated and is succeeded by Vice-President Theodore Roosevelt

1902

	EUROPE		AMERICAS
Apr	• Peasant revolt in Russia suppressed	Dec	• Venezuela blockaded by Britain and Germany over non-payment of international debt
June	• Triple Alliance of Germany, Austria and Italy renewed		
Dec	• Secondary education provided by the state in England and Wales		

1903

	EUROPE		AMERICAS
Jan	• Ownership of land for peasants in Ireland as the landlords are gradually bought out	Jan	• Alaska frontier question settled between USA and Canada
Apr	• Massacre of Russian Jews at Kishinev, Bessarabia	Nov	• US–Panama treaty places Panama Canal Zone in US hands
Aug	• Pope Pius X succeeds Pope Leo XIII (died July)	Nov	• Panama declares itself independent of Colombia
Nov	• Russian Social Democratic Party splits into Mensheviks and Bolsheviks		

1904

	EUROPE		AMERICAS
Feb	• Outbreak of Russo–Japanese War	Nov	• Theodore Roosevelt elected President of USA
Apr	• Entente Cordiale between Britain and France following agreement on territorial disputes over Morocco, Siam (Thailand), Newfoundland and Egypt		
Oct	• Russian fleet mistakenly fires on British trawlers at Dogger Bank in North Sea		

1905

	EUROPE		AMERICAS
Jan	• Russian Revolution follows 'Bloody Sunday' massacre (22nd) in St Petersburg		
June	• Norway declares independence from Sweden		
July	• Separation of Church and State in France		
Oct	• First of Russian soviets (councils) formed in St Petersburg under Leon Trotsky		
Nov	• Foundation of Sinn Féin ('Ourselves Alone') party in Ireland		
Dec	• Uprising in Moscow crushed by government troops		

1906

	EUROPE		AMERICAS
Jan	• Liberal landslide in British general election leads to sweeping social reforms	Apr	• Earthquake in San Francisco kills more than 1,000 people
Mar	• Algeçiras Conference: Spain and France confirm Morocco's independence	July	• Peace treaty ends war between Guatemala, El Salvador and Honduras
May	• First meeting of Duma (elected parliament) in Russia	Oct	• Insurrection in Cuba on President Palma's re-election; Roosevelt intervenes to establish provisional government to carry out reforms
June	• Anti-Semitic pogroms in Russia		
July	• Russian Duma dissolved and martial law declared		
Nov	• Leon Trotsky exiled to Siberia		

1907

	EUROPE		AMERICAS
Aug	• Anglo-Russian agreement defines spheres of influence in central Asia and Persia	Nov	• Oklahoma becomes state of USA

AFRICA, ASIA, AUSTRALASIA

Jan	● British Protectorate established over northern Nigeria
Feb	● Boer War in South Africa: relief from Boer siege of Ladysmith by British forces
May	● Orange Free State annexed by Britain
May	● Mafeking relieved by British forces after 217 days siege
May	● Russians occupy Manchuria and massacre 45,000 Chinese
June	● Boxer Rebellion in China

Jan	● Foundation of Commonwealth of Australia, with Edmund Barton as first Prime Minister
Feb	● North West Frontier Province created in India between Afghanistan and Punjab
Sept	● Peace Protocol between China and European powers ends Boxer Rebellion
Sept	● Ashanti kingdom annexed to British Gold Coast colony

Apr	● Russo–Japanese Convention: Russia agrees to evacuate Manchuria
May	● Peace of Vereeniging ends Boer War
Sept	● White settlement of Kenya highlands begins

Feb	● Kano, Nigeria, submits to Britain
Mar	● British occupation of northern Nigeria complete

Feb	● Russo–Japanese war begins as Japanese attack Russian fleet
Aug	● British troops, led by Francis Younghusband, arrive in Tibet
Oct	● Revolt of Hereros and Hottentots against Germans in South-West Africa (until 1908)
Oct	● Reorganization of French possessions as French West Africa, with capital at Dakar

May	● Destruction of Russian fleet by Japanese at Tsushima
July	● Muslim uprising in German East Africa
Sept	● Treaty of Portsmouth (US): Japan establishes protectorate over Korea and secures leasehold of Port Arthur and Sakhalin Island after its defeat of Russia
Nov	● Government of Papua transferred from Britain to Australia

Mar	● Britain pays compensation for damage caused in the Boer War
Dec	● Aga Khan founds All-India Muslim League
Dec	● Transvaal colony is granted self-government in South Africa

Mar	● Anarchy in Morocco: French troops move in
July	● Orange River colony gains autonomy as Orange Free State
Sept	● Revolt of Hereros crushed by German troops
Sept	● New Zealand receives dominion status

SCIENCE & CULTURE

- ● Giacomo Puccini *Tosca*
- ● Edward Elgar *Dream of Gerontius*
- ● First Zeppelin flight in Germany
- ● Quantum theory is formulated by Max Planck
- ● Browning revolver invented by John M Browning
- ● Sigmund Freud *Interpretation of Dreams*
- ● Second Modern Olympic Games are held in Paris

- ● Ragtime jazz develops in USA
- ● Sergei Rachmaninov 2nd Piano Concerto
- ● First Nobel prizes awarded
- ● Trans-Siberian railway completed
- ● Adrenalin discovered by Jokichi Takamine
- ● Guglielmo Marconi achieves first transatlantic radio transmission

- ● Claude Debussy *Pelléas et Mélisande*
- ● Completion of Aswan Dam in Egypt
- ● Hormonal action demonstrated by William Bayliss and Ernest Starling

- ● Jack London *The Call of the Wild*
- ● Henry James *The Ambassadors*
- ● Leos Janáček *Jenufa*
- ● Ford Motor Company formed in Detroit, USA
- ● Wright brothers make first successful flight in aeroplane with petrol engine

- ● Joseph Conrad *Nostromo*
- ● Auguste Rodin *The Thinker*
- ● Rolls-Royce company formed
- ● Giacomo Puccini *Madame Butterfly*
- ● Abbey Theatre, Dublin opened
- ● Anton Chekhov *The Cherry Orchard*
- ● New York Broadway subway opens with first electric trams
- ● Silicone developed by F S Kipping

- ● Claude Debussy *La Mer*
- ● First cinema opens in Pittsburgh, USA
- ● Theory of Relativity formulated by Albert Einstein
- ● Antonio Gaudi builds Casa Mila in Barcelona
- ● Les Fauves (Wild Beasts) group led by Henri Matisse and André Derain

- ● Gamma rays discovered by Joseph Thomson
- ● Vitamins discovered by Frederick Gowland Hopkins
- ● Roald Amundsen crosses North West Passage and determines position of magnetic North Pole

- ● Mahler 8th Symphony ('Symphony of a Thousand')
- ● Pablo Picasso *Les Demoiselles d'Avignon*
- ● Ivan Pavlov studies conditioned reflexes
- ● Pablo Picasso and Georges Braques evolve Cubist Movement

EUROPE	AMERICAS

EUROPE

Feb	● Assassination of Carlos I and Crown Prince of Portugal
July	● 'Young Turk' revolutionaries promise elections in Ottoman Empire
Oct	● Bulgaria declares its independence from Turkey
Oct	● Austria annexes Turkish provinces of Bosnia and Hercegovina
Dec	● Disastrous earthquake in south Calabria (Italy) and Sicily

Apr	● Sultan Abdul Hamid II of Turkey deposed by 'Young Turks': Muhammad V succeeds until 1923
Aug	● Anti-government revolutionary rising in Barcelona, Spain, crushed

May	● Edward VII of Britain dies and is succeeded by George V
Sept	● Italy declares war on Turkey
Oct	● Revolution in Portugal: Manuel II abandons throne, Portugal is declared a republic

Aug	● Strikes and industrial unrest in Britain
Nov	● Italy annexes Turkish province of Tripoli
Nov	● Suffragette riots in Whitehall, London

Jan	● German elections leave Socialists the largest single party in the Reichstag
May	● Italy bombards Dardanelles and seizes Rhodes
May	● Greece signs anti-Ottoman alliance with Bulgaria (joined by Serbia in July)
Oct	● Treaty of Ouchy ends Italo–Turkish war: Italy secures Tripoli
Oct	● First Balkan War: Serbia, Montenegro, Greece and Bulgaria drive Turkey out of Macedonia

Jan	● German Army Bill expands size of German army
May	● Albania declares its independence from Turkey
June	● Second Balkan War: Bulgaria fights Serbia, Turkey, Greece and Romania, but loses substantial territory in peace settlement (in Aug)
Aug	● Treaty of Bucharest ends Second Balkan War

Mar	● Curragh 'mutiny' of British Army against Home Rule in Ulster
May	● Irish Home Rule Act introduces self-government for all of Ireland
June	● Assassination of Archduke Francis Ferdinand, heir to the Austro-Hungarian throne, at Sarajevo in Bosnia

AMERICAS

May	● North Carolina becomes a 'dry' (no-alcohol) state
Aug	● Cuba holds first general election under US supervision: Liberal victory, with José Gomez as President (until 1913)

Dec	● Dr José Madriz elected in Nicaragua to succeed ousted President Zelaya

May	● Mexican Civil War: Porfirio Díaz overthrown, Francisco Madero becomes President

Jan	● New Mexico and Arizona (Feb) become states of USA
Apr	● *SS Titanic* sinks, drowning 1,500 people
May	● US marines land in Nicaragua to prevent renewal of civil war

Jan	● Woodrow Wilson becomes President of USA
Feb	● General Victoriano Huerta takes power in Mexico and murders Madero. Wilson refuses recognition and US arms embargo ensues

Jan	● President Oreste of Haiti abdicates during revolt and US marines land to preserve order
Mar	● Unrest in Brazil: Rio de Janeiro in state of siege
Mar	● President Wilson sends US troops into northern Mexico to crush bandits
Apr	● Civil government established in Panama Canal Zone
Apr	● General civil disorder in Mexico: many local dictators: Aluaro Obregon is dictator of three-quarters of Mexico
July	● President Huerta succeeded by Venustiano Carranza
Aug	● Universal Negro Improvement Association and African Committees formed in Jamaica

AFRICA, ASIA, AUSTRALASIA

May	• Pan-Islamic Hijaz railway opened in Arabia as far as Medina
Aug	• Léopold II hands over control of the Congo to Belgian government
Nov	• Labour government elected in Australia

Oct	• Prince Ho Hirobumi assassinated after establishing Japanese control in Korea
Dec	• Union of Cape Colony, Transvaal and Orange Free State

Jan	• French Congo reorganized as French Equatorial Africa
May	• Louis Botha and James Hertzog found South African Party and win first elections
July	• Cape Colony, Natal, Orange Free State and Transvaal form independent Dominion of South Africa

Mar	• French troops occupy Fez, Moroccan capital, after tribal revolt
July	• Agadir crisis in Morocco with arrival of German gunboat, *Panther*, to protect its interests in Morocco
Sept	• Italo–Turkish War begins in Libya
Oct	• Famine and revolution in China: Manchu dynasty overthrown (Dec)
Nov	• French protectorate imposed on Morocco

Jan	• Chinese republic proclaimed under leader Sun Yixian (Sun Yat-sen)
Feb	• Sun Yixian replaced by General Yuan Shikai
Apr	• Tibetans expel Chinese troops from Lhasa
Aug	• Japan and Russia reach agreement over spheres of influence in Mongolia and Manchuria

July	• China agrees to grant Mongolian independence
Nov	• Mohandas Gandhi, leader of Indian Passive Resistance Movement in South Africa, is arrested after protesting against Transvaal government's discrimination against its Indian population

Jan	• Northern and Southern Nigeria united as single British colony
Dec	• Egypt declared British protectorate

SCIENCE & CULTURE

• Ford Motor Company produces first Model 'T'
• Béla Bartók 1st String Quartet

• Robert Peary reaches North Pole
• Sergei Diaghilev launches *Ballets Russes* in Paris

• Vasili Kandinsky *Improvisation XIV* one of the paintings to herald the start of purely abstract painting
• Excavation of Knossos and discovery of Minoan culture by British archaelogist Arthur Evans
• Edward Elgar Violin Concerto
• Igor Stravinsky *The Firebird*

• First fighter plane built by Anton Fokker
• Aircraft first used for offensive measures by Italians in Libya
• Roald Amundsen reaches South Pole
• Georges Braque *Man with a Guitar*
• Richard Strauss *Der Rosenkavalier*

• Robert Scott and companions die after reaching South Pole
• Glenn Curtiss constructs first sea-plane
• Stainless steel invented by Howard Brearley
• Maurice Ravel *Daphnis et Chloé*
• Arnold Schoenberg *Pierrot Lunaire*

• First Charlie Chaplin motion picture
• D H Lawrence *Sons and Lovers*
• Marcel Proust first part of *À La Recherche du Temps Perdu* (completed 1927)
• Igor Stravinsky *Rite of Spring*
• Thomas Mann *Death In Venice*

• See page 35

THE WAR TO END ALL WARS

A relatively stable order was smashed in an orgy of blood and violence.

On the outbreak of the First World War in 1914, Sir Edward Grey, the British Foreign Secretary, remarked to a friend that "the lamps are going out all over Europe. We shall not see them lit again in our life-time." In retrospect many contemporaries shared Grey's view that a relatively stable order, one marked by continuous progress and prosperity, had been smashed in an orgy of blood letting and violence. The resurgence of European intellectual culture and a vibrant experimental art that had occurred before the war – itself the origin of the post-war modern movement – was swamped under a tide of jingoism and militarism.

The pre-war pageantry of the ruling classes – the balls, fêtes, spas and country houses of the well-to-do, the poetry and literature of the younger intellectuals – had always been merely a veneer masking profound social unease. All countries experienced increasing labour unrest, strikes and riots in the years prior to 1914. Britain faced civil war in Ireland and suffragette violence in England. Revolutionary outbreaks in Russia culminated in the assassination of the Prime Minister, P.A. Stolypin, in 1911, while increasing nationalist fervour throughout Europe and virulent anti-Semitism in both Austria–Hungary and Russia disfigured what often seem in hindsight to have been peaceful and civilized societies. At the same time the rise of the socialist movement in Europe terrified the propertied classes.

Nor was the likelihood of a long and destructive war lacking its prophets. Ivan Bloch, a Polish banker, in a vast study written during the 1890s, warned his readers that gigantic strides in modern military technology, allied to the conscription of millions of young adult males, would cause the next war to be a long drawn-out, bloody stalemate, leading eventually to revolution and the collapse of Western civilization. Norman Angell, a British writer, believed that the intricate peace-time mechanism of international finance, investment and trade would collapse on the outbreak of war, leading to immense suffering and chaos. Such forebodings were dismissed by European generals, who planned to wage a short, victorious war, brevity made necessary, in their view, by the colossal expense of the undertaking. In the event Bloch was proved to have been largely accurate

in his prophecy. During the war the trenches, barbed wire, machine guns and artillery dominated the battlefield, cutting a swathe of death and mutilation through an entire generation of young men.

The war did, however, bring some transient benefits to previously deprived elements in all the belligerent nations. Governments found themselves forced to intervene industrially and socially in an unprecedented fashion to mobilize all their resources to meet the insatiable demands of the war machines. The effort created conditions of almost full employment, and the working classes were now in a position to bargain for improved wages and better working conditions. Women had to be called upon in large numbers to replace the men who had gone to fight, and many left domestic service, the chief source of female employment before 1914, to work in the new munitions factories or in non-combatant roles in

The Russian Revolutions of 1917

In February 1917 the Tsarist regime collapsed in Russia, a victim of its own incompetence in managing a world war. The transport system was in chaos, there were acute shortages of food and clothing, and munitions were not reaching the war fronts. In addition, the armies were demoralized by a long succession of defeats and large number of casualties.

The revolution began when strikers demonstrating about food shortages in Petrograd (then the capital) were joined by the Petrograd military garrison which had been ordered to crush them. The Tsar's ministers were arrested and the Tsar was forced to abdicate on 2 March. The insurrectionists then set up soviets, or workers' and soldiers' councils, to monitor events and the Duma (parliament) which met on 27 February, fearing mob rule, hastily set up a Provisional government consisting of liberal politicians under Prince Lvov. It was hoped that this government would administer the country until a Constituent Assembly, elected by the Russian people, could be established. The soviets and the Provisional government co-existed uneasily until the Bolshevik revolution in October.

Imprisoned members of the various revolutionary parties, including the Bolsheviks, an extreme Marxist group, were released, while the German government, anxious to disrupt Russia's war effort further, allowed Vladimir Illyich Lenin, the Bolshevik leader, to travel in a sealed train from his exile in Switzerland across Germany to Petrograd. The Bolsheviks soon began to penetrate the soviets. The Provisional government meanwhile announced that it would continue to prosecute the war, and prepared for a new Russian offensive in the summer. This decision was not popular with the mass of the population, which was suffering from food shortages and war weariness. Meanwhile, the peasants were clamouring for the seizure of the estates of the nobility and their redistribution, which the government insisted must be done legally through an eventual Constituent Assembly. When A.F. Kerensky, the Minister of Justice, replaced Lvov in July, all he could offer was a more vigorous prosecution of the war. His position was further weakened when General Kornilov, the Army Supreme Commander, attempted unsuccessfully to overthrow the government in July. As the economy continued to deteriorate, and with the transport system at a complete standstill, Russia's armies, after further defeats during the summer, began to disintegrate as troops deserted in large numbers. The Provisional government staggered on until after an almost bloodless coup in October, Lenin and the Bolsheviks seized power in Petrograd. They had triumphed as a minority party because of Lenin's shrewd tactical skill in striking at the most favourable moment, because of the divisions among their opponents, and because of the disorder and confusion inside Russia.

◄ With the majority of men called-up to fight, young women and the elderly formed the workforce in munitions factories.

the armed services. (Many of these gains were lost during the post-war slump as demobilized ex-servicemen swelled the unemployed, although British women were given the vote. Dissatisfaction with the meagre results of war-time sacrifices became widespread after the war.)

The length of the war did encourage the growth of a strong popular movement in the West, spearheaded by the US President, Woodrow Wilson, which called for a new morality in politics and international affairs. War should be outlawed and conflicts prevented by a world founded on the principle of national self-determination, with an international organization to arbitrate disputes and maintain peace. This system was to replace the pre-1914 balance of power politics and alliance systems, and prevent the frenzied arms races associated with them, which many felt had been responsible for the war.

Wilson's vision was challenged, however, by an alternative programme put forward by Vladimir Illyich Lenin and the Bolsheviks, who had seized power in Russia in 1917. The European socialist movement had disintegrated on the outbreak of war, with the majority of socialists in every country supporting their governments' war efforts. However, Lenin's revolutionary Marxist party was bitterly hostile to moderate socialism, which had failed to act internationally to prevent the war and which had showed itself to be the ally of capitalism. Lenin's communist ideology envisaged a peaceful world based not upon capitalist exploitation and violence but on the victory of the proletariat worldwide. Communist propaganda seeking to undermine the loyalty of the proletariat in the West to the existing order terrified the bourgeoisie, and at the end of the war added a new and menacing source of instability to an irreparably fissured world order.

The Causes of World War I

Legend:
- International boundary 1914
- Central Power at outbreak of war
- State later allied to Central Powers
- Entente Power at outbreak of war
- Ally or associate of Entente Powers
- Neutral State later allied to Entente Powers
- Neutral throughout the war
- → Schlieffen plan
- Slav—inhabited areas of Austria-Hungary
- Ottoman lands gained by Balkan states 1913

0 km 400
0 mls 300

SWEDEN
NORWAY
FINLAND
L. Lado
Bergen
Christiania
Stockholm
St. Petersb
NORTH SEA
Glasgow
Edinburgh
DENMARK
BALTIC SEA
Riga
Belfast
UNITED KINGDOM
Gothenburg
Dublin
Manchester
Copenhagen
Danzig
Königsberg
Mins
Birmingham
Hamburg
NETHERLANDS
Amsterdam
Berlin
Warsaw
London
G E R M A N
Cologne
Leipzig
Oder
Vistula
Brussels
BELGIUM
Frankfurt
Breslau
ATLANTIC OCEAN
Brest
E M P I R E
Prague
Krakow
Lemberg
Seine
LUX.
Rhine
Paris
Reims
ALSACE-LORRAINE
Nuremberg
A U S T R I A -
Dn
Loire
Munich
Danube
Vienna
Tours
Berne
Budapest
Tisza
Yassy
FRANCE
SWITZERLAND
H U N G A R Y
Bordeaux
Lyon
Milan
Trieste
Sava
ROMAN
Rhône
Turin
Venice
BOSNIA
Belgrade
Bucharest
Toulouse
Annexed by
Austria 1908
Danube
Var
Marseille
Florence
Sarajevo
SERBIA
BULGARIA
PORTUGAL
SPAIN
ITALY
ADRIATIC SEA
MONTENEGRO
Sofia
Lisbon
Tagus
Madrid
Barcelona
Corsica
Rome
Cetinje
Üsküb
Durazzo
Tangier
Gibraltar (Br)
Balearic Is.
Naples
ALBANIA
Salonica
Gall
SPANISH MOROCCO
Algiers
Sardinia
Palermo
GREECE
Aegean Sea
MOROCCO (Fr)
ALGERIA (Fr)
Tunis
Sicily
Athens
TUNISIA (Fr)
Malta (Br)
MEDITERRANEAN SEA
Crete
Tripoli
LIBYA (Italian)

The immediate cause of the First World War was the murder of the heir to the Austrian throne, Francis Ferdinand, by Serbian-backed terrorists in Sarajevo, the capital of the Austrian province of Bosnia, on 28 June 1914. This assassination brought to a head the hatreds which had long poisoned great power relations. In 1914 Europe was divided between two hostile alliance systems: Germany and Austria–Hungary on the one hand, and France, Britain and Russia on the other. In 1904 Britain, increasingly suspicious of Germany's ambitions, had abandoned its policy of 'Splendid Isolation' and had aligned itself with France and, in 1907, with Russia to form the Triple Entente. Any conflict between two rival powers was therefore likely to involve the whole of Europe in a major war. An arms race, together with a series of international crises after 1900, had raised tensions to boiling point.

While Germany was by 1914 the strongest industrial and military power in Europe, it remained restless and insecure. It watched with increasing foreboding the growth of Russia's military power, and its fears for future security were enhanced with encirclement by the Triple Entente, and the growing enfeeblement of its only reliable ally, Austria–Hungary. Serbia was actively conspiring against Austria to bring about its disintegration and the absorption of the South Slavs into a greater Serbia. Serbian complicity in the murder of Francis Ferdinand provided Austria with the opportunity to crush Serbia before it was too late, and Germany urged Austria to act decisively.

Germany hoped that the ensuing conflict could be localized, but its own military and diplomatic strategy made this impossible. Faced by a war on two fronts against France and Russia, its generals had devised a war plan that would enable the main German armies to march through Belgium and defeat France before Russia could mobilize its forces and launch an offensive in the east. Once the French army had been annihilated Germany's main armies would then be switched to crush Russia. This necessitated immediate war with France in the event of a conflict with Russia, since the latter could be allowed no time to complete its laborious mobilization.

When Austria finally declared war on Serbia on 28 July, Russia, acting in defence of fellow Slavs, mobilized on 31 July as a warning to Austria not to go too far. Germany thereupon declared war on Russia on 1 August, and on France on 3 August. Its invasion of Belgium on 4 August brought Britain into the war in defence of Belgian neutrality, and a British force crossed the Channel to fight alongside the French army. All the major powers except Italy, which remained neutral until 1915, were now at war.

The Western Front

Bruges
Ghent
Brussels
BELGIUM
Meuse
Nieuport
FLANDERS
Lys
Namur
Dunkirk
Charleroi
Dinant
Passchendaele
July–Oct 1917
Menin
Escaut
Sambre
Ypres
29 Oct–11 Nov 1914
22 Apr–24 May 1915
Mons
23 Aug 1914
Givet
Messines
Lille
Strait of Dover
Calais
Armentières
Maubeuge
Neuve Chapelle
ARTOIS
La Bassée
No military activity–
actual front line indeterminate
Lens
Douai
Le Cateau
26 Aug 1914
Mézières
Vimy
Arras
Cambrai
20 Nov–7 Dec 1917
Boulogne
Bapaume
Guise
Flers
The Somme
June–Sept 1916
St. Quentin
Rethel
Albert
Péronne
PICARDY
Laon
CHAMPAGNE
Somme
Aisne
Amiens
Moreuil
Roye
Oise
Chemin des Dames
Reims
Noyon
Montdidier
Soissons
Maximum German advance
June–July 1918
Marne
Epernay
Compiègne
Belleau Wood
5–11 June 1918
Villers-Cotterets
Château Thierry
FRANCE
Mont mirail
Chantilly
Meaux
The Marne
5–10 Sept 1914
Paris
Coulommiers
Seine

Front lines 1914–1918

- 5 Sept 1914
- Jan 1915
- Feb 1916
- Aug 1918
- Nov 1918
- ⊗ Major battle

0 km 80
0 mls 50

With the outbreak of war in August 1914, powerful German armies thrust through Belgium and into northern France. By 5 September the Germans were 20 miles from Paris on the River Marne. Here the French rallied and forced the Germans to retreat to the River Aisne. After heavy fighting the front stabilized in northern France in November; a continuous line of trenches stretched from the North Sea coast of Belgium to the Swiss border, dividing the two sides. Repeated Franco–British offensives, notably at Ypres in 1915, on the River Somme in 1916 and again at Ypres in 1917, failed to move the front line more than a few miles.

The belligerents attempted to overcome the trench deadlock by using gas, tanks and aeroplanes, but artillery, machine guns and barbed wire remained the predominant weapons in this war of attrition. Attempts by the Allies to find alternative fronts to relieve pressure on the Western front, notably at Gallipoli in 1915, met with little success, and by the end of 1917 the Allied cause in the West had made little progress. Nor did Britain's naval superiority

enable it to defeat Germany at sea. The German navy only ventured out in force once, in May 1916, but the ensuing battle of Jutland was indecisive. In 1917 the Germans, in retaliation for the British blockade of their sea-born commerce, declared unrestricted submarine warfare against British and neutral shipping. The adoption of the convoy system in 1917 saved Britain from starvation, and the submarine campaign also brought the United States into the war against Germany in April 1917.

With the removal of Russia from the war in March 1918, the Germans switched the bulk of their forces to the Western front. By July the Germans had once more reached the River Marne. Heavy German casualties, and increasing shortages of food and raw materials resulting from the Allied blockade, enabled the Allies, reinforced by a million fresh US troops, to launch a counter-offensive in July which by October had driven the Germans back towards the German border. With its armies in retreat and its allies defeated, Germany signed an armistice on 11 November 1918.

German advance to 5 Sept 1914

— 22 Aug — 3 Sept

— 30 Aug — 5 Sept

◄— German advances

World War I: Other Fronts

SWEDEN

DENMARK

GERMANY

Berlin •

Munich •

SWITZERLAND

Alps

ITALY

Milan •

Venice

BALTIC SEA

Memel

Königsberg

Thorn

Breslau

Prague

AUSTRIA-

Vienna •

HUNGARY

Budapest •

Danube

Po

Petrograd

○ Riga
Sept 1917

Dvina

○ Vitebsk

○ Vilnius

○ Minsk

RUSSIAN

EMPIRE

○ Orel

○ Voronezh

Don

⊗ Gumbinnen
Aug 1914

○ Grodno

Augustow

Masurian Lakes
Sept 1914

⊗ Baranovichi

Pinsk

Pripet

Pripet Marshes

○ Gomel

○ Kharkov

Tannenberg
Aug 1914

Vistula

Brest-Litovsk

○ Kiev

Dnieper

○ Yekaterinoslav

Rostov

Warsaw
Oct–Nov 1914

POLAND

⊗ Lutsk

UKRAINE

Lodz

⊗ Krasnik

Lemberg
(Lvov)

○ Tarnopol

Krakow

Tarnow

GALICIA

Limanowa
Dec 1914

Gorlice

Przemysl
Mar 1915

Carpathians

Dniester

○ Czernowitz

○ Jassy

Odessa

Crimea

Sevastopol

BLACK SEA

Sinope

Tisza

Danube

ROMANIA
conquered 1917

Bucharest •

○ Constanta

○ Varna

OTT

Ankara

Caporetto
Oct 1917

⊗ Isonzo
1915–16

○ Trieste

Vittorio Veneto
Oct 1918

Sarajevo ○

Spalato ○

Belgrade

SERBIA
conquered
Nov 1915

MONTE-
NEGRO

ADRIATIC SEA

Nish
Oct 1915

Skopje

Monastir

ALBANIA

BULGARIA

Sofia •

Salonika
Allied landing
Oct 1915

GREECE

Athens ○

AEGEAN
SEA

Bosporus

Constantinople
(Istanbul)

Dardanelles

Limnos

Gallipoli Peninsula
Apr 1915–Jan 1916

Izmir

MEDITERRANEAN SEA

Alexandria

Legend

	Allied Powers
	Central Powers
⊗	Major battle

Italian Front

Front line

June 1916

Nov 1917

4 Nov 1918 at Armistice

Lines of advance

→ Central Powers, Oct–Nov 1917

→ Allies, Oct–Nov 1918

Eastern Front

Furthest extent of Russian forces, Aug 1914

Furthest extent of Romanian forces, Sept 1916

Front line at Armistice, Dec 1917

Lines of advance

→ Allies

→ Central Powers

→ Brusilov Offensive, Aug 1916

Boundary of Russian territory occupied by Central Powers after Treaty of Brest-Litovsk, Mar 1918

Given the vast spaces, the fighting in the East was much more fluid than in the West. Russia faced two enemies, Germany and Austria–Hungary. An initial Russian advance into East Prussia was repulsed by the Germans who destroyed the Second Russian Army at Tannenberg in late August 1914. Thereafter, despite inflicting defeats on the Austro–Hungarian armies in Galicia, Russia was steadily pushed out of Poland, while a Russian offensive in 1916 led by General Brusilov failed to regain much ground. The two Russian revolutions of 1917 weakened Russian resolve and led to a cease-fire with Germany and Austria–Hungary in December, in turn leading to the peace treaty of Brest–Litovsk in March 1918, which took Russia out of the War.

At the end of 1914 Turkey declared war on the Allies, and invaded Russian Armenia. Russian appeals for Allied assistance led in 1915 to an Anglo–French attempt to seize Constantinople and force Turkey out of the war. Having failed to take the Dardanelles Straits by naval action in March, the Western Allies landed troops on the Gallipoli Peninsula. The Allied troops were then tied down in trenches in the foot hills facing tenacious Turkish resistance from the high ground above. The expedition was evacuated in January 1916. An Anglo–French–Italian force occupied the Greek city of Salonika in December 1915, but did not break out and defeat Bulgaria until 1918. Italy had joined the Allies in May 1915 but failed to smash the Austro–German front despite a series of offensives along the Isonzo river. Italy suffered a major defeat at Caporetto in late 1917, rallied in 1918 and then defeated the demoralized Austro–Hungarian army at Vittorio Veneto in October.

In the Middle East, British troops attempted to advance from the Persian Gulf and take Baghdad in 1915 but were besieged by the Turks at Kut on the Tigris river and forced to surrender ignominiously early in 1916. Not until 1917, after Lawrence of Arabia had led an Arab guerrilla campaign against the Turks in Arabia, and British expeditions were mounted from Egypt and the Persian Gulf, did the tide turn against the Turks, who were driven out of Mesopotamia and Syria before they surrendered on 30 October 1918. Elsewhere, Britain, Australia, New Zealand, South Africa and Japan occupied Germany's colonies in China, the Pacific and in Africa, although a German force in German East Africa managed to evade the British until the end of the war in November 1918.

Middle East
— Furthest advance of Russian forces
— Front lines at Armistice, 31 Oct 1918
Lines of advance
→ Turks, Feb 1915
→ Allies
→ Arabs, Dec 1916 – Oct 1918

Making Peace

NORWAY

Bergen

Oslo
(Christiania)

SWEDEN

FINLAND
1917/20

L. Onega

L. Ladoga

Helsinki
(Helsingfors)

Leningrad
(Petrograd)

BLACK SEA

Sino

Stockholm

Gulf of Finland

Tallinn
ESTONIA
1918/20

L. Pskov

NORTH
SEA

Gothenburg

Ankara

Moscow

DENMARK

Copenhagen

Riga

LATVIA 1918/20

LITHUANIA
1918/20

Smolensk

TURKEY

Kay

SCHLESWIG
To Den. 1920
to Germany 1920

Hamburg

Elbe

Stettin

Memel Terr.
Autonomous regime
1924

Memel

Danzig
Free city controlled
by League of Nations

Königsberg

Kaunas

Grodno

to Poland
1920

Minsk

USSR

Adana

Alexandrett

NETHERLANDS

Amsterdam

Brussels

BELGIUM

Malmédy
to Belg. 1920

Cologne

Eupen

LUX.

Dortmund

Berlin

GERMANY

Leipzig

to Poland 1919

Oder

Vistula

to Germany 1920

Warsaw

POLAND
1916

Brest-Litovsk

Kiev

Dnieper

Cyprus
British Colony 1925

TEF
O
ALAW

LEBANON

Beirut

Damasc

SAAR
controlled by
League of Nations
1920-35

Rhine

Frankfurt

Nuremberg

Breslau

to Germany
1921

to Poland
1921

Bug

Haifa

ALSACE-
LORRAINE
to France
1919/20

FRANCE

Strasbourg

Berne

Danube

Prague

CZECHOSLOVAKIA
1918/19

Munich

Krakow

Lvov
(Lemberg)

TESCHEN
to Poland 1920

Dniester

Bug

PALESTINE

Jerusalem

Am

Dead
Sea

TRA
JORD

Lyon

LIECH

SWITZERLAND

to Italy
1919/20

to Aust.
1920

Vienna

Klagenfurt

AUSTRIA

Sopron
to Hung. 1921

Tisza

Budapest

HUNGARY
1918/19

to Romania
1919/20

Iași
(Yassy)

BESS-
ARABIA
to Romania
1918/20

Odessa

Sevastopol

BLACK
SEA

Aqaba

Sinai

Milan

Po

Turin

Venice

to Italy
1919/20

ITALY

Trieste

Fiume
free city 1920
to Italy 1924

Sava

Zara
to Italy 1920

Sarajevo

Belgrade

to Yug.
1919

Danube

BULGARIA

Sofia

Bucharest

ROMANIA

Marseille

KINGDOM OF
SERBS, CROATS
AND SLOVENES
1918

to Yug.
1919

Varna

Rome

ADRIATIC SEA

Durrës
(Durrazo)

Tirana

to Yug.
1919

Salonica

AFRICA

Naples

ALBANIA

Aegean
Sea

Togoland
Br/Fr
Mandate

Cameroons
French
Mandate

Palermo

GREECE

Athens

German
East Africa
British
Mandate

Sicily

Malta
(Br)

Crete

German South-
West Africa
Union of S.Africa
Mandate

IND

MEDITERRANEAN
SEA

Boundaries of Germany,
Austria-Hungary and
Russia 1914

Territory ceded by

Austria-Hungary

Bulgaria

Germany

Russia

Demilitarized Rhineland,
eastern boundary

Allied occupation with
bridge-heads

Under French occupation
1923-25

Plebiscite area

1916   Year of independence

International boundary 1926

0 km   400

0 mls   300

The peace conference which convened in Paris in January 1919 to determine the fate of Germany and its allies was dominated by the five major victor powers – the British Empire, the United States, France, Italy and Japan. The conference was divided from the outset by the rivalry between the peace aims of the US President, Woodrow Wilson, and those of the other great powers. Wilson's post-war policy was based on his Fourteen Points speech of January 1918, which called for a future world order governed by the principles of national self-determination and the prevention of future wars by a world-wide League of Nations. His idealism conflicted with the ambitions of the other four powers, which had made arrangements to annex German and Turkish territories.

French demands, however, caused the most controversy. Conscious of its weakness *vis à vis* Germany, France insisted that the peace settlement should permanently weaken Germany. Britain and the United States successfully resisted the demand for the severance of the Rhineland from Germany, but did agree to a 15-year Allied occupation and permanent demilitarization of the Rhineland and the virtual disarmament of Germany. France also called for the imposition of a reparations bill on Germany to compensate the Allies for damage caused by the war.

Five peace treaties were signed at the end of the war. The main treaty with Germany was signed at the Palace of Versailles, outside Paris, on 28 June 1919. It was followed on 10 September by the Treaty of St Germain with Austria, on 27 November by the Treaty of Neuilly with Bulgaria, on 4 June 1920 by the Treaty of Trianon with Hungary, and finally on 10 August 1920 by the Treaty of Sèvres with Turkey. From these treaties arose the new nations of Poland, Czechoslovakia and Yugoslavia, joining Finland, Estonia, Latvia and Lithuania, which had emerged from the wreckage of the Russian Empire in 1917. Austria and Hungary were divided, Romania was enlarged and Germany was reduced in size. Where disputes arose as to ownership, plebiscites were held by the League of Nations to consult the local populations, although some disputes, notably at Teschen and Fiume, were resolved by force.

Outside Europe, the Allies secured the bulk of their territorial and colonial demands, as German colonies and Turkey's former possessions in the Middle East were handed over to them. Japan took the former German concession of Shandong, amid strong Chinese protests. The entire peace settlement failed to satisfy many nationalist aspirations in Europe and the Middle East, but objections were brushed aside, only to reappear later in new and more threatening guises.

The Costs of the War

3,800,000

36.2
UNITED STATES

13,250,000

9,500,000

49.6
BRITISH EMPIRE

47.0
GERMANY

8,200,000

380,000
BELGIUM

28.2
FRANCE

13.
AUSTR

MO

5,600,000

100,000
PORTUGAL

14.7
ITALY

Europe 1914–18

Allied Powers

Central Powers

Neutral

Symbol represents
total number of
men mobilized

Wounded

Killed

13.4 War expenditure $bn

13,000,000

9,000,000

16.3

RUSSIA

1,000,000

NGARY

1,000,000   950,000

ROMANIA

000

RO

SERBIA   BULGARIA

GREECE

2,840,000

OTTOMAN EMPIRE

In 1914 millions of young men were conscripted into the armies of the belligerent nations and sent to the front lines. The Allies mobilized about 11 million troops in August 1914 and the Central Powers about eight million. In the long and bloody battles that ensued, in which the results of a half century of advanced military technology were fully employed, the number of casualties suffered on all sides was devastating. Indeed, in the case of Russia it was impossible to calculate a reliable figure. Of the other major powers, French deaths in the field of battle numbered about 1,400,000, German about 1,800,000, Austro–Hungarian some 1,300,000, British and British Empire 900,000, Italian 600,000 and American about 120,000.

In addition the war left behind an enormous legacy of indebtedness. In the Allied countries direct and indirect taxes were raised to unprecedented levels to help pay for the war, while Britain was forced to liquidate many overseas investments, suffering an outflow of gold reserves as it borrowed heavily from New York banks to sustain itself and its Allies in the struggle. By 1919 a complex structure of interlocking loans had been built up. Britain was owed at least $11 billion by other countries, and owed about $4.7 billion to the United States. France owed the United States and Britain a total of $7 billion. The war converted the United States from a debtor into a rich creditor nation, while Britain was now a new debtor whose plight was made worse by the loss of a considerable portion of its pre-war export trade to the United States, Japan and other countries, whose internal economies had not been badly affected by the war. After the war Britain and France pressed the United States to write off their debts as their contribution to the war effort. When the United States refused and turned down a request for reconstruction credits, the Allies sought to recoup their losses from Germany in the form of reparations. The French secured German deliveries of timber and other materials to assist them in the reconstruction of the shattered industries and mines of northern France.

Germany had paid for the war by borrowing heavily from the German people, and from using resources plundered from conquered territories, but by 1918 it, too, was economically exhausted and saddled with a huge internal debt it could not hope to repay. Germany was thus in no mind to pay the massive $32 billion demanded by the Allied Reparation Commission in 1921.

Chronology 1914–1918

EUROPE	AMERICAS

EUROPE

July • Austria–Hungary declares war on Serbia
July • Italy declares its neutrality
Aug • Germany declares war on Russia and France, and invades Luxembourg and Belgium
Aug • Britain and Belgium declare war on Germany
Aug • Germans defeat Russians at the Battle of Tannenberg
Aug • Japan declares war on Germany
Sept • Trench warfare begins on Aisne salient
Sept • Allies halt German advance on Paris at the Battle of the Marne
Sept • Russians invade Hungary
Oct • (to Nov) Battle of Ypres halts German advance
Nov • Britain, France and Russia declare war on Turkey

Jan • Britain announces naval blockade of Germany
Feb • German submarines begin blockade of Britain
Apr • Allies land on Gallipoli peninsula, Turkey
Apr • Germans use poison gas at the Second Battle of Ypres
May • Sinking of British liner, *Lusitania*, by German U-boat off Irish coast
May • Italy denounces Triple Alliance and declares war on Austria
Sept • British–French offensive in Champagne and Flanders fails to break German front
Oct • Bulgaria joins Central Powers and launches offensive against Serbia with Austria and Germany

Feb • (to July) German offensive on western front at the Battle of Verdun causes terrible losses
Apr • Easter Rebellion in Dublin
May • Battle of Jutland, the only major naval battle in the war between Britain and Germany
June • Brusilov offensive by Russians in Galicia
July • (to Nov) Over one million killed at the Battle of the Somme
Aug • Romania declares war on Germany
Oct • Greek fleet surrenders to Allies at Athens
Nov • Central Powers proclaim independence of Poland

Feb • Revolution in Russia leads to abdication of Tsar (Mar) and establishment of Provisional government
June • Sinn Féin riots in Dublin
July • Major Allied offensive at the Third Battle of Ypres (Passchendaele)
Aug • Revolt in Spain over home rule for Catalonia
Oct • Italians defeated by Austrians at the Battle of Caporetto
Oct • Russian Revolution: Bolsheviks led by Lenin seize power

Jan • Russia proclaimed Union of Soviet Socialist Republic
Mar • Treaty of Brest–Litovsk: Russia withdraws from the war
Aug • Allied offensive on western front breaks through Hindenburg line of defences
Oct • Italian victory at the Battle of Vittorio Veneto: Austria–Hungary surrenders
Oct • Czechoslovakia proclaimed independent republic
Nov • German navy mutinies
Nov • Kaiser Wilhelm II abdicates and Germany is proclaimed a republic
Nov • Armistice signed between Germany and Allies
Nov • Poland proclaimed a republic
Dec • Bolshevik rule in Estonia
Dec • Serbo-Croat-Slovene Kingdom of Yugoslavia proclaimed

AMERICAS

Aug • USA proclaims itself neutral
Aug • Panama Canal opened to commerce
Dec • British defeat German fleet at Battle of Falklands

Jan • House of Representatives defeat proposal for women's suffrage in USA
Jan • Pancho Villa of Mexico signs treaty with USA, halting border conflict
July • Revolution in Haiti: US troops occupy Haiti to 1934
Sept • USA loans $500 million to Britain and France

Mar • US punitive expeditions to Mexico continue
Apr • Nicaragua grants the USA the right to build trans-isthmian canal
June • Battle of Carrizal between US and Mexican troops
Nov • Woodrow Wilson, Democrat, re-elected US President
Nov • Jeanette Rankin, Montana, becomes first woman member of Congress

Mar • US marines land at Santiago, Cuba, at request of civil government
Apr • Following sinking of six US ships, USA, Cuba and all South American states (except Brazil) enter First World War on side of Allies
June • Brazil revokes its neutrality and seizes German ships
June • First US troops arrive in France
Dec • Prohibition in Canada

Jan • First US oil pipeline begins operation in Wyoming
Jan • Congress passes law in favour of women's suffrage
May • Nicaragua and Costa Rica declare war on Central Powers
June • New York ports close after sinking of nine ships by U-boats off Atlantic coast
Aug • USA severs relations with Russia

AFRICA, ASIA, AUSTRALASIA

Aug	• British forces capture German Togoland
Aug	• Japan declares war on Germany and seizes German interests in China
Oct	• Boer rebellion under Christiaan de Wet against British in South Africa crushed
Nov	• Anzac (Australian and New Zealand Army Corps) troops occupy Samoa and German New Guinea
Nov	• Indian troops occupy Basra in Persian Gulf
Dec	• Mahatma Gandhi returns to India from South Africa and supports government

Jan	• In response to Japan's '21 demands', China cedes all German interests in southern Manchuria and Inner Mongolia to Japan but rejects Japanese demand for virtual protectorate over China
Jan	• South African troops occupy Swakopmund in German South-West Africa
Feb	• Turks repulsed from Suez Canal
May	• Louis Botha occupies Windhoek, capital of German South-West Africa
July	• German forces in South-West Africa surrender to Botha
Sept	• British forces advance against Turks in Mesopotamia
Nov	• Chinese princes vote for establishment of a monarchy, with Yuan Shikai as emperor

Feb	• British, French and Belgian forces complete conquest of German Cameroons
Apr	• British surrender Kut-el-Amara to Turks
June	• Arab revolt in Hijaz begins as the Grand Sheriff of Mecca revolts against Turkey
June	• T E Lawrence leads Arab forces against the Turks
June	• Jan Smuts captures Wilhelmsthal in German East Africa
Aug	• New British offensive in Mesopotamia
Sept	• British troops take Dar-es-Salaam

Mar	• British capture Baghdad
Aug	• China declares war on Germany and Austria
Oct	• Germans renew offensive in East Africa at Battle of Mahiwa
Nov	• British defeat Turks at Gaza, Jaffa and Jerusalem (Dec)
Nov	• Balfour Declaration promises to establish Jewish 'national home' in Palestine

Feb	• Australians occupy Jericho
Aug	• Japanese advance into Siberia
Sept	• Islamic riots in Calcutta
Oct	• British and Arab forces occupy Damascus
Oct	• Turkey surrenders to Allies
Nov	• German troops surrender in Northern Rhodesia

SCIENCE & CULTURE

• James Joyce *Dubliners*
• Ernest Shackleton leads Antarctic expedition

• Albert Einstein extends his Theory of Relativity
• John Buchan *The Thirty-Nine Steps*
• Virginia Woolf *The Voyage Out*
• Outbreaks of tetanus in trenches controlled by serum injections
• Hugo Junkers makes first all-metal aeroplane
• Alfred Wegener publishes theory of continental drift
• Marcel Duchamp paints first Dada-style picture, *The Bride Stripped Bare*
• D H Lawrence *The Rainbow*
• Gustav Holst *The Planets* suite
• *SS Campania* converted into first aircraft carrier

• First tanks used in Battle of the Somme by British forces
• Typhus disease first isolated
• Refrigeration of blood for transfusion
• Margaret Sanger opens first birth control clinic in USA
• Claude Monet *Water Lilies*
• Dadaist anti-art cult flourishes in Zurich, headed by Tristan Tzara, Hans Arp and Giacomo Balla
• Jazz sweeps USA

• 100-inch telescope built at Mount Wilson in California
• First jazz recording by the Original Dixieland Jazz Band
• T S Eliot *Prufrock and Other Observations*
• The Gotha biplane is the first aircraft specially designed for bombing
• Women in munitions factories cut their hair short as safety measure, and 'bobbed hair' becomes fashionable in Britain and USA

• Béla Bartók *Bluebeard's Castle*
• James Joyce *The Exiles*
• Lytton Strachey *Eminent Victorians*
• Paul Nash exhibits paintings of Western Front Battlefields

THE NEW WORLD ORDER

Nationalist passions increased tension and instability during the inter-war period.

The end of the First World War saw the establishment of a new order across the world. In 1919 the United States and Japan had emerged as leading world powers and, with Britain, France and Italy, were to form the Big Five at the Paris Peace Conference. Russia was torn by revolution and civil war, Austria–Hungary had disappeared from the map of Europe, while Germany was at the mercy of the victorious powers.

The United States was, by 1919 a superpower, her industry and trade having expanded enormously as a result of her relative immunity from the 1914–18 conflict. Britain hoped that the post-war order would be based on Anglo–American collaboration to maintain world peace and stability, but any possibility of this was wrecked when the United States repudiated the Treaty of Versailles and withdrew into isolationism after 1920. The maintenance of the post-Versailles order now depended on Britain and France: Italy, dissatisfied with her gains in 1919, could not be relied upon to support them, and Japan took little interest in European issues.

Britain and France, however, soon quarrelled over the future of Germany. By 1920 the intense war-time anti-German feelings in Britain were subsiding, and a recession and increasing unemployment encouraged the British government to look to the economic recovery of Germany as a means of reviving British industry. France, on the other hand, fearful of the resurgence of Germany's industrial and military power, insisted on Germany's fulfilment of the punitive clauses of the Versailles Treaty, and particularly on the payment in full of its reparations obligations, seen by many French politicians as a means of impeding Germany's economic revival. France and Britain clashed repeatedly in the early 1920s over this and other issues as Britain sought to reduce the reparations burdens on Germany, a course which France rejected. This dispute culminated in a Franco–Belgian occupation of the Ruhr, Germany's main industrial region, when Germany defaulted on its reparations payments in 1923.

The new balance of power was thus inherently unstable, with the United States, the only power capable of mediating between Britain and France, remaining aloof. A shaky compromise was patched together between the two European powers in 1924 and 1925, when France was persuaded to reduce its reparations demands and withdraw from the Ruhr, while a series of multilateral treaties signed at Locarno guaranteed the western frontiers of France, Germany and Belgium. Germany then re-entered the concert of powers and for the remainder of the decade Europe remained relatively peaceful.

Outside Europe, the new world order faced a different set of problems, for while the First World War had led to the success of nationalist particularism in Europe, it had also generated intense

The Exploited Continent

▲ **Crowds gather during the Irish Free State elections in August 1923 in which de** **Valera's wing of Sinn Féin sought complete independence from Britain.**

Although South America was composed of independent republics, its resources had always been developed with outside capital. Most South American economies were controlled by overseas entrepreneurs, who helped between the wars to develop new industries based on the exploitation of tin, oil, copper, rubber and guano. Cattle, grain, coffee and bananas were also produced in abundance, mostly on large estates, but there was no developed peasant agriculture and the Indian tribes were pushed further into the hinterland.

After 1920 relations between the separate states of Latin America remained generally peaceful, although there was intermittent conflict between Bolivia and Paraguay over a border dispute after 1928, Bolivia being defeated in 1935. The Pan-American Congress, set up in 1889, was dominated by the United States, which intervened in Central America seven times between the wars to protect its trade and investment, notably in Nicaragua and Cuba. The Congress met every five years, but United States domination was resented in South America, and many South American states joined the League of Nations in the vain hope that it would provide a counterweight to the United States. The Congress organized binding arbitration in the case of border disputes in 1936, and in 1928, 21 American states signed a peace pact. South America remained neutral in the developing world tension after 1931, but the United States became concerned about the growth of fascist influence in the German communities in Argentina and Brazil.

nationalist feelings in the overseas empires of the victorious Western European powers.

The British Empire emerged from the war greatly enlarged as a result of its seizure of Germany's former colonies and its occupation of Mesopotamia and Palestine after the collapse of the Ottoman Empire. However, this outwardly imposing structure concealed serious weaknesses which were ultimately to destroy it. The cost of policing and administering the diverse and increasingly restive populations of the Empire was to become an ever increasing burden on an already strained exchequer. Furthermore, the extended nature of the Empire, dependent on the sea for its protection and commerce, posed equally expensive problems for its defence during the 1930s against hostile Japan and Italy. French and Dutch colonies in the Far East were to face similar problems including those of internal security and external defence during the period.

While paying lip service to Woodrow Wilson's principle of national self-determination in 1919, British, French and Italian politicians had no intention of applying this to their existing colonies or to their newly acquired territories; although they agreed to administer the latter under League of Nations mandates to create an illusion of international surveillance, the League's powers were minimal. Supplicants from Ireland and other disaffected nationalities in the British Empire were refused a hearing at the Paris Peace Conference.

The 'white' British dominions – Canada, Australia, New Zealand and South Africa – had already achieved self-government and autonomy from close Whitehall control, and the 1931 Statute of Westminster gave their independence legal validity. After a bitter struggle with Britain, southern Ireland achieved dominion status and virtual independence in 1921. However, for the most part the Western powers did not believe that colonial peoples were yet ready for self-government and even the governments of the Arab countries in the Middle East which had emerged after the war were deemed to require considerable European vigilance and the presence of European army and air bases to ensure their good behaviour. It was felt that the education of the indigenous inhabitants of colonial territories in the intricate arts of democratic government and administration would entail a long process of instruction.

The Far East

After 1914 Japan took advantage of the preoccupation with the war in Europe of its rivals in the Far East and seized Germany's Chinese concession in Shandong and its islands in the north Pacific. Japan also sought to increase its influence over the Chinese government by presenting 21 demands to Beijing in March 1915, which not only called for Chinese recognition of Japan's concessions in Manchuria and Shandong but would also have placed the whole of China under a virtual Japanese protectorate. Anglo–American pressure forced Japan to abandon the more far-reaching demands, but Japanese ambitions in China were to resurface in the 1930s. Japan also took the opportunity afforded by the Bolshevik revolution in Russia to occupy Vladivostock and eastern Siberia temporarily.

At the Paris Peace Conference, despite US protests, Japan retained Germany's former economic concession in Shandong – the United States had wanted the province to be restored to China in its entirety. In 1921 American and Canadian pressure forced Britain to abandon the 1902 alliance with Japan in return for US agreement to limit its naval building, with which Britain was finding it financially difficult to compete. The agreement provided for a 5 : 5 : 3 ratio in battleship strengths between Britain, the United States and Japan, which left Japan (with no global naval responsibilities)

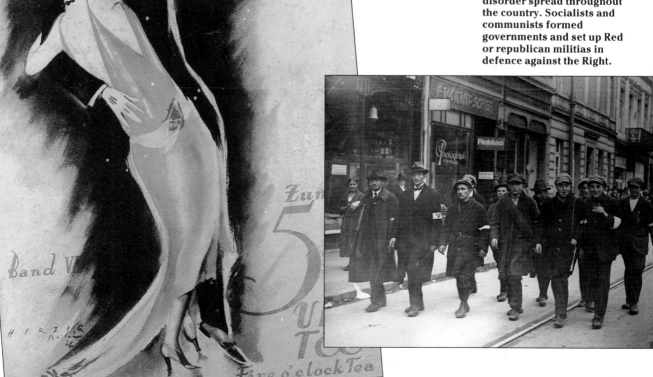

◀ A song sheet illustrates the elegance and daring of the 'Roaring Twenties'.

▼ With the collapse of the German economy in 1923, disorder spread throughout the country. Socialists and communists formed governments and set up Red or republican militias in defence against the Right.

supreme in Far Eastern waters. The Anglo–Japanese alliance was replaced by innocuous multilateral treaties providing for cooperation between the great powers in the Pacific area in the event of problems arising there, and a pledge that they would respect China's integrity. Japan also withdrew its troops from Siberia. The result of the loss of the alliance was that Japan no longer needed to respect Britain's views about its activities in China. Both Australia and New Zealand had pressed Britain to maintain the alliance, since they, like many British politicians, had little confidence in American willingness to join with the other powers in deterring any future Japanese advances in the Far East. In the last resort Britain, anxious to avoid a major breach with the United States, and conscious of America's financial strength, gave way to American pressure. However, until 1931, the civilian government in Tokyo was in full control of the Japanese military and pursued a relatively peaceful policy towards China, despite frequent Chinese nationalist interference with Japan's commerce and concessions in China. After 1931 the situation changed dramatically as Japan launched an all-out assault on China's territorial integrity while the other powers looked on helplessly.

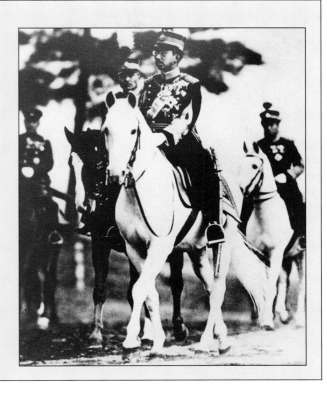

▶ **Hirohito became Emperor of Japan in 1926.**

The Western powers were faced with the greatest challenge to their domination in the Far East, where Moscow-backed communist parties and Japanese-financed propaganda in India, China, Indo-China and Indonesia sought to undermine the loyalty of the inhabitants to their European rulers. The nationalist parties were led by Western-educated middle-class intellectuals, who saw themselves as the natural liberators of their countries from foreign control and who demanded independence on the basis of those very democratic principles which the 1919 peace-makers extolled. Britain evolved a policy of granting limited self-rule to Indian assemblies, but nationalist discontent during Gandhi's non-violent civil disobedience campaigns, and the reluctance of many moderate nationalists to compromise themselves in the eyes of their supporters by associating with 'puppet' governments, enabled the British to delay any real transfer of power in India until 1947. In Palestine the situation was complicated by the influx of Jewish refugees from Europe, enticed there by Britain's 1917 promise of a 'National Homeland' for the Jews in Palestine. Their arrival was bitterly resented by the resident Arab population, and this resulted in increasing anti-Jewish violence during the 1930s which necessitated the despatch of strong British troop reinforcements to maintain order.

Nationalist passions created increasing tension and instability in Europe during the inter-war period.

In Germany resentment at the allegedly harsh and vindictive Versailles Treaty exploded in the 1930s into the extremism and excesses of Hitler's national socialism, which was determined to overthrow the entire European status quo in Germany's favour. In Eastern and Central Europe, Yugoslavia and Czechoslovakia struggled, and ultimately failed, to create unified states out of their ethnically diverse peoples. Poland, which had absorbed Ukrainians, Lithuanians and Germans during and after 1919, sought to maintain its integrity in the face of the demands of a resurgent Germany and an increasingly powerful Soviet Russia during the late 1930s for the incorporation of their fellow nationals into their own countries. After Stalin's rise to power, the non-Russian peoples of the Soviet Union, who had achieved a degree of autonomy in the early 1920s, were gradually brought under Moscow's control and cultural and linguistic separatism was suppressed.

In Turkey the nationalists, led by Mustapha Kemal, sought to modernize and secularize the country after its humiliating defeat in 1918. The attempt to reconstruct a solely Turkish Republic as a cohesive state brought the nationalists into bitter conflict with Greece in Smyrna and Thrace and a near war with Britain in 1922 at Chanak. Eventually Turkey succeeded in its endeavour: it was the only country in south-eastern Europe to preserve its independence and unity during the Second World War.

The League of Nations

GREENLAND
(Denmark)

ICELAND

NORWAY

SWEDEN

FINLA
192

CANADA

UNITED
KINGDOM

DENMARK

Danzig

EIRE
1923

GERMANY
1926 **1933**

POLAND

CZECH.

1 NETHERLANDS
2 BELGIUM
3 LUXEMBOURG 1929
4 SWITZERLAND
5 AUSTRIA 1920
6 HUNGARY 1922
7 YUGOSLAVIA
8 ALBANIA

FRANCE

ITALY
1937

ROMA

BU

UNITED STATES

SPAIN
1939

PORTUGAL

GREECE

EG

MEXICO
1931

CUBA

DOMINICAN
REPUBLIC
1924

HAITI

HONDURAS **1936**

GUATEMALA **1936**
EL SALVADOR 1924 **1937**

NICARAGUA **1936**

COSTA RICA 1924

PANAMA

VENEZUELA
1938

COLOMBIA

LIBERIA

(Br and Fr)

(Br and Fr)

ECUADOR
1934

BRAZIL
1926

PERU
1939

BOLIVIA

PARAGUAY
1935

(S.Afr)

CHILE
1938

ARGENTINA

URUGUAY

SOUTH
AFRICA

▇	Founder member
�	State admitted in 1920 by invitation
□	State subsequently admitted
▨	Colony of member state
▧	Mandated territory
▨	Non-member
1924	Date of joining
1937	Date of leaving

40

The United States repudiation of the Covenant of the League of Nations in 1920 was a major blow to the effectiveness of the League as an international organization. Given America's isolationism and Japan's lack of interest in events outside China and the Pacific, Britain and France were the only powers concerned with upholding the League as a peace-keeping organization.

During the early 1920s the League – which had its headquarters in Geneva – attempted to formulate arms limitation and collective security agreements as required by the Covenant, but these efforts foundered on the mutual suspicions and hostilities of the powers. The Disarmament Conference, convened in 1932, collapsed in 1934, chiefly as a result of Germany's demand for parity in armaments with the other powers and France's refusal to agree to this unless it received further guarantees of its security.

The League, which supervised the system of mandates and controlled the Free City of Danzig (Gdansk) in what is now Poland was presented with a first major challenge in 1931–2 when China appealed to the League against Japan's invasion of Manchuria. The United States refused to apply sanctions and Britain did not wish to become involved in war with Japan. As a result, the resolutions passed by the League failed to deter Japan's takeover of Manchuria. The impotence of the League was demonstrated in 1935, when despite the imposition of sanctions, it failed to prevent Italy's conquest of Abyssinia. The British government, caught between its unwillingness to fight and public indignation at Italy's aggression, adopted a pusillanimous policy which destroyed the League's effectiveness.

Japan and Germany left the League in 1933, and Italy in 1937, losses balanced to some extent by the accession of the Soviet Union in 1934. But its final act before it was overwhelmed by the Second World War, was to expel the Soviet Union following the latter's invasion of Finland in 1939.

China in Turmoil

Occupied by Japanese forces by 1933

Occupied by Japanese forces, 1933–38

Communist revolutionary bases, 1934–36

Main communist base from 1936

Central Red Army ('The Long March')
Oct 1934 – Nov 1935

4th Front Army

2nd Front Army

0 km ————— 800
0 mls ————— 500

USSR

MONGOLIA

Amur

Qiqihaer

Haerbin

MANCHURIA
Invaded, 1931

MANCHUKUO
Puppet state, 1933

Songhua

Shenyang

CHAHAR

JEHOL

KOREA
(Jap)

Port Arthur

INDIA

BUR

XINJIANG

SUIYUAN

Baotou

Beijing

Tianjin

HEBEI

NINGXIA

Ningxia

Huang

Taiyuan

SHANXI

Ji'nan

SHANDONG

Qingdao

YELLOW SEA

BUR

GANSU

Lanzhou

Yan'an

SHAANXI-GANSU-
NINGXIA R.B.

QINGHAI

SHAANXI
Xi'an

HUBEI-HENAN-
SHAANXI R.B.

Huang

Kaifeng

HENAN

JIANGSU

Nanjing

Pasi

C   H   I   N   A

SICHUAN-SHAANXI R.B.

ANHUI

Shanghai

Ganze

XIKANG

SICHUAN

Chengdu

HUBEI

HENAN-HUBEI-
ANHUI R.B.

Hankou

Hangzhou

Yangzi

ZHEJIANG

EAST CHINA SEA

Luding

Chongqing

HENAN-HUBEI-SICHUAN-
GUIZHOU R.B.

HENAN-HUBEI-
JIANGXI R.B.

FUJIAN-ZHEJIANG-
JIANGXI R.B.

Yalung

Yangzi

Zunyi

Changsha

Nanchang

Guiyang

HUNAN

JIANGXI

Kunming

YUNNAN

Guilin

HUNAN-
JIANGXI R.B.

CENTRAL
REVOLUTIONARY
BASE

FUJIAN

Fuzhou

GUANGXI

Xi

Nanning

GUANGDONG

Guangzhou

Hong Kong (Br.)

Formosa (Jap.)

BURMA

FRENCH INDO-CHINA

THAILAND

SOUTH CHINA SEA

Hainan

V
PE

Rise of the Guomindang
1932

rlords, 1926

undary of Warlord area, 1926

a controlled by Guomindang, 1926

a coming under effective Guomindang
trol at date shown

a coming under nominal Guomindang
trol at date shown

thern expedition, 1926–27

upied by Japan, 1931

USSR

Amur

MANCHURIA

Haerbin

ZHANG ZUOLIN
1928
Shenyang

FENG YUXIANG

Beijing

Port Arthur

KOREA
(Jap.)

YAN
XISHAN

SHANDONG
1930
Qingdao
under Japanese control
1927–29
subsequently
HAN FUZHU

Huang

Xi'an
1930

Kaifeng

C H I N A

Nanjing
Shanghai

8 SICHUAN
WARLORDS
Chongqing

Yangzi

Hankou
1926–27
1929

WU PEIFU
SUN
CHUANFANG

Hangzhou

Changsha

Fuzhou
1929

TANG JIYAO
Kunming

GUANGXI
CLIQUE

GUOMINDANG
Guangzhou

Formosa (Jap.)

FRENCH
INDO-CHINA

750
m

Hong Kong (Br.)

subsequently
ZHEN JIDANG
1929

nls
500

**General
Jiang Jieshi
(Chiang Kai-shek).**

After the 1911 revolution that overthrew the Qing dynasty, and the disappearance of the unifying Manchu bureaucracy, China sank into chaos. A semi-parliamentary government at Nanjing was established by the Nationalist party, or Guomindang, led by a Western-educated intellectual, Sun Yixian (Sun Yat-sen). It was opposed by a conservative regime at Beijing in the north led by General Yuan Shikai. After Yuan's death in 1916 the north–south divide became even more pronounced. In 1921–2 civil war broke out in the north between various warlords, while in Guangzhou (Canton) Sun Yixian secured Soviet assistance in strengthening his military forces and in reorganizing the Guomindang. His death in 1925 opened the way for increasing Chinese Communist party and Soviet influence on the Guomindang movement, which manifested itself in anti-foreign strikes and riots, a boycott of foreign goods and a campaign for the abolition of the privileges which foreign powers had extracted from China in the 19th century. At the same time the Guomindang army, led by Jiang Jieshi (Chiang Kai-shek), who had served in the Japanese army and had trained with the Red Army in Moscow, marched against the northern warlords, capturing Hankou, Nanjing and Shanghai by 1927, and simultaneously thwarting a communist take-over of the Guomindang.

By 1928 the Guomindang armies had defeated all the northern warlords and entered Beijing. A national government was set up and the nationalists were in control of much of China. By 1930 Jiang had become the real power in the Nationalist party. However, the new government's writ was a tenuous one. The Japanese had reacted violently to nationalist encroachments on their concessions in Shanghai, Manchuria and Shandong, and this boded ill for the future. Widespread banditry occurred after the disbandment of soldiers from the various civil war armies, famine was endemic, and a Communist government had established itself in Jiangxi in the south.

In 1934 Jiang's forces drove the communists out of Jiangxi. Mao Zedong (Mao Tse-tung) and more than 100,000 men and their dependents trekked 8,000 miles on the Long March north-west to Yan'an in Shaanxi province, 6,000 survivors arriving in October 1935, to set up a guerrilla regime there. The nationalist hope for a peaceful and modernized China with a strong central government eventually succumbed to the twin impacts of Japanese aggression and communist penetration of the Chinese interior. The invasion by Japanese forces, however, led to a truce between the Guomindang and the communists as they joined forces in the fight against Japan in 1937.

THE CONFLICT OF IDEOLOGIES

Both fascism and communism weakened the will-power of bourgeois governments.

The length and destructiveness of the First World War was largely responsible for the rise of both communism and national socialism in Europe. The chaos the war caused in Russia enabled the Bolsheviks to seize power in November 1917, with Lenin as Chairman of the Council of People's Commissars. The Bolsheviks appreciated as much as the fascists that they needed at least the tacit support of the masses to succeed, and Lenin's slogan 'bread, land and peace' appealed to Russian peasants, workers and soldiers alike. All the resources of the Bolshevik state were employed to consolidate the revolution at home and propagate it abroad – the Red Army, the secret police, political agitation, propaganda, subversion, diplomacy, and financial and political aid and advice to dissident elements abroad. Compromises with the capitalist enemy were regarded as tactical manoeuvres, designed to keep capitalism off-guard until such time as the onward march of the revolution could be resumed. Force and violence, both in word and deed, were the prime methods by which communism defended itself, and all anti-Bolshevik parties in Russia were ruthlessly crushed. The Soviet Union was a one-party state, and party membership was small and tightly controlled. Yet, while its revolutionary propaganda overseas alarmed the ruling classes, communism posed no real threat to the status quo in Europe between 1918 and 1939, and after the collapse of short-lived communist regimes in Hungary and Bavaria in 1919, no country became communist. However, the bitter division between the socialists and communists in Germany in the 1920s helped ease Hitler to power.

Fascism was also a product of the war's violence, although it also drew much of its inspiration from pre-war ideologies and insecurities, which manifested themselves in violent nationalism and anti-Semitism. Fascism capitalized on the dissatisfaction and unrest of demobilized ex-servicemen, of lower-middle classes made even more insecure by war-induced changes in society, and of ultra-nationalists and others who were bitterly opposed to the peace settlements. Since it was based essentially on the state, its ideology was not uniform throughout Europe, although it was anti-communist, anti-Semitic (except in Italy where there were few Jews), anti-liberal and anti-parliamentarian. It demanded the dissolution of the allegedly corrupt and inefficient existing order and its replacement by a new, vigorous and disciplined system which in its corporate aspects would control both capital and labour for the benefit of the nation. The very dynamism of fascism had widespread appeal since it promised renewal and revival after the post-1918 disillusionment. In Germany and Hungary, fascism

Inflation in the 1920s

capitalized on the bitterness of defeat and the harshness of the peace treaties, in Italy on the dissatisfaction with Italy's meagre territorial gains. In every country it harked back to a supposed former greatness. By 1939 it had captured Italy and Germany, but fascist parties in France, Belgium, Holland and Britain, the Falange in Spain, and the Iron Guard in Romania did not survive.

Both fascism and communism sowed dissension and discord, undermining the existing order, and helping to weaken further the will-power of bourgeois governments, particularly in France, to resist Hitler. During the 1930s, Stalin sought to forge a united front of the left to resist fascism and encouraged the formation of Popular Front governments in France and Spain for this purpose. But the suspicions of communism which had been aroused in the middle classes during the 1920s worked against the success of such experiments, while Hitler played on their fears for his own purposes.

Although both Britain and France suffered inflationary pressures after the war, it was Germany, Russia and Central and Eastern Europe that suffered the most. In these states inflation had a catastrophic effect. Russia's banknote issue increased fivefold during the war, but the value of the rouble was maintained by Allied credits and by making exporters take roubles rather than foreign currency. The Provisional government increased the money supply by five and a half times in six months in 1917, but following the October revolution economic activity came to a halt during the civil war and as a result of communist seizure of property and industries. The expropriation of foreign investments meant that the Soviet government was refused foreign credits. By June 1919, ninety per cent of Soviet expenditure was met by printing banknotes: inflation became uncontrollable.

The Weimar Republic, forced to pay reparations and committed to welfare schemes, began to print money to meet the cost. The Franco–Belgian occupation of the Ruhr, Germany's main industrial region, resulted in the Ruhr workers refusing to work the mines and factories from 1923–25, and output collapsed. The Berlin government resorted to the printing press to pay for essential services, and eventually the currency collapsed completely. By November 1923 the mark was worth one-trillionth of its 1914 value, and workers were paid daily, only to find that the mark had depreciated further by the time they came to spend it. Pensions and savings became worthless and businesses were wiped out. Although the currency was stabilized after 1925, the middle and lower-middle classes, who had suffered so much from this hyper-inflation, turned to the national socialists in large numbers when depression led them to fear renewed inflation in 1930.

Italy: the First Fascist State

Benito Mussolini was a journalist and former anti-war socialist, who had, during the First World War, become a fervent supporter of Italy's intervention on the side of the Entente. He owed his political triumph in Italy to his clever manipulation of Italy's disappointment at the meagre territorial gains in 1919 and of the distress which resulted from the post-war economic crisis in Italy. He set up the *Fasci di Combattimento* in Milan in 1919, a semi-military organization calling for the satisfaction of Italy's imperialist claims and for numerous internal reforms. After the war anarchy had spread across Italy as peasants seized land and workers occupied factories. Communist encouragement of these outrages alarmed the middle classes, who feared that the country was on the brink of a Bolshevik takeover. The fascists played on these fears, securing subsidies from industrialists and landowners and arms from a sympathetic Italian army. In October 1922 the fascists organized their forces for a march on Rome to overthrow the government, while Mussolini took advantage of the rising tension to bully the king into appointing him Prime Minister. Over the next four years he gradually consolidated his power by absorbing nationalists into the Fascist party. He secured centre party support for changes in the electoral law in 1923 which enabled the fascists to gain sweeping victories in the 1924 elections, and then took advantage of the uproar resulting from the murder by fascist thugs of the socialist Giacomo Matteotti to impose a fascist totalitarian regime. All other political parties were then banned.

The Russian Civil War

SWEDEN

FINLAND

Stockholm

L. Onega

Petrozavodsk

Archangel

Entente forces 1918

Feb 1920

Shenkursk

Helsinki

L. Ladoga

Vyborg

Tallinn (Reval)

Kronstadt

Narva

Petrograd

Yudenich 1919

ESTONIA

Dorpat

Novgorod

Maloya Vishera

Vologda

BOLSHEVIK

Vyatka

Glazov

Pe

BALTIC SEA

Valka

Psków

Yaroslavl

Kostroma

Kolchak 1918–19

Riga

LATVIA

Dvina

Volga

Tver

Ivanovo

Izhevsk

LITHUANIA

Dvinsk

Vitebsk

Smolensk

Moscow

Nizhniy Novgorod

Kazan

Königsberg

Kaunas

EAST PRUSSIA

Vilna

RUSSIA

Vistula

Aug 1920

Minsk

Mogilev

Kaluga

Simbirsk

Volga

Oct 1919

Warsaw

POLAND

Brest-Litovsk

Gomel

Tula

Penza

Samara

Pripet

Poles 1920

Orel

Tambov

Orenb

Lvov

Zhitomir

Aug 1920

Kiev

Oct 1919

Kursk

Voronezh

Saratov

Ural

UKRAINE

Denikin 1919–20

Kharkov

Don

Dniester

Bug

Dnieper

Poltava

Jan 1920

Tsaritsyn

Cossacks 1918–20

ROMANIA

Kishinev

BESSARABIA

Yekaterinoslav

Odessa

Nikolayev

Wrangel 1920

Nov 1920

Mariupol

Novocherkassk

Rostov

Volga

Astrakhan

Bucharest

Danube

Crimea

Simferopol

Mar 1920

Cossacks 1917–19

BULGARIA

Sevastopol

Novorossiysk

Piatigorsk

BLACK SEA

Sochi

Grozny

CASPIAN SEA

Entente forces

Vladikavkaz

Constantinople

Feb 1921

Caucasus

Apr 1920

TURKEY

Batumi

Tiflis

Kars

Baku

Entente forces

Krasnov

46

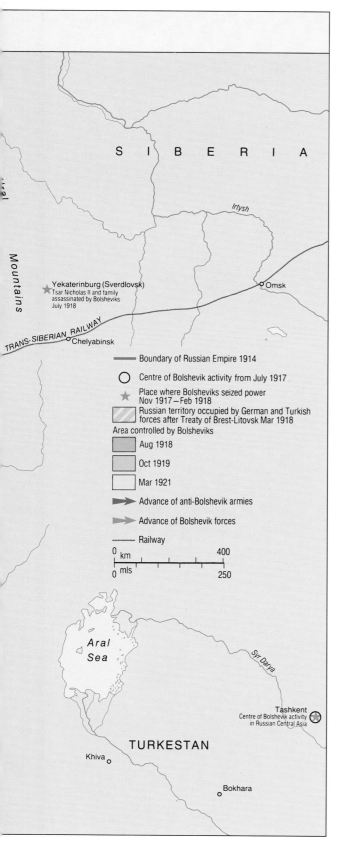

Boundary of Russian Empire 1914

○ Centre of Bolshevik activity from July 1917

★ Place where Bolsheviks seized power Nov 1917 – Feb 1918

Russian territory occupied by German and Turkish forces after Treaty of Brest-Litovsk Mar 1918

Area controlled by Bolsheviks

Aug 1918

Oct 1919

Mar 1921

➤ Advance of anti-Bolshevik armies

➤ Advance of Bolshevik forces

Railway

0 km 400
0 mls 250

The Russian civil war began in May 1918 when the Czechoslovak Corps (ex-prisoners of war who were travelling on the Trans-Siberian railway towards Vladivostok and evacuation) clashed with Soviet troops in the Urals and proceeded to occupy the railway. This occupation enabled counter-revolutionary forces (or Whites) to organize anti-Bolshevik armies in western Siberia. White forces also began to establish themselves in those areas of European Russia which the Germans occupied in March 1918. Although, during 1918, a small detachment of British troops landed at Archangel, Murmansk and in the Transcaucasus in support of the Whites, and French troops occupied Odessa, Allied intervention was at most half-hearted. By the end of 1919 they had evacuated their troops from Russia.

The Bolsheviks were threatened from all sides. In the Ukraine the Germans set up a Ukrainian separatist government, while in the south, a former Tsarist general, Denikin, formed a volunteer army consisting mainly of Cossacks and drove the Reds out of the Caucasus. In the Urals and Siberia, an ex-Tsarist admiral, A.V. Kolchak, raised an army and proclaimed himself Supreme Ruler of Russia in November 1918. Both these White armies met with initial successes in 1919. In the spring Kolchak nearly reached the Volga while Denikin's forces had advanced to within 240 miles of Moscow by October 1919. However, Red Army counter-offensives in the autumn drove Kolchak's forces back into Siberia and by March 1920 his army was crushed. The same fate was suffered by Denikin's Volunteer Army by the spring of 1920 and by his successor, General Wrangel, in the Crimea. A White army under former Tsarist general, Yudenich, which had begun advancing from Estonia towards Petrograd during the summer of 1919 was also defeated. The last major threat was Poland's invasion of the Ukraine in April 1920. This was repulsed by the Red Army, which drove the Poles back to the Vistula. Warsaw was saved by spirited Polish resistance. In October the two sides signed an armistice.

With the defeat of the Whites, the Bolsheviks were able to establish their control over other regions of Russia which had broken away after the revolution. The last outpost of resistance, Vladivostok, was recovered when a Japanese garrison, which had occupied the port in 1918, departed in October 1922.

The victory of the Bolsheviks was the product of a number of factors: the organizing abilities of the Commissar for War, Leon Trotsky, who recruited former Tsarist officers and built up the Red Army into a formidable fighting force; their control of the central Russian war industries; and the flexibility which Moscow's radial communications gave their forces.

Soviet Foreign Policy

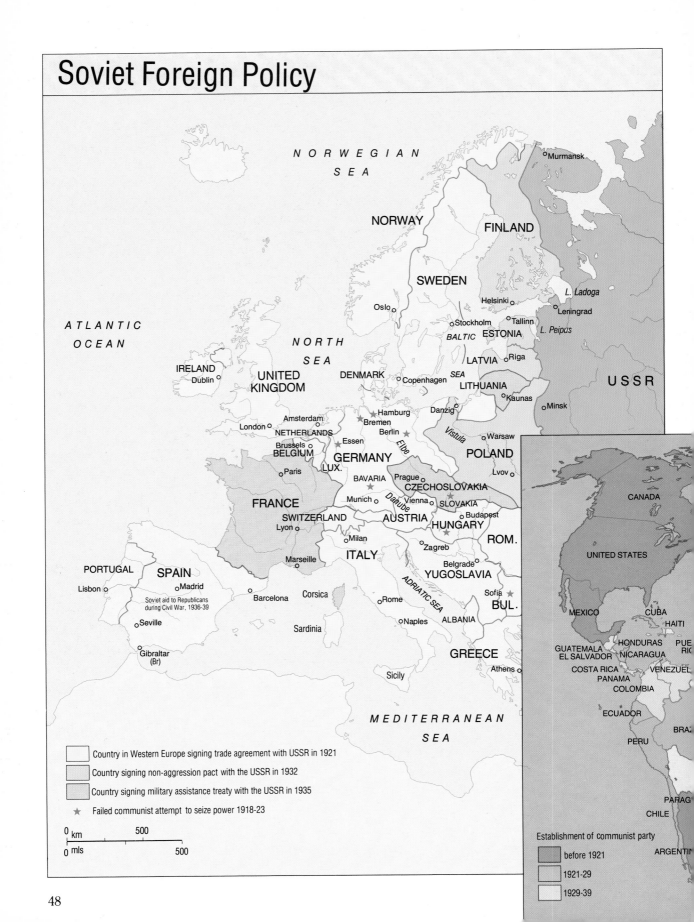

NORWEGIAN SEA

NORWAY

FINLAND

SWEDEN

ATLANTIC OCEAN

NORTH SEA

Oslo

Murmansk

L. Ladoga
Leningrad
L. Peipus

Helsinki
Stockholm
Tallinn
ESTONIA

BALTIC SEA

USSR

IRELAND
Dublin

UNITED KINGDOM

DENMARK

LATVIA   Riga

LITHUANIA

Copenhagen

Kaunas

Minsk

Danzig

London
Amsterdam
NETHERLANDS
Brussels
BELGIUM
LUX.

Hamburg
Bremen
Berlin

GERMANY

Elbe

Vistula

Warsaw

POLAND

Lvov

Paris

BAVARIA
Prague
CZECHOSLOVAKIA

FRANCE

Munich
Danube
Vienna
SLOVAKIA

SWITZERLAND
Lyon

Milan

AUSTRIA
Budapest
HUNGARY

ROM.

PORTUGAL
Lisbon

SPAIN
Madrid

Soviet aid to Republicans
during Civil War, 1936-39

Seville

Barcelona

Corsica

Marseille

ITALY

Zagreb
Belgrade
YUGOSLAVIA

ADRIATIC SEA

Rome

Sofia
BUL.

Naples   ALBANIA

Sardinia

GREECE

Gibraltar
(Br)

Sicily

Athens

MEDITERRANEAN SEA

Country in Western Europe signing trade agreement with USSR in 1921

Country signing non-aggression pact with the USSR in 1932

Country signing military assistance treaty with the USSR in 1935

★ Failed communist attempt to seize power 1918-23

0 km   500
0 mls   500

CANADA

UNITED STATES

MEXICO   CUBA
HAITI
HONDURAS   PUE
GUATEMALA   RIC
EL SALVADOR   NICARAGUA
COSTA RICA   VENEZUEL
PANAMA
COLOMBIA

ECUADOR

BRA

PERU

PARAG
CHILE

ARGENTIN

Establishment of communist party

before 1921
1921-29
1929-39

The Bolshevik victory in the Russian civil war in 1921 left the new regime ostracized by the outside world. The 1921 famine led the Bolsheviks to seek to restore trade links with the West. However, the results of these efforts were negligible. The Soviets refused to repay the Allied loans to the Tsarist regime which had been sequestrated after the revolution and so further Allied investment was not forthcoming. The activities of the Moscow-controlled Third Communist International or 'Comintern', which had been set up as an agency to spread revolutionary propaganda, further alienated the West. It fostered working class unrest in Western Europe and nationalist outbreaks in India, China and elsewhere in Asia as well as setting up and supporting communist parties around the world. The West would not accept the communist fiction that the Comintern was independent of the Soviet government. However, the failure of Comintern-inspired revolutions in Germany in 1923 discredited it in the eyes of Soviet leaders, and with Stalin's rise to power after 1924, the Comintern was brought more closely under party control. After 1927 Stalin launched an industrialization programme and the Soviet Union began to pay less attention to external revolutionary activity. A more peaceful Soviet Union

was then able to sign non-aggression and trade pacts with many of its neighbours.

After 1933, alarmed by the threats posed by resurgent Germany and Japan, Stalin became a leading exponent of collective security against fascist aggression. The Soviet Union joined the League of Nations in 1934 and signed an alliance with France the following year. Britain remained aloof, its hostility increased by Soviet aid to the Spanish republicans during the civil war, which led to fears in London of a Bolshevik Spain. Stalin's purges of the Red Army High Command in the mid-1930s convinced many in the West that the effectiveness of that army had been gravely weakened. Britain preferred to conciliate Germany, and when Moscow was not consulted in 1938 over the fate of Czechoslovakia, with whom the Soviet Union had an alliance, Stalin began to despair of his efforts to build up an anti-fascist front. In August 1939 Stalin signed a non-aggression pact with Germany, which in return for Russia's neutrality promised it eastern Poland. Stalin had achieved his ambition of keeping the Soviet Union out of war, but the cost was to be a heavy one for his country.

1 DENMARK
2 NETHERLANDS
3 BELGIUM
4 GERMANY
5 SWITZERLAND
6 ITALY
7 AUSTRIA
8 CZECHOSLOVAKIA
9 HUNGARY
10 YUGOSLAVIA
11 BULGARIA
12 GREECE

Russia under Stalin

BARENTS SEA

Novaya Zemlya

○ Murmansk

L. Ladoga

Leningrad

Archangel

L. Onega

○ Vorkuta

Ural Mountains

Ob

S

Minsk

Smolensk

N. Dvina

Yaroslavl

Moscow

Tula

Gorkiy

Kiev

Don

Kazan

Molotov

Sverdlovsk

Ob

Odessa

Kharkov

Dnepropetrovsk

Dneiper

Dnieper

Stalino

Volga

Kuybyshev

Ufa

Chelyabinsk

Magnitogorsk

TRANS-

SIBERIAN

Sevastopol

BLACK SEA

Stalingrad

Omsk

Novosibirsk

Stal

Astrakhan

Karaganda

Semipalatinsk

Tbilisi

Irtysh

Baku

Aral Sea

Syr Darya

L. Balkhash

CASPIAN SEA

Amu Darya

Frunze

Alma Ata

Tashkent

Ashkhabad

Collectivization of peasant holdings, 1933

Over 70%

50-70%

Under 50%

◯ Main industrial areas

■ Industrial cities

▨ Areas containing labour camps

ARCTIC OCEAN

Kolymskaya

Kolym

Indigirka

Magadan

Igarka

SEA OF
OKHOTSK

Lena

Yakutsk

B   E   R   I   A

Lower Tunguska

Upper Tunguska

Angara

Lena

LWAY

Krasnoyarsk

L. Baykal

Amur

Blagoveshchensk

Khabarovsk

Chita

Irkutsk   Ulan Ude

Vladivostok

The 1921 famine in Russia led the Communist party to allow the re-emergence of free enterprise in the agricultural sector. Lenin's New Economic Policy enabled the peasantry to market their produce and retain any profits that accrued. As a result, agricultural production increased significantly during the 1920s.

After Lenin's death in January 1924, Josef Stalin triumphed over Leon Trotsky in the struggle for Soviet leadership. Stalin then sought to strengthen the Soviet Union as the bastion of communism by a vigorous programme of industrialization and modernization under the slogan 'Socialism in One Country'. This was inaugurated in 1928 by the first Five Year Plan. Short

of capital and overseas credits the plan could only be successful through ruthless exploitation of the peasantry. After 1928 the peasants were forced to sell their produce to the state at controlled prices. They were herded into collective farms, and the richer peasants were deported to forced labour camps. Detachments of secret police enforced obedience to the system and, as a result, agricultural production collapsed and a terrible famine gripped the Soviet Union in 1932. Industrialization and urbanization, on the other hand, proceeded rapidly during the 1930s, and both output and gross national product doubled as new industrial areas were opened in the mineral-rich Urals and western Siberia.

The Rise of Nazism

to Oldenburg

SCHLESWIG-
HOLSTEIN

MECKLENBURG-
SCHWERIN

Hamburg

OLDEN
BURG   Bremen

HANOVER

Hanover

Brunswick   Magdeburg

Goslar   LOWER

ANHALT

SAXONY

WESTPHALIA

Düsseldorf

Cologne

RHINELAND

H
E
S
S
E

Frankfurt

to Oldenburg

SAAR   PFALZ

BADEN

WURTTEMBERG

Stuttgart

Leipzig

Weimar

THÜRINGIA

Nuremberg

BAVARIA

Munich

POMERANIA

Stettin

BRANDENBURG

Berlin

Frankfurt

Dresden

UPPER
SAXONY

Breslau

SILESIA

Königsberg

EAST PRUSSIA

German general election, 20 May 1928
Majority party by constituency

Social Democratic Party

Centre Party &
Bavarian People's Party

German National
People's Party

Communist Party

German People's Party

People's Party &
Agrarian Party

National Socialist German
Workers' Party (Nazis)

0 km ————————— 200

0 mls ————————— 15●

Percentage of votes cast

Centre Party
& Bavarian
People's
Party

German
National
People's
Party

Social Democratic
Party

Communist Party

German People's Party

People's Party &
Agrarian Party

German Democratic Party

Middle Class Party

National Socialist German
Workers' Party (Nazis)

Others

Nuremberg Party Day 1933.

The National Socialist German Workers' (Nazi) Party was marked by its virulent anti-Semitism and anti-communism. It was led by Adolf Hitler, an Austrian malcontent who had joined the German army in 1914. As a leader Hitler had charisma and was a compelling orator. After an unsuccessful Nazi coup against the Bavarian government in 1923, for which Hitler was subsequently imprisoned, his movement remained insignificant during the post-1925 years of economic recovery in Germany. It was given a new lease of life by the onset of the depression in 1930. The Nazis capitalized on the widespread unemployment that ensued – it reached five million in September – by promising to restore the economy and create full employment. It also drew on German feelings of superiority – the myth of the 'master race' – and dissatisfaction with the punitive terms of the Treaty of Versailles in order to increase its strength. At the general election of 14 September 1930 the Nazi party increased its share of votes from 810,000 in 1928 to 6.4 million, rising from 12 seats to 107 in the Reichstag, more than the Socialist and Communist parties combined, although no party possessed an overall majority. The Conservative and Nationalist politicians who surrounded the ageing President Hindenburg sought to use the Nazis for their own ends. Despite a set-back in the November 1932 elections, when the Nazis lost 34 of the 230 Reichstag seats won in July, former Chancellor Franz von Papen persuaded Hindenburg to appoint Hitler as Chancellor of a coalition government of National Socialists, Conservatives and Nationalists, with von Papen as Vice-Chancellor, on 30 January 1933. The Third Reich had begun.

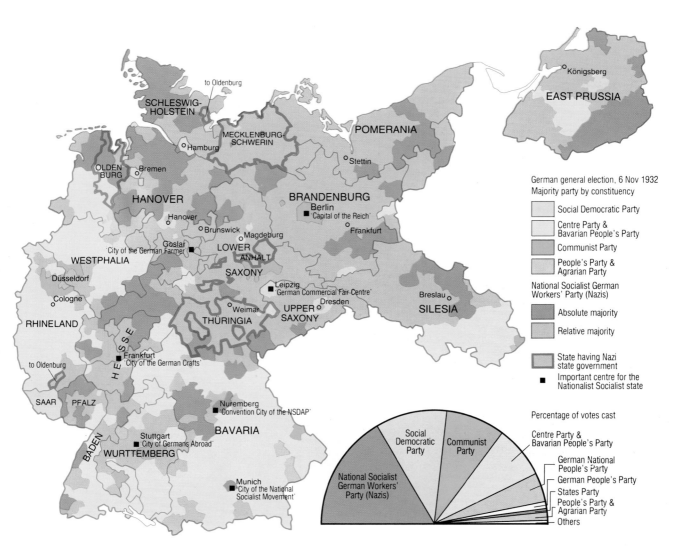

German general election, 6 Nov 1932
Majority party by constituency

- Social Democratic Party
- Centre Party & Bavarian People's Party
- Communist Party
- People's Party & Agrarian Party

National Socialist German Workers' Party (Nazis)

- Absolute majority
- Relative majority
- State having Nazi state government
- ■ Important centre for the Nationalist Socialist state

Percentage of votes cast

- National Socialist German Workers' Party (Nazis)
- Social Democratic Party
- Communist Party
- Centre Party & Bavarian People's Party
- German National People's Party
- German People's Party
- States Party
- People's Party & Agrarian Party
- Others

THE CRISIS YEARS

Membership of fascist parties escalated as the poverty-stricken flocked to their ranks.

During the 1930s the world order created in 1919 gradually collapsed under the impact of economic crisis and political extremism. The Depression, which began in the United States in 1929, and spread to Europe in the following year, created heavy unemployment and immense distress as banks closed, industrial production slumped and markets for agricultural products and raw materials collapsed. The imposition of high tariff walls by the United States and Britain made the situation even worse. The disaffected elements which had emerged in every society after the First World War, especially in Germany, Italy and Japan, but which had been contained by a measure of economic prosperity and political stability after 1925, became active once more during the Depression. Membership of fascist and crypto-fascist parties escalated as the unemployed and the poverty-stricken lower-middle classes flocked to their ranks. Ultimately the impotence of the German government in the face of the Depression and the electoral strength of the National Socialist party propelled Hitler to power in 1933. After 1930 fascist Italy emerged as a threat to the status quo in the Adriatic and Mediterranean. Japan was hard hit by the

Depression, especially as much of the trade vital to its survival was shut out of the American market by tariffs. The only outlet for Japanese trade and investment lay in Manchuria and north China, rich in agriculture and minerals, and it was in this area, weakened by civil war and revolution, that younger officers in the Japanese army saw Japan's economic salvation. They were behind the seizure of Manchuria in 1931 in defiance of their own government and the League of Nations. By 1934 the Japanese were encroaching on the rest of northern China and in 1937 full scale war broke out between Japan and China.

Nazi Germany also embarked on an aggressive foreign policy. On coming to power Hitler had inaugurated a massive rearmament programme, which he confirmed publicly in 1935, when Germany denounced the disarmament clauses of the Versailles Treaty. He took advantage of the breach between France and Britain on the one hand and Italy on the other over the latter's seizure of Abyssinia in 1935, to draw Italy into close alignment with Germany. The British Prime Minister, Neville Chamberlain, believed that if Germany's grievances could be rectified, it would become stable and peaceful. Britain and

◀ Sacred cows form the vanguard of a peaceful demonstration in Delhi. Between the wars, Britain also faced problems in India. The Indian National Congress campaigned for Indian independence throughout the 1920s, led by Mahatma Gandhi who adopted a policy of civil disobedience. During 1930 and 1931 the British met with Congress and Indian minority groups but no agreement was reached and, in 1932, Gandhi was arrested and Congress banned. Congress later agreed to cooperate with Britain's Government of India Act in 1935 which established Indian provincial administrations and a federal parliament.

▶ Nazi propaganda celebrates the Third Reich and Austria's union with Germany.

▶▶ Crowds mass in Lustgarten, Berlin, in 1936 to hear Hitler give his May Day address.

France did nothing to hinder Germany's remilitarization of the Rhineland in 1936 or its seizure of Austria early in 1938. Indeed, later in the same year Chamberlain supported Hitler's demand for the annexation of German Sudetenland, on the grounds of self-determination, thus destroying Czechoslovakia as a viable military and economic power.

Britain and France were also badly hit by the Depression. The weak Labour government in Britain collapsed in 1931 and was replaced by a Conservative-dominated coalition. This government, concerned at the fragility of Britain's economy during the 1930s, and conscious of its military weakness, pursued a cautious policy at home and abroad, hoping to avoid any collision that would bring it into conflict with a possible combination of Germany, Italy and Japan, which Britain could not hope to defeat. France, even more timid in dealing with Hitler, was bitterly divided politically and threatened internally by a combination of right-wing extremists and fascists who nearly brought down the Third Republic in 1933. However, democracy survived, as it did in the United States, despite the devastating effects of the Depression on that country's economy. Franklin Delano Roosevelt's election to the presidency in 1932 resulted in a vigorous assault on unemployment and economic distress – the New Deal – which, while only partly successful, saved the country from extremism. The Depression made the United States even more determined to remain free of international entanglements so it avoided any involvement in the dramatic events that were unfolding in Europe.

The Soviet Union was unaffected by the Depression. Stalin's alarm at the threatening behaviour of Nazi Germany and Japan in the 1930s led him to approach Britain and France to join the Soviet Union in an anti-fascist coalition. Western distrust of Soviet Russia was too strong to allow this, and Moscow was not consulted about the fate of Czechoslovakia in 1938. As a result Stalin, in disgust, turned to Germany in 1939 as a means of avoiding war, while Hitler sought further gains at the expense of Czechoslovakia and Poland. The stage was set for the Second World War, the conclusion, in W. H. Auden's words, of 'a low dishonest decade'.

The Third Reich

When Hitler became Chancellor of Germany in 1933 he began to consolidate all power in the hands of the National Socialist (Nazi) party. After the Reichstag fire on 27 February 1933 emergency decrees led to the arrest of communists, socialists and other opponents of the regime and their incarceration in concentration camps. The National Socialists gained a 52 per cent majority in the Reichstag elections of 5 March, and immediately passed an act enabling the government to rule for four years without calling parliament. Thereafter the freedom of the press was abolished, Jews were deprived of their employment, and the trade union movement and all other political parties were banned. When the Brownshirts, the paramilitary wing of the Nazi party, became critical of the slow progress of the Nazi revolution and demanded their incorporation into the army, Hitler acted on 30 June 1934 – 'the night of the long knives'. Brownshirt leaders were rounded up and shot, while a number of other opponents of the regime were also eliminated. When President Hindenburg died on 2 August 1934, Hitler took over the powers of the presidency, including that of Commander-in-Chief of the army, and he made the German army swear an oath of allegiance to himself as *Führer* or leader.

By 1937 many in the army leadership had become alarmed over Hitler's rash foreign policy. In January 1938 Hitler sacked the Army chief of staff and the Defence Minister, purged the High Command of anti-Nazi officers and replaced the remaining conservatives in his government with Nazis. He also became Supreme Commander of the Armed Forces and abolished the War Ministry.

Europe between the Wars

FINLAND

NORWAY

SWEDEN

76

NORTH
SEA

ESTONIA

93

115

Refug
revol

DENMARK

LATVIA

UNITED
KINGDOM

164

LITHUANIA

IRELAND

Germans from
former colonies

177

Elbe

Germans
1919-23

2236

NETHERLANDS

Vistula

ATLANTIC

OCEAN

36

GERMANY

Poles
1918-19

POLAND

BELGIUM

845

Oder

Germans

33

LUX.

SAAR

Refugees from Nazis
1933-39

CZECHOSLOVAKIA

Austria,
Czechoslovakia
and Hungary

Germans
1919-21

Germans

9

SWITZ.

414

AUSTRIA

Hungarians
1919-24

FRANCE

97

HUNGARY

ROMANIA

Turks
1913-3

PORTUGAL

Refugees
1922-39

Hungarians
1919-24

Bulgarians

YUGOSLAVIA

Turk
1913-

1013

Refugees from
civil war 1936-39

ITALY

Turks

BULGARIA

692

SPAIN

Corsica

1605

Bulgarians

ALBANIA

Bulgarians

Sardinia

Balearic Is.

GREECE

Turks

Sicily

MEDITERRANEAN

SEA

It took several years after 1919 before Europe began to recover from the devastating economic effects of the Great War. For a short period, between 1925 and 1929, the European economy recovered as international trade expanded and American investment began to pour into Europe. It is impossible to establish a definite connection between the economic wellbeing of communities and emigration, but during the 1920s emigration from Europe to the United States and Britain's White Dominions increased rapidly. On the other hand it fell markedly during the depressed 1930s. Following the treaties made after the First World War there was a great movement of people within Europe itself. With the drawing of new boundaries many people found themselves living under alien rule and vast numbers of refugees moved to escape from foreign powers and fascist and Bolshevik leaders.

With the October 1929 New York stock market crash, the post-1925 recovery was abruptly thrown into reverse and the capitalist economies of Europe suffered severely. As a means of overcoming the crisis they sought balanced budgets, deflation and public expenditure cuts which worsened the situation by further reducing purchasing power. Most European powers raised tariffs as a means of excluding foreign competition. Britain's system of imperial preference enabled an expansion of trade with the Dominions, while Germany arranged barter deals with Eastern Europe whereby she purchased their agricultural produce in return for manufactured goods. Unemployment levels in Germany remained relatively low partly as a result of the exodus of foreign workers after 1933. Everywhere, emigration fell markedly after 1930.

Unemployed workers in 1939 in Britain.

United States: The Great Depression

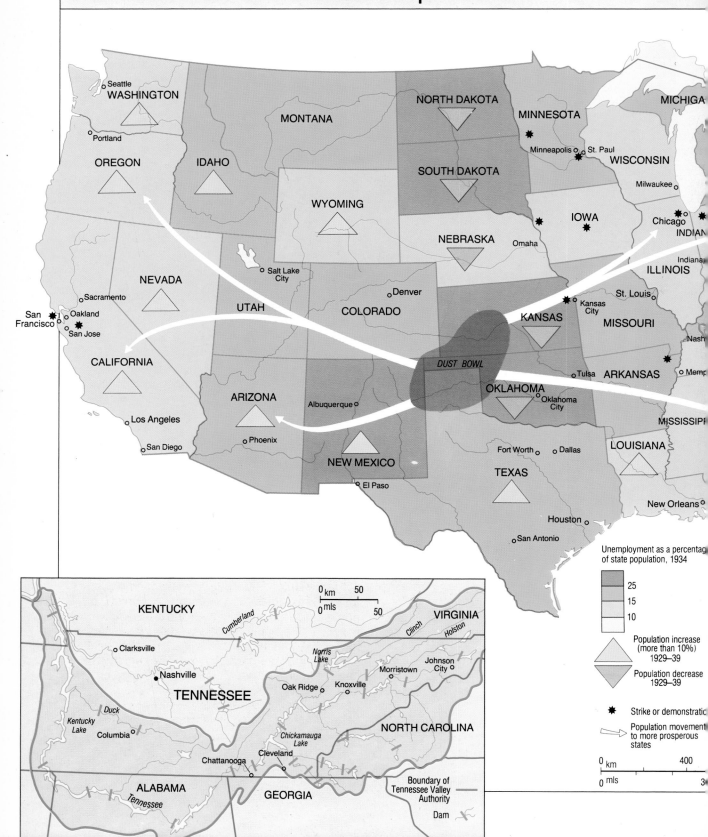

Seattle
WASHINGTON
Portland

MONTANA

NORTH DAKOTA

MINNESOTA
Minneapolis St. Paul
WISCONSIN
Milwaukee

MICHIGA

OREGON
IDAHO

SOUTH DAKOTA

WYOMING

NEBRASKA
Omaha

IOWA

Chicago
INDIAN

Indiana
ILLINOIS

NEVADA
Sacramento

Salt Lake City
UTAH

Denver
COLORADO

KANSAS
Kansas City

St. Louis
MISSOURI

Nash

San Francisco Oakland
San Jose

DUST BOWL

Tulsa ARKANSAS

Memp

CALIFORNIA
Los Angeles
San Diego

ARIZONA
Phoenix

Albuquerque

OKLAHOMA
Oklahoma City

MISSISSIPP

NEW MEXICO
El Paso

Fort Worth Dallas

LOUISIANA

TEXAS

Houston
San Antonio

New Orleans

Unemployment as a percentag
of state population, 1934

25
15
10

Population increase
(more than 10%)
1929–39

Population decrease
1929–39

* Strike or demonstratio

Population movement
to more prosperous
states

0 km   400
0 mls   3

KENTUCKY
Cumberland
Clarksville
Nashville
TENNESSEE
Duck
Kentucky Lake
Columbia

0 km   50
0 mls   50

Norris Lake
Oak Ridge Knoxville
Morristown
Johnson City

Clinch
Holston
VIRGINIA

NORTH CAROLINA

Chickamauga Lake
Cleveland
Chattanooga

ALABAMA
GEORGIA
Tennessee

Boundary of
Tennessee Valley
Authority

Dam

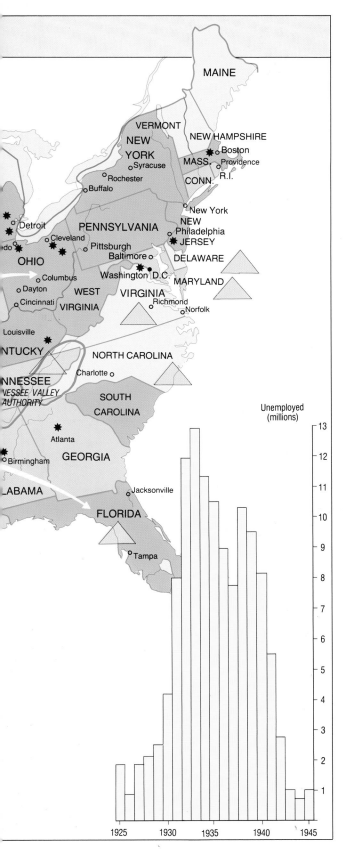

The beginning of the Great Depression is associated with the New York stock market crash (the 'Wall Street Crash') of October 1929. The immediate effects of the Wall Street Crash were a collapse in share prices, a withdrawal of credit, rising unemployment and the closure of many banks. At first, the US government appeared powerless in the face of such economic calamity. But the election of a new president in 1932 marked a new era in economic management.

President Franklin Delano Roosevelt's 'New Deal' involved intervention in the economy on an unprecedented scale and directly challenged the American tradition of orthodox budgetary management and free enterprise. During the so-called 'Hundred Days', from March to June 1933, he secured Congressional enactment of 75 laws, all of which sought to reinvigorate the economy. He restored confidence in the banking system, guaranteed farm prices, and tried to freeze agricultural production by paying farmers a subsidy for not planting their land. Attention was also paid to the problems of farmers affected by the creation of a Dust Bowl in the Prairie States after 1934 caused by overfarming of the arid soil. The Tennessee Valley Authority, intended to build dams to provide cheap hydro-electricity and to develop the resources of impoverished Tennessee and neighbouring states, was created in 1933. The National Recovery Administration was set up to aid businessmen, raise wages and cut hours. Later, unemployment benefit and old age pensions were introduced.

Industrial production rose steadily after 1935 and by early 1937 production was back to 1929 levels. High unemployment and unrest persisted however, as did the social dislocation caused by mass migration out of the Dust Bowl and other poor States to California and elsewhere in search of work, and many of Roosevelt's measures were declared unconstitutional by the Supreme Court. In 1937, concerned about budget deficits, he cut expenditure sharply. This resulted in a new recession in mid-1937, with two million being added to the unemployment totals. His policies were running into increasing opposition from businessmen and conservatives who were reacting against excessive state intervention and higher taxes on the rich. However, the 'New Deal' stablized the country politically and economically and provided work and basic security for many employees, farmers and home owners. The unemployment problem was not, however, finally solved until the United States began to rearm in 1940.

Democracies in Danger

Europe 1925

Authoritarian regime

`1923` Date of commencement of authoritarian regime

Parliamentary regime

Monarchy

0 kms 600
0 mls 400

FINLAND

NORWAY

SWEDEN

ESTONIA

DENMARK

LATVIA

LITHUANIA

IRELAND

EAST PRUSSIA (GER.)

USSR `1921`

UNITED KINGDOM

NETH

BELG LUX.

GERMANY

POLAND

FRANCE

CZECHO-SLOVAKIA

SWITZ. AUSTRIA HUNGARY

ROMANIA

PORTUGAL

SPAIN `1923`

ITALY `1922`

YUGOSLAVIA

BULGARIA `1923–30`

ALBANIA `1925`

TURKEY `1922`

GREECE

Europe 1926–39

Authoritarian regime

`1934` Date of commencement of authoritarian regime

Parliamentary regime

Country governed by Popular Front, with date

Monarchy

0 kms 600
0 mls 400

FINLAND

NORWAY

SWEDEN

ESTONIA `1934`

DENMARK

LATVIA `1934`

IRELAND

LITHUANIA `1936`

EAST PRUSSIA (GER.)

USSR

UNITED KINGDOM

NETH

BELG LUX.

GERMANY `1933`

POLAND `1926`

CZECHO-SLOVAKIA

FRANCE
June 1936 – Apr 1938

SWITZ. AUSTRIA `1933` HUNGARY

ROMANIA `1938`

PORTUGAL `1926`

SPAIN `1923–30` `1939`
Feb 1936 – Mar 1939

ITALY `1929`

YUGOSLAVIA

BULGARIA `1934`

from 1928

ALBANIA
Italian prot. 1927

from 1935

GREECE `1936`

TURKEY

In the 1920s the economic weakness of many of the newly independent Central and Eastern European states bred political instability, and in Poland, Romania, Hungary, Yugoslavia and Bulgaria conservative authoritarian regimes soon replaced the fragile democracies that had been established in 1919. Czechoslovakia was an exception in that it maintained its democratic constitution until 1939, but the country was much more economically and industrially advanced than any of the others. Austria depended on foreign loans for its very survival during the 1920s but its democratic system fell apart in the early 1930s. Romania, Czechoslovakia and Yugoslavia were reluctantly forced into a degree of political cooperation by the threat of a Habsburg restoration in Hungary in 1921, but they had few other interests in common: Czechoslovakia feared the revival of Germany, Romania of Russia and Bulgaria, while Yugoslavia was apprehensive of Italian ambitions along the Dalmatian coast. Poland remained apart: it had serious boundary disputes with Czechoslovakia and Lithuania, and dreaded the resurgence of Russia and Germany.

The weaknesses and divisions of these four states made them tempting targets for German economic and political penetration during the 1920s and 1930s. Faced with threats of a resurgent Germany and a communist Soviet Union, the four states allied themselves with Germany's traditional enemy, France. During the 1920s, Poland, Czechoslovakia, Yugoslavia and Romania all signed treaties with France which were designed both to secure the Versailles settlement and to enhance French security against Germany. France, however, was a far from stable partner in these alliances.

Between 1918 and 1940 the Third Republic in France saw more than 40 governments. However, the threat to French democracy was more apparent than real, since the Radical Socialist party was the mainstay of most French cabinets during the period, its ministers merely exchanging offices when governments changed. The French civil service provided the state with administrative continuity, while the French army was loyal to the Republic. The Republic's existence was only seriously challenged in 1934, when the suicide of Serge Stavisky, a fraudulent Jewish businessman, exposed a major financial scandal, the latest in a long series, in which many cabinet ministers and parliamentary deputies were implicated. This scandal coincided with the worst effects of the depression on France. As a result a number of extreme right-wing groups and the communists joined together to assault the discredited democratic system, and in so doing aroused considerable anti-Semitic feeling. After demonstrations in Paris on 6 February, a large crowd of rioters attempted to storm the Chamber of Deputies, but were eventually dispersed by the police. While there was much support for the extremists, the various right-wing leagues lacked a single leader or a unifying ideology: they were variously fascist, monarchist or Catholic. The election of a Popular Front government, which had communist support in 1936 alarmed the bourgeoisie but it collapsed in April 1938, and was succeeded by a Radical Socialist cabinet which remained in power until May 1940, when the Republic finally collapsed amid German conquest.

Percentage of votes cast for the
Popular Front in France, 26 April 1936
(by department)

60   52·5   45   37·5   30   22·5

The Spanish Civil War

French naval patrol

British naval patrol

El Ferrol
La Coruña
Gijón
Oct 1937
Oviedo
Oct 1936
Bilbao
June 1937
Guernica
Destroyed
in bombing raid
27 Apr 1937
San Sebastián
Sept 1936
Frontier closed
by France
13 July 1938

Pontevedra
León
Pamplona
Logroño
Huesca

Vigo
Orense
Burgos
Nationalist
Headquarters
Ebro
Zaragoza

CAT

Porto
Valladolid
OLD CASTILE
Duero
Lérida
Mar 1938

Salamanca

PORTUGAL
Madrid
Falls to Nationalists
28 Mar 1939
Teruel

Cáceres
Tagus
Toledo
Sept 1936
NEW CASTILE
Cuenca
Castellón
June 1938

Lisbon
Badajoz
Aug 1936
Ciudad Real
Mass execution carried out
by Republicans, 1936
Jucar
Valencia
Mar 1939

Albacete
Headquarters of the
International Brigade

Guadiana
Alicante

Córdoba
Jaén
Cartagena

Nationalist supply route (from Hamburg)
Guadalquivir
ANDALUSIA

Huelva
Seville
Granada

Almeria

German naval patrol

Málaga
Feb 1937

Cadiz
Gibraltar (Br.)
British naval patrol

Ceuta
French naval patrol

Tangier
60,000 Rif
mercenaries
recruited by Franco

Melilla

SPANISH MOROCCO

FRENCH
MOROCCO

Area under Nationalist control by

- July 1936
- Oct 1937
- July 1938
- Mar 1939

Nationalist supply route
Republican supply route
○ Nationalist base
● Republican base

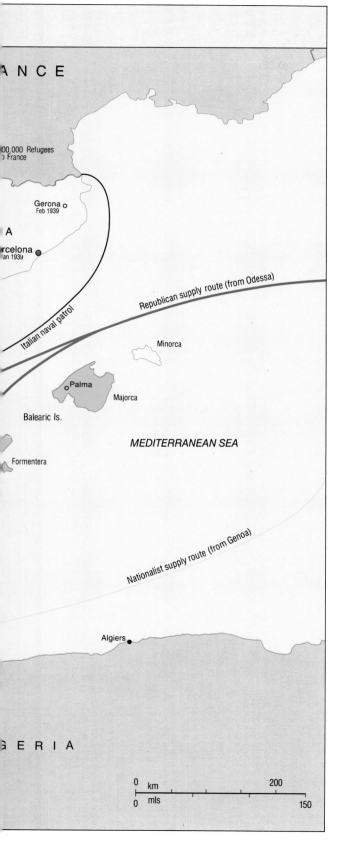

N C E

100,000 Refugees
to France

Gerona o
Feb 1939

A

rcelona ●
an 1939

Italian naval patrol

Republican supply route (from Odessa)

Minorca

o Palma

Majorca

Balearic Is.

Formentera

MEDITERRANEAN SEA

Nationalist supply route (from Genoa)

Algiers ●

G E R I A

| 0 | km | | 200 |
| 0 | mls | | 150 |

In the 1930s Republican Spain was polarized not only between Left and Right, but between monarchists and republicans, fascists and communists, traditionalists and modernists, anarchists and conservatives. Violence and disorder were endemic. The elections of February 1936 resulted in a Popular Front government, led by Manuel Azana, consisting of liberals, socialists, communists and anarchists. Many people feared either a right-wing coup or a bloody revolution. The middle classes and landowners in particular feared that the new government would expropriate their property, while the government itself seemed unable or unwilling to stem the general disorder which spread across the country. On 17 July 1936 the Spanish army, led by General Francisco Franco, intervened, bringing troops over from Spanish Morocco to crush the government. Franco had no clear programme beyond overthrowing the Republic, but by 1937 he had brought the other right-wing parties, including the Falange, under army control and into an amorphous Nationalist movement.

The civil war was marked by fearful violence and atrocities on both sides. On the Republican side, especially in the early days, violence was spontaneous and personal. Large numbers of priests were tortured and murdered, 'class enemies' were shot out of hand. Nationalist violence consisted of more organized massacres of prisoners and political opponents. Public opinion outside Spain was, initially, largely against the Republicans, and many saw the situation as another Bolshevik revolution. Britain and France adopted a policy of non-intervention, fearing that great power involvement might result in a major war. However, Italy sent military assistance to Franco, while Germany provided his forces with tanks, aircraft and advisers. The Soviet Union provided aid to the Republicans, and thousands of volunteers joined 'International Brigades' to fight on the Republican side. The war became a great ideological crusade for the Left.

At the outset the Spanish government controlled the east and centre of Spain and the Basque country in the north. The war lasted three years, with Franco's forces gradually getting the upper hand. The Nationalist victory, in March 1939, was based on its superior resources and unity of command. The Republicans suffered from deep divisions within their ranks, and inadequate supplies; by the end of the war their centres of power had been isolated by the Nationalists. The legacy of the civil war was oppression, bitterness or exile. Nationalist reprisals after the war were severe, but Franco established an uneasy peace and by keeping Spain out of the Second World War laid the foundations for gradual recovery.

The Path to War

SWEDEN

DENMARK

NORTH SEA

• Copenhagen

BALTIC SEA

Königs

Danz

UNITED KINGDOM

• Kiel

Hamburg •

Stettin •

• Bydgoszcz

• London

Amsterdam •

NETHERLANDS

Hanover •

Brunswick •

Berlin •

• Poznan

Lodz

Vistula

Ems

Magdeburg •

• Brussels

BELGIUM

Essen •

GERMANY

Breslau •

Oder

Cologne •

Kassel •

Leipzig •

Elbe

Rhine

Dresden •

Kat

Demilitarized Rhineland occupied Mar 1936

LUXEMBOURG

Frankfurt •

Ceded to Germany by Czechoslovakia at Munich agreement Oct 1938

SUDETENLAND

Prague •

SUDETEN-LAND

Krak to Polar Czechos Sept

• Paris

Würzburg •

Pilsen •

BOHEMIA-MORAVIA
Invaded Mar 1939

Saarbrücken •
SAAR to Germany by plebiscite Mar 1935

Nuremberg •

• Brno

SLOVAK
Satellite, Mar

Karlsruhe •

FRANCE

• Stuttgart

Danube

Bratislava •
Oct 1938

Rhine

Augsburg •

Linz •

Vienna •

Budapest •

HUNGA

• Berne

Munich •

SWITZERLAND

• Salzburg

AUSTRIA
Annexed Mar 1938

Graz •

Tisza

Innsbruck •

Drava

Drava

Suba

Milan •

Zagreb •

Venice •

Trieste •

Sava

ITALY

YUGOSLAVIA

Florence •

Nazi Germany, 1933-35

Territory gained

1935-36

1938

1939

Boundary of Germany
1 Sept 1939

Other international boundaries,
1 Sept 1939

Autobahns 1939

Constructed

planned

Under the impact of Hitler's moves in Europe, Mussolini's seizure of Abyssinia in 1935–6 and Albania in 1939, and Japan's advance into China after 1931, the 1930s witnessed the gradual disintegration of the world order established in 1919. The first major blow to the Versailles system was Germany's remilitarization of the Rhineland on 7 March 1936. Beyond making diplomatic protests, Britain and France did nothing to resist Hitler's move. Indeed, when Neville Chamberlain became British Prime Minister in 1937, he adopted a policy of conciliating or appeasing Hitler in the hope that if the Western democracies satisfied Germany's legitimate demands for territorial revision it might settle down to become a peaceful member of the European community. In this policy Chamberlain gravely miscalculated, since Hitler was not interested merely in alterations to the status quo in Europe: he wanted to overthrow it altogether in Germany's favour. Thus Britain and France again did nothing when Hitler forced Austria into union with Germany (the *Anschluss*) – forbidden under the Versailles Treaty – in March 1938. He next demanded, on the grounds of national self-determination, the severing of Sudetenland, with its German population, from Czechoslovakia and its incorporation with Germany. At the Munich Conference on 29 September 1938, Britain and France acceded to this demand, although the loss of Sudetenland destroyed Czechoslovakia's defences and demoralized the Czechoslovak army. In March 1939 German troops occupied the rest of Czechoslovakia. Chamberlain reacted by guaranteeing Poland's independence – after Hitler demanded the transfer of Danzig and the Polish Corridor to Germany – and joined France in mutual support of Poland. Chamberlain also opened negotiations in Moscow for an alliance with the Soviet Union. These measures failed to prevent war: on 23 August Hitler and Stalin signed a non-aggression pact, and confident that Britain and France would not now intervene, Germany invaded Poland on 1 September. Britain and France declared war on Germany on 3 September.

None of the Western democracies emerged with much credit from these events. An earlier and more determined Allied response might have stopped Hitler but by 1939 he was buoyed up by his previous successes and convinced that he had little to fear from France and Britain. The United States remained aloof from Europe, and did nothing to resist acts of aggression which would ultimately threaten American security. Indeed, during the 1930s, Congress strengthened isolationism by passing neutrality legislation making it impossible for the Allies to raise American loans in the event of war.

Chronology 1919–1939

EUROPE	AMERICAS

1919

EUROPE

- May • Bavarian government troops capture Munich from communists: civil war breaks out and a right-wing government is established
- June • Peace Treaty signed at Versailles, after German–Austrian protests over its terms
- June • German fleet scuttled at Scapa Flow
- Aug • Hungarian Socialist regime under Béla Kun overthrown by Admiral Horthy
- Dec • German troops evacuate Latvia and Lithuania

AMERICAS

- Mar • Bankruptcy of Canadian Grand Trunk Pacific Railway
- Apr • Rioting against conscription in Quebec
- June • Nicaragua asks USA for protection against Costa Rica
- July • Race riots in Chicago
- Sept • Steel strike in USA
- Dec • US House of Representatives moves to curtail immigration

1920

EUROPE

- Apr • Russo–Polish war (to Oct)
- Nov • First full-time session of League of Nations

AMERICAS

- Jan • Prohibition of alcohol in USA
- May • Venustiano Carranza, President of Mexico, deposed and replaced by General Aluaro Obrezon

1921

EUROPE

- Jan • Paris Conference: Germany to pay £11,300 million in reparations over 42 years
- Mar • Treaty of Riga ends Soviet–Polish war
- Dec • Anglo–Irish Treaty creates the Irish Free State

AMERICAS

- Mar • Warren Harding (Republican) becomes US President
- Aug • USA makes peace treaties with Germany, Austria and Hungary

1922

EUROPE

- Mar • End of civil war in USSR
- Apr • Civil war in Ireland (to Apr 1923)
- Aug • Greco–Turkish war ends in Greek defeat (Sept)
- Oct • Italian fascists march on Rome and Benito Mussolini becomes Italian Prime Minister

1923

EUROPE

- Jan • Default by Germany on reparation payments
- Feb • France and Belgium occupy Ruhr to obtain reparations from Germany
- July • Non-fascist parties dissolved in Italy
- Nov • Failure of Adolf Hitler's coup d'état in Munich

AMERICAS

- Aug • Calvin Coolidge (Republican) becomes President of USA on sudden death of Harding
- Sept • USA resumes relations with Mexico

1924

EUROPE

- Jan • First British Labour government formed under Ramsay Macdonald
- Oct • 'Zinoviev letter' allegedly urging revolution in Britain brings down Labour 1924

AMERICAS

- Feb • US troops land in Honduras
- July • Elias Calles elected President of Mexico

1925

EUROPE

- July • France and Belgium evacuate Ruhr after Dawes Plan proposals compromise on reparations
- Oct • Adolf Hitler publishes *Mein Kampf*
- Oct • Treaty of Locarno guarantees Germany's western frontiers

AMERICAS

- Dec • Freehold of oil companies in Mexico abolished, replaced by 50-year leases

1926

EUROPE

- May • General strike in Britain
- May • General Pilsudski instigates coup d'état in Poland
- Sept • Germany admitted to League of Nations

AMERICAS

- May • Mexico nationalizes minerals and oils
- July • Anti-church legislation in Mexico

1927

EUROPE

- July • Socialist riots in Vienna following acquittal of Nazis for political murder

AMERICAS

- Apr • Carlos Ibanez assumes dictatorship in Chile and is elected President (May)

1928

EUROPE

- Jan • Leon Trotsky deported to Siberia: Stalin emerges as sole ruler in USSR

AMERICAS

- July • Carlos Ibanez, President of Chile, resigns and is succeeded by Montero (Oct)
- Nov • Herbert Hoover (Republican) elected President of USA

1929

EUROPE

- Feb • Vatican City becomes independent state within Italy
- May • General Election in Britain won by Labour: Ramsay MacDonald forms his second administration (to 1931)
- Dec • Unemployment in Germany exceeds three million

AMERICAS

- Sept • Peace between Paraguay and Bolivia
- Oct • Wall Street Crash: 'Black Friday' heralds beginning of world economic crisis
- Nov • Ortez Rubio elected President of Mexico

AFRICA, ASIA, AUSTRALASIA

Mar	• Nationalist riots in Cairo against British rule following deportation of Said Zaghul Pasha
Apr	• Amritsar massacre in Punjab as British troops fire on nationalist rioters
May	• War between British India and Afghanistan (to Aug)
Aug	• Anglo–Persian agreement at Tehran to preserve integrity of Persia
Aug	• Treaty of Rawalpindi ends Afghan War
Sept	• China ends war with Germany
Mar	• Western Allies occupy Constantinople (Istanbul)
Apr	• British civil administration of Palestine under League of Nations mandate
Aug	• Treaty of Sèvres: Turkey loses its former Arab territories and is confined to Anatolia
Jan	• First Indian Parliament meets
July	• Mongolia declares its independence from China
July	• Communist party formed in China
Aug	• End of British mandate in Iraq after uprising: Hashemite kingdom established (to 1958)
Feb	• Nine-Power Treaty secures independence of China: Japan restores Shandong
Mar	• Britain recognizes independence of Egypt
Nov	• Turkish Republic proclaimed, bringing end to Ottoman Empire
May	• Britain declares independence of Transjordan
Aug	• Treaty of Lausanne with Turkey revises Sèvres treaty in Turkey's favour
Oct	• Kemal Ataturk becomes first President of Turkey, with Ankara as new capital
June	• Britain declines Egyptian demand for evacuation of Sudan
Nov	• Soviet advisers help reorganize Guomindang (Nationalist) party in south China: Jiang Jieshi (Chiang Kai-shek) becomes leader
Jan	• Ibn Saud proclaimed king of Hijaz: name of state changed to Saudi Arabia
May	• Lebanon proclaimed a republic
June	• Chinese Nationalist government established at Hankou
July	• Chinese Guomindang expels communists from its ranks
July	• Jiang Jieshi (Chiang Kai-shek) becomes president of China after defeating insurgents
Aug	• Coup d'état in Ethiopia: Ras Tafari (Haile Selassie) takes control
Aug	• Arab–Jewish disturbances in Palestine
Dec	• All-India National Congress demands independence

SCIENCE & CULTURE

- Ernest Rutherford splits the atom
- Alcock and Brown make first trans-Atlantic non-stop flight from Newfoundland to Ireland
- First successful helicopter flight
- Rupert Brooke *Collected Poems*
- Daily London–Paris air service begins
- Preventative serum produced to combat yellow fever
- Edward Elgar Cello Concerto
- André Gide *La Symphonie Pastorale*

- D H Lawrence *Women In Love*

- Invention of Thompson sub-machine gun
- Aldous Huxley's first novel *Chrome Yellow*
- Irving Berlin first of 'Music Box Revues'

- British Broadcasting Company founded
- Howard Carter discovers tomb of Tutankhamen
- Vaughan Williams *Pastoral Symphony*
- James Joyce *Ulysses*
- T S Eliot *The Wasteland*

- Le Corbusier *Towards a New Architecture*

- George Gershwin *Rhapsody in Blue*
- Thomas Mann *The Magic Mountain*

- Rudolf Valentino stars in *The Son of the Sheik*
- Alban Berg *Wozzeck*
- Sergei Eisenstein *Battleship Potemkin*
- Robert Millikand discovers cosmic rays
- F Scott Fitzgerald *The Great Gatsby*

- Television invented by John Logie Baird
- T E Lawrence *Seven Pillars of Wisdom*
- Charleston dance becomes new craze
- Fritz Lang produces the film *Metropolis*
- William Walton *Façade* suite

- Charles Lindbergh flies solo from New York to Paris
- *The Jazz Singer* the first talking picture, with Al Jolson
- Hermann Hesse *Steppenwolf*

- Maurice Ravel *Boléro*
- Alexander Fleming discovers penicillin
- Walt Disney produces *Plane Crazy*: first Mickey Mouse cartoon
- Bertolt Brecht and Kurt Weill *The Threepenny Opera*

- Airship *Graf Zeppelin* flies round world
- Invention of the iron lung by Cecil Drinker
- Ernest Hemingway *A Farewell to Arms*

EUROPE	AMERICAS

1930

Sept • German elections: 107 Nazis win seats in Reichstag	Jan • War breaks out again between Paraguay and Bolivia Sept • Revolution in Argentina: Hipólito Irigoyen deposed: succeeded by General José Uriburu Oct • Revolution in Brazil (to Nov): Getúlio Vargas becomes President (to 1945)

1931

Apr • Revolution in Spain: Republican constitution replaces monarchy Aug • National Government formed in Britain following severe financial crisis	

1932

May • President Doumer of France assassinated: Albert Lebrun succeeds Oct • British Union of Fascists formed by Sir Oswald Mosley Oct • Hunger marches by unemployed in Britain	July • Uprising in São Paulo, Brazil (to Oct) Nov • Franklin Delano Roosevelt wins US Presidential election (to 1945)

1933

Jan • Hitler becomes German Chancellor and Reichstag burned Jan • Beginning of systematic persecution of German Jews July • Germany becomes one-party state under Nazis	Feb • US Bank crisis June • Roosevelt enunciates 'Good Neighbour' policy: aid sent to Central and South America and US troops withdrawn from Nicaragua Aug • Uprising in Cuba: Fulgencio Batista seizes power

1934

June • 'Night of the Long Knives' in Germany July • Austrian Chancellor Dollfuss murdered by Nazis Aug • President Hindenburg dies: Hitler becomes Chancellor of Germany Dec • Purge of Bolsheviks in Russia begins	May • Cuba abrogates US right of intervention Nov • Lázaro Cardenas becomes President of Mexico

1935

Mar • Germany reintroduces conscription and repudiates military clauses of Versailles Treaty Apr • New constitution in Poland: Smigly-Ridz becomes virtual dictator	June • Armistice between Bolivia and Paraguay ends Gran Chaco War Dec • Death of Juan Gomez, President of Venezuela since 1908: subsequent riots in Caracas: military intervene: Eleazar Contreras succeeds

1936

Feb • General Franco rebels against new Spanish Republican government, starting Spanish Civil War Mar • German troops occupy demilitarized Rhineland Nov • Rome–Berlin anti-communist axis proclaimed	Nov • F D Roosevelt re-elected US President • Rearmament begins in Canada

1937

Apr • German bombers destroy Guernica May • Neville Chamberlain succeeds Baldwin as British Prime Minister Oct • Nationalist forces take Gijón and complete conquest of north-west Spain	Mar • Cardenas assumes control of Mexico's oil resources and nationalizes the largely foreign-owned railways July • Military coup d'état in Bolivia Nov • New constitution of Brazil promulgated Dec • All parties dissolved in Brazil

1938

Mar • Austria declared part of German Reich after German occupation Apr • Franco's forces enter Catalonia Oct • German troops occupy Sudeten territory in Czechoslovakia after Anglo–French agreement	Mar • All British and US oil companies expelled from Mexico and oil nationalized May • Nazi movements in Chile and Brazil suppressed Oct • Labour Standards Act passed in USA to regulate minimum wages and maximum hours

1939

Mar • Hitler occupies Czechoslovakia Mar • Madrid's surrender to General Franco ends Spanish Civil War Mar • Britain and France pledge to support Poland Apr • Hitler denounces Germany's pact with Poland Apr • Italy invades Albania May • Hitler and Mussolini sign the 'Pact of Steel' Aug • Attempts by Chamberlain and French premier Edouard Daladier to negotiate with Hitler fail Aug • USSR–German non-aggression pact signed	Mar • US ambassador recalled from Berlin Apr • Roosevelt makes peace plea to Hitler June • Brazil allows entry of 3,000 German Jewish refugees July • President Cardenas of Mexico offers 50 acres to each peasant

AFRICA, ASIA, AUSTRALASIA	SCIENCE & CULTURE
Mar • Gandhi begins civil disobedience movement (to 1931) **June** • Rebellion in Lower Burma led by Saya San (to 1932) who was later hanged: 10,000 rebels die **Nov** • Ras Tafari becomes Haile Selassie I of Ethiopia	• Amy Johnson flies solo from Britain to Australia in 19.5 days • W H Auden *Poems 1930* • First World Cup in soccer, won by Uruguay • Discovery of planet Pluto
Sept • Japan invades Manchuria	• ICI produce petrol from coal • Walt Disney's first colour film, *Flowers and Trees* • Boris Karloff stars in film *Frankenstein* • Virginia Woolf *The Waves* • William Walton *Belshazzar's Feast*
Jan • Indian Congress declared illegal: Gandhi arrested **Feb** • Manchukuo Republic proclaimed in Manchuria by Japanese **Mar** • Ex-Chinese emperor, Pu Yi, becomes President of Manchukuo	• Karl Jansky pioneers radio astronomy • Aldous Huxley *Brave New World* • Vitamin D discovered
Feb • Japanese occupy China north of Great Wall **Mar** • Japan leaves League of Nations after League condemns its actions in China	• Richard Strauss *Arabella* • George Orwell *Down and Out in Paris and London* • Garcia Lorca *Blood Wedding* • The film *King Kong* • Marx Brothers star in *Duck Soup*
May • Six Week War between Saudi Arabia and Yemen (until June) **Oct** • Mao Zedong (Mao Tse-tung) leads Chinese Communists on the Long March (to Nov 1935)	• Evelyn Waugh *A Handful of Dust* • Dmitri Shostakovich *Lady Macbeth of Mtensk* • Paul Hindemith *Mathis der Mahler*
Oct • Italy invades Ethiopia: Italy condemned by League of Nations and sanctions imposed	• George Gershwin *Porgy and Bess* • Pan-American Airways begin trans-Pacific service from California • First radar equipment built for detecting aircraft • Fred Astaire and Ginger Rogers dance in *Top Hat*
May • Italians take Addis Ababa, and Ethiopia is formally annexed by Italy	• Sergei Prokofiev *Peter and the Wolf* • Margaret Mitchell *Gone with the Wind* • Olympic Games are held in Berlin
Apr • Burma becomes separate entity in British Empire **July** • Beginning of war between China and Japan after Likouchiao incident **Dec** • Japanese take Nanjing and Shanghai: Chinese government moves capital to Chongqing	• *Pithecanthropus* skull discovered in Java (Java Man) • Alban Berg *Lulu* • Frank Whittle builds first jet engine • John Steinbeck *Of Mice and Men* • Nazi exhibition of 'Degenerate Art' in Munich
Apr • Civil disobedience campaign in Tunisia against French rule organized by Habib Bourguiba	• Ballpoint pen patented by Ladislao Biro • J P Sartre *La Nausée* • Christopher Isherwood *Goodbye to Berlin*
Feb • Japanese troops occupy Chinese island of Hainan **May** • Fighting (until Sept) between Japanese and Russians on border of Manchukuo and Mongolia: Japanese repulsed	• Otto Hahn achieves nuclear fission by bombarding uranium with neutrons • John Cobb at Bonneville Salt Flats, Utah, drives at 369.74 mph (595.04 kmh) • DDT is invented by Paul Muller • *Gone With The Wind* film released • John Steinbeck *The Grapes of Wrath* • Popular songs of the period include *Roll Out The Barrel*, and *We'll Hang Out the Washing on the Siegfried Line*

THE GLOBAL WAR

After the Japanese attack on Pearl Harbor the war became a world-wide struggle.

The Second World War originated in Europe and remained confined to that continent until the Soviet Union, Japan and the United States became involved in 1941. What gave the war a global dimension in 1939 was the commitment to the struggle of the entire British Empire and the Dominions, together with France's overseas colonies.

Britain and France declared war on Germany on 3 September after Hitler's forces invaded Poland. They remained on the defensive in September while Germany defeated Poland and divided that country with the Soviet Union. There was no fighting on the Western Front during the so-called 'phoney war' until May 1940, but Germany invaded Denmark and Norway in April 1940 and defeated an Anglo–French force which landed in Norway. On 10 May 1940 Germany launched an all-out assault on Holland and Belgium and Anglo–French armies sent to defend Belgium were defeated by a German panzer assault across the Ardennes to the French coast, the remnants of the British and French forces being evacuated by sea to Britain from Dunkirk. When the Germans invaded France in June the demoralized French agreed to an armistice on 22 June. Italy declared war on France and Britain on 20 June.

Britain was now alone, facing a Germany dominant on the Continent. However, during the summer and early autumn of 1940 the Royal Air Force Fighter Command defeated a German aerial assault on Britain's aerodromes and aircraft factories (the Battle of Britain) and Hitler postponed a sea-borne invasion of the British Isles indefinitely. Thereafter, until June 1941, fighting was concentrated in the Balkans, in the Mediterranean and in North Africa, where Italy was saved from defeat by the despatch of German troops to Tripoli early in 1941. When Germany invaded Greece in April, a British Expeditionary Force sent to assist the Greeks was defeated and evacuated from Greece and then finally from Crete, by 1 June.

With Germany's invasion of the Soviet Union on 22 June 1941 and Japan's attack on Pearl Harbor on 7 December (which was followed by a German declaration of war on the United States), the war became a world-wide struggle. The Russians, taken entirely by surprise, were driven out of western Russia

Total War

to the gates of Leningrad and Moscow by the end of the year, with heavy losses of men and equipment. However, both cities held out. The Japanese sank part of the American fleet at Pearl Harbor. Simultaneously Japanese forces attacked British and Dutch possessions in the Far East, capturing the Dutch East Indies, Singapore, Malaya and most of Burma.

The year 1942 represented the furthest limit of the Axis advance. Once the United States had geared up its war industries, supplied substantial quantities of military aid to Russia and Britain and built up its own armed forces, the Allies reasserted themselves. At the end of 1942 and in early 1943, Axis forces in North Africa were routed by a two-pronged Allied advance – the British from Egypt and an Anglo–American amphibious force which had landed in Algeria and Morocco. After July 1943 the Allies seized Sicily and advanced into southern Italy. The Italian government signed an armistice in September 1943.

► Members of the French Resistance, or 'Maquis' watch for German forces at Montrachet. Resistance to the German occupation of Europe varied from country to country. In France, the Resistance impeded the movement of German reinforcements to Normandy and prepared the way for Allied armies.

During the Second World War civilians experienced the death and destruction of war on a scale never before seen in history. It was the result not only of the fighting which took place across Europe and South-East Asia, and the miseries of occupation, but also of the aerial bombing of towns and cities – intended to destroy civilian morale as well as eliminate industrial targets. The *Luftwaffe* bombed Warsaw in 1939 and Rotterdam in 1940 to force the inhabitants to surrender. From late 1940 and 1941 onwards, during the 'Blitz', German bombers attacked British towns and cities, including the industrial town of Coventry which suffered immense destruction in November 1940. In 1944 and 1945 German V1 flying bombs and V2 rockets were launched on England killing thousands. After 1942 Royal Air Force bombers pounded German population centres by night and the American Army Air Force attacked German industrial and communications targets by day. This campaign culminated in the destruction of Dresden on 13 February 1945. Some 600,000 German civilians died as a result of this bombing campaign. For six months before the dropping of the atomic bombs on Japan during August 1945, Japanese cities had also been the targets of an American air assault in which 260,000 civilians were killed.

▲ General Patch and the US 7th Army crossed the Rhine at Worms in 1945 after defeating the Germans in Alsace and the Saar.

In the Pacific the Japanese fleet suffered a series of defeats at the hands of American carrier-borne aircraft and Japan was gradually driven from its Pacific island outposts.

The Red Army forced a German army corps investing Stalingrad to surrender in February 1943 after five months of heavy fighting. Despite many set-backs and appalling losses on both sides the Red Army drove the Germans back to their 1939 frontiers by the end of 1944. In the West after 1943 British and American bombers pounded German cities and industries, while at sea the German U-boat threat to Allied merchant shipping, which had caused grievous Allied losses, was finally smashed in 1944.

By 1944 the Germans and Japanese were in retreat everywhere. On D-Day – 6 June 1944 – an Anglo–American amphibious assault on Normandy from Britain secured bridgeheads, and after heavy fighting the Germans were driven out of France and Belgium during the late summer. Despite numerous disasters, such as a nearly successful German counter-offensive against Allied positions in Belgium between December 1944 and January 1945, Germany was gradually occupied by Soviet and Allied forces, and after the suicide of Hitler on 30 April the German High Command surrendered on 8 May 1945.

In the Pacific bitter fighting continued as the Japanese clung tenaciously to the outlying islands of Iwo Jima and Okinawa before being pushed back to their home islands in June. British and Indian forces drove the Japanese from Burma in the spring of 1945. Expecting suicidal Japanese resistance and massive Allied losses if the Allies invaded Japan, President Truman authorized the dropping of two atomic bombs on Hiroshima and Nagasaki on 6 and 9 August 1945, while the Soviet Union declared war on Japan and defeated its forces in Manchuria. The Japanese agreed to surrender on 14 August.

The German Advance

Legend:
- Axis territory, 1 Sept 1939
- German gains to end 1939
- Axis gains to end 1940
- Axis gains to end 1941
- Axis gains to Nov 1942
- Allied territory Nov 1942
- Vichy France and territories
- Neutral
- → Axis advance
- ★ City bombed during Battle of Britain 1940
- — International boundary 1 Sept. 1939

0 km 400
0 mls 300

FINLAND
Allied with Axis

Ceded to L
Mar 194

Hel

NORWAY
Invaded April 1940
Oslo

SWEDEN
Stockholm

Gulf of Finland

ESTO
Riga
LAT

B A L T I C   S E A

LITHUANIA
Kauna

Danzig
EAST PRUSSIA

NORTH SEA

DENMARK
Invaded April 1940
Copenhagen

Hamburg

Glasgow ★
Edinburgh
Belfast ★
UNITED KINGDOM
Newcastle ★
Dublin
Liverpool ★
Hull ★
Sheffield ★
IRELAND
Coventry ★
Bristol ★
London ★
Plymouth ★
Southampton ★

English Channel

NETHERLANDS
Amsterdam Invaded May 1940
Dunkirk
Brussels
BELGIUM
LUX.

Cologne
Berlin
GERMANY
Frankfurt
Elbe
Oder
Vistula
Bug
Warsaw
Annex
by US
Sept 1

POLAND
Invaded Sept 1939

Prague
BOHEMIA-MORAVIA
Protectorate Mar 1939
Krakow
Lvov

SLOVAKIA
Satellite Mar 1939
Chernov

Paris
FRANCE
Invaded May 1940
Loire
Meuse
Maginot Line
Rhine
Nuremberg
Danube
Munich
Vienna

ATLANTIC OCEAN

Bay of Biscay

Bordeaux
Vichy
VICHY FRANCE
Neutral June 1940-Nov 42
Co-operation with Germany
Rhône
Marseille

SWITZERLAND
A l p s

AUSTRIA
Annexed Mar. 1938

Budapest
HUNGARY
Allied with Axis

ROMAN
Allied with Ax

Milan
Po
Zagreb
Belgrade
Bucha
Danube

YUGOSLAVIA
Invaded April 1941
Divided up between Axis states

Sofia

PORTUGAL
Lisbon
Madrid
SPAIN

Corsica
ITALY
Rome

ADRIATIC SEA

BULGARI
Allied with Axis

Naples
ALBANIA
Occupied by Italy 1939

Sardinia

GREECE
Invaded April 1941
Ath

Aege

Tangier
Gibraltar (Br.)
SPANISH MOROCCO
Rabat
Casablanca

Algiers
Oran

Tunis
Sicily
Malta (Br.)

MEDITERRANEAN SEA

Crete
Invaded
May 194

MOROCCO
(Vichy France)

ALGERIA
(Vichy France)

Sfax
Gabes
TUNISIA
(Vichy France)
Invaded Nov 1942

Tripoli

Benghazi
Tobruk

LIBYA

72

In 1940 and 1941 the German army won a
remarkable series of victories which resulted in
Germany's domination of the European continent.
These victories were not achieved by greater
manpower or superior equipment, for in May 1940
France, Britain and Belgium fielded as many troops
as the German *Wehrmacht*, and although the French
air force was extremely weak, French tanks were of
better quality than their German equivalents.

When Germany invaded Belgium and Holland on
10 May 1940 Anglo–French forces advanced into
Belgium and established a continuous front with the
Maginot Line. However, the Germans had already
planned to send armoured or panzer divisions
through the lightly defended Ardennes Forest towards
the French coast, encircling the main Allied armies in
Belgium. The panzers, a unique combination of
tanks, aircraft and motorized infantry, moving at high
speed, crossed the Meuse near Sedan on 13 May and
by 25 May had reached Calais. The out-manoeuvred
Allies fell back on Dunkirk, and although about
340,000 troops were evacuated by every available
ship to England, they lost all their weapons and
equipment. Germany then overran France, which
signed an armistice on 22 June 1940. Germany had
won because of its superior operational skills and
command system. This defeat was a major example
of what has been described as Blitzkrieg or lightning
war. Germany next planned a victory by cross-
Channel invasion of Britain, but the *Luftwaffe*, while
attempting to knock out the Royal Air Force in
preparation for such an assault, was defeated by
Fighter Command in the Battle of Britain during the
summer and autumn of 1940. Germany then turned its
attention to the Balkans, North Africa and Russia in
1941. Yugoslavia and Greece were conquered in April
and a British Expeditionary Force, sent to help the
Greeks, was forced to evacuate in May. When
Germany sent Erwin Rommel and his Afrika Korps to
help the Italians in North Africa, Britain faced another
formidable enemy, who drove them back into Egypt
by the summer of 1942.

On 22 June 1941 Germany invaded Soviet Russia
– Operation Barbarossa – designed to conquer
European Russia to the Urals within a few months.
Spearheaded by the panzers, the German armies
swept into Russia in three directions, towards
Leningrad, towards Moscow, and towards the
Ukraine, the Caucasus and the Crimea. They
advanced 50 miles a day, capturing entire Soviet
armies and cities, but the onset of the harsh winter of
1941 slowed up their advance. By December they had
besieged Leningrad, occupied the Ukraine and most
of the Crimea, but were unable to take Moscow. Most
importantly, they had not defeated the Russians.

The Japanese Advance

USSR

MONGOLIA

TIBET

INDIA

Calcutta

C H I N A

Chongqing
Yangzi

MANCHUKUO
(MANCHURIA)

Mukden

Amur

Beijing

Vladivostok

KOREA

JAPAN

Tokyo

Hankou
Nanjing
Shanghai

Nagasaki

Sakhalin

Kuril Is.

Ryukyu Is.
Okinawa

Bonin Is.

Mario

BURMA
Invaded Dec 1941

Rangoon

THAILAND
Allied to Japan

Andaman Is.

Bangkok

Hanoi

Guangzhou

Hong Kong
Invaded
8-25 Dec 1941

Formosa
(Taiwan)

Hainan

FRENCH
INDO-
CHINA

Mekong

Luzon

Manila

PHILIPPINE
ISLANDS (US)
Occupied 6 May 1942

P A C I F I C

Iwo Jima

Mariana
Is.

Guam (US)

MALAYA
Invaded Dec 1941

Singapore
Occupied
15 Feb 1942

Sumatra

INDIAN
OCEAN

SOUTH CHINA SEA

BRUNEI

BR.
N. BORNEO

SARAWAK

Kuching

BORNEO

Mindanao
Davao

Yap

Palau Is.

C a r o l i n e
I s l a n d s

Tru

Celebes

Banjarmasin

Batavia

Java

Makassar

Bali

DUTCH EAST INDIES
Invaded Dec 1941

Amboina

Timor

NORTH-EAST
NEW GUINEA

New Guinea

PAPUA

New Britain

Rabaul

	Japanese Empire 7 Dec 1941
	Japanese occupied territory 7 Dec 1941
	Japanese occupied territory to 6 Aug 1942

— Limit of Japanese expansion 6 Aug 1942

➤ Japanese advance

— International boundary 7 Dec 1941

0   800
km

0   600
mls

Darwin

AUSTRALIA

CORAL SEA

Guadalca

Battle of the Co
4-9 May 19

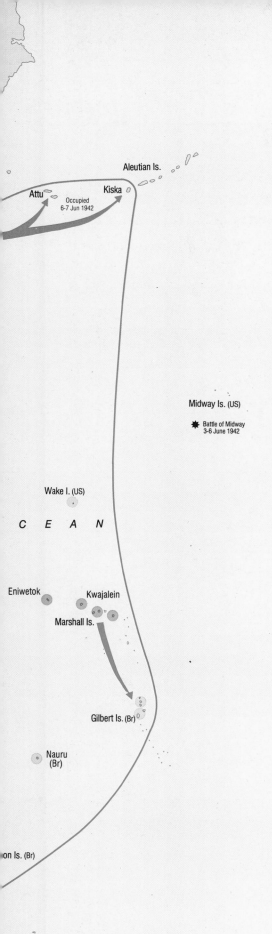

Aleutian Is.

Attu
Occupied
6-7 Jun 1942
Kiska

Midway Is. (US)

Battle of Midway
3-6 June 1942

Wake I. (US)

C E A N

Eniwetok
Kwajalein

Marshall Is.

Gilbert Is. (Br)

Nauru
(Br)

on Is. (Br)

The Japanese attack on the American naval base at Pearl Harbor on 7 December 1941 was intended to destroy the American Pacific Fleet and prevent any effective American intervention against Japan in the Far East. Inevitably this unprovoked assault caused intense anger and indignation in the United States and President Roosevelt had no difficulty in securing a declaration of war against Japan from Congress. During December the Japanese also attacked the Dutch East Indies, Hong Kong, the Philippines, Malaya, Singapore and islands in the Pacific Ocean, and sank two British battleships, the *Prince of Wales* and the *Repulse*, which had been sent to defend Singapore and Malaya. All these territories fell to the Japanese by early 1942, with an entire British Imperial army of about 80,000 men surrendering to a much smaller Japanese force besieging Singapore on 15 February. In December 1941 the Japanese invaded Burma, which they conquered by April: British casualties of 14,000 men were twice those of the Japanese. The British had now been forced back to the borders of India. Elsewhere the Japanese invaded New Guinea and occupied the northern half of the island, leading to fears in Australia of an imminent invasion. General Douglas MacArthur, former American commander in the Philippines, took command of Australian forces and repulsed a Japanese attack on Papua. In May 1942 American and Japanese carrier-borne aircraft fought in the Coral Sea, off the north-east coast of Australia, and although this was a drawn battle – both sides lost two carriers each – it prevented Japanese reinforcements reaching Papua. The Japanese tried to capture the Midway Islands, hoping to use them as a base from which to threaten America's Pacific coast. They failed, and the Americans gained the initiative. However, they still faced ferocious fighting. From August 1942 to February 1943 both sides fought for the possession of Guadalcanal, one of the Solomon Islands, which the Japanese finally abandoned after inflicting and receiving some appalling losses. Nevertheless, by January 1943 the Japanese were in occupation of a vast area in the Asian-Pacific region, from the southern Aleutian Islands in the north, through Wake Island in the east to northern New Guinea in the south and up through the Dutch East Indies, Malaya and Burma, eastern China and Manchuria to Sakhalin off the coast of Russia. They hoped to organize this area into a 'Greater South-East Asian Co-Prosperity Zone', although in practice this meant the exploitation of the human and natural resources of the conquered territories as a means of building up Japan's strength against the United States and her allies.

The World at War

GREENLAND

Murmansk

ICELAND
Reykjavik

SWEDEN
FINLAND
Archangel

NORWAY

U.S.S.R.

U.K.
Liverpool

DEN.

EIRE

NETH.
BELG.
L.

GERMANY POLAND

SLOVAKIA
FRANCE
HUNG.
SWITZ.
ROM.
ITALY
BULG.
GREECE
TURKEY

CANADA

Québec

St. Johns

Halifax

New York

UNITED STATES

NORTH ATLANTIC
OCEAN

PORT. SPAIN

SYR.
LEB.
PAL.
IRAQ
TRANS-
JORD.
IRAN
AFGHANI.

MOROCCO

LIBYA
EGYPT
SAUDI ARABIA
K.
Q.
OMAN

MEXICO

CUBA
HAITI

DOM.
REP.

ALGERIA

ADEN
PROT.

BR. HOND.
HOND.

GUAT.
EL SALV.
NIC.

C.R.

PANAMA

Port of Spain
VENEZUELA

COLOMBIA

Br
Dutch Fr
GUIANA

SP.
SAHARA

GAMBIA
PORT.
GUINEA
SIERRA LEONE

FRENCH WEST AFRICA

NIGERIA
GOLD
COAST
TOGO
Lagos
LIBERIA
Takoradi
CAMEROONS
SPANISH
GUINEA

ANGLO-
EGYPTIAN
SUDAN

ERIT.
YEM.

ETHIOPIA

SOMALILAND

UGANDA
KENYA

ECUADOR

PERU

Natal

Ascension I.

BRAZIL

FRENCH EQUAT. AFRICA

BELGIAN
CONGO

TANGANYIKA

ANGOLA

N.
RHODESIA

NYASALAND

MOZAMBIQUE
MADAGASCAR

BOLIVIA

Rio de Janeiro

PARAGUAY

PACIFIC
OCEAN

SOUTH ATLANTIC
OCEAN

S.
RHODESIA

SOUTH-
WEST
AFRICA

BECHUANA-
LAND

Lourenço
Marques

INDIA

UNION
OF
S. AFRICA

CHILE

URUGUAY
Montevideo

ARGENTINA

A Japanese ship under attack in the Battle of Midway, 1942.

The 1939–1945 war was truly a global one. Most countries were eventually drawn into the conflict; none could escape its effects. The most outstanding example was the worldwide assault on international commerce. The British imposed a maritime blockade on Germany in 1939 and in 1942 the United States navy began to destroy Japan's sea-going commerce. In 1941 Germany launched a submarine (U-boat or *Unterseeboot*) campaign designed to wipe out Britain's merchant shipping fleet and starve it of food and raw materials. The submarine blockade was first set up on western approaches to Britain, and later, once moved into the mid-Atlantic, it lay beyond the reach of Allied land-based craft. When the United States entered the war, the German long-range U-boats were soon to endanger shipping in US waters too. In 1942, at the height of the Battle of the Atlantic, 7.8 million gross tons of Allied merchant shipping was sunk with the loss of 26,000 merchant seamen. However, Allied counter-measures gradually defeated the submarine menace in 1943 with the breaking of Germany's radio codes by British signal intelligence, the availability of more long-range patrol aircraft and escort vessels for convoys and a massive expansion of American shipbuilding capacity. In the Far East American surface vessels and aircraft had, by 1944, destroyed Japan's merchant fleet, American signals intelligence having also broken the Japanese naval codes. Japan was accordingly cut off from vital imports.

MONGOLIA

MANCHUKUO

JAPAN

CHINA

TIBET

BHUTAN

PAL

Calcutta

BURMA

TAIWAN

THAI-LAND

FR. INDO-CHINA

PHILIPPINE IS.

Colombo

CEYLON

MALAY STATES

PACIFIC OCEAN

NEW GUINEA

DUTCH EAST INDIES

EAN

AUSTRALIA

Perth

Sydney

NEW ZEALAND

Allied states

Territory under Axis control, 1942

Neutral

Sea route

Zone of Allied air cover

Area of U-boat activity

Nazi Europe

REICHSKOMMISSARIAT
NORWAY

SWEDEN

FINLAND

Leningr

NORTH
SEA

UNITED
KINGDOM

DENMARK

BALTIC SEA

Klooga ◇ Tallinn ◇ Vaivara

Riga

REICHSKOMMISSARIAT
OSTLAND

Kaunas

Minsk

Smol

London

REICHSKOMMISSARIAT
NETHERLANDS
Amsterdam ○

Hamburg ◇ Neuengamme

Bergen-
Belsen ◇

Niederhagen

G E R M A N Y

Danzig ◇ Stutthof

Vistula

Bialystok

Treblinka ◆

Brussels ○
BELGIUM
50

Ravensbrück ◇
Sachsenhausen-Oranienburg ◇
◇ Berlin

POLAND

Warsaw ○

Cologne ○

565

◆ Chelmno

3,500
GENERAL
GOVERNMENT
OF POLAND

Sobibor ◆

Paris ◇ Drancy

Frankfurt ○

Rhine

Flossenburg ○

Buchenwald ◇

Gross Rosen ○

Theresien-
stadt

Prague ○

◆ Majdanek

Belzec ◆

FRANCE
150

Natzweiler ◇

350

Auschwitz-
Birkenau ◆

○ Krakow
Stryzow

Kiev ○

Lvov ○

REICHSKOMMISSA
UKRAINE

Balanov

Dachau ◇ ○ Munich

Danube

Mauthausen ◇

Vienna ○

Plaszow ◇

Dniester

SWITZERLAND

AUSTRIA
300

SLOVAKIA

Edineti ◇

Odessa ○

Vichy ○

VICHY FRANCE
Occupied Nov 1942

Milan ○

Budapest ○

HUNGARY
500

ROMANIA

834

Bucharest ○

Les
Milles ◇
Marseille ○ ◇ Nice

Venice ○

Jasenovac ◇

Belgrade ○

Danube

Corsica

45

ITALY

Rome ○

CROATIA
64

SERBIA

MONTENEGRO
(to Italy)

○ Sofia

BULGARIA
46

Sardinia

Naples ○

ALBANIA
(to Italy)

Istanbul ○

MEDITERRANEAN
SEA

GREECE
110

ALGERIA
(Vichy France)

TUNISIA
(Vichy France)

Sicily

Athens ○

Boundary of Germany 1937

Boundary of Greater Germany 1942

Other international boundaries 1942

Territory under German rule

Territory under German occupation

States allied with Germany

Major population movements 1939-44

Germans

Poles

Russians and Ukranians

Pre-war Jewish population (in thousands)

Concentration camp

Extermination camp

0 km 400
0 mls 300

Moscow

Deportations to Siberia

U S S R

Don

Volga

Kharkov

Stalingrad

2,700

petrovsk

Rostov

Sea of Azov

Stavropol

Crimea

Grozny

Sevastopol

ACK SEA

Tiflis

Ankara

TURKEY

The so-called German 'New Order' in Europe was a system of economic exploitation devoted to the needs of Germany and its armed forces. Initially, the Germans plundered raw materials and machinery from conquered countries, dismantling factories and shipping them back to the Reich. Later, however, they permitted Western European industries to remain in production although the bulk of their output was sent to Germany. Agricultural produce was also requisitioned. As more Germans were drafted into the army, workers in occupied countries were forcibly recruited to work in German factories, while Soviet and Polish prisoners of war were transported to work in munitions factories and mines. Large numbers died of starvation and ill-treatment.

Hitler had preached anti-Semitism since 1920, developing the theory of an 'Aryan' master-race so that anti-Semitism and racism became the rallying cries of his regime. The Nazis' 'Final Solution' of the Jewish question began in 1939 with the occupation of Poland. Polish Jews were rounded up into ghettos, a pattern repeated in other Nazi-occupied countries. The mass murder of Jews was placed on a more systematic basis following the Wannsee Conference of leading *Schutzstaffeln* (SS) officials on 20 January 1942. An official, Adolf Eichmann, was put in charge of the transport of Europe's Jews from their homelands to the death camps in the East. In the wake of the German armies, special SS Task Forces were sent to root out and kill Jews, Gypsies, Soviet commissars and educated Slavs. The SS had already experimented with poison gas to asphyxiate their victims and mobile gas vans had been deployed in captured towns and villages for this purpose. Now specially constructed death camps were set up in Poland in which thousands of Jews were gassed daily. During the war between four to six million Jews were murdered by the Nazis.

After 1942 European resistance movements proliferated, assisted by the British Special Operations Executive and the American Office of Strategic Services. Across Europe, partisans sabotaged factories, roads and railways and ambushed German troop and supply convoys. German reprisals were savage: often, the populations of entire villages were exterminated. In 1943 heavy fighting broke out between Tito's partisans in Yugoslavia and German troops. As with similar conflicts elsewhere in Europe, the more numerous and better-equipped Germans prevailed. In July 1944 the Polish Underground Home Army seized two thirds of Warsaw, anticipating assistance from the Red Army outside the city. Stalin refused to help them however, and in October the Germans ruthlessly crushed the revolt.

The Allied Counter-offensive

Legend:
- Allied territory Nov. 1942
- Areas liberated by Allies to July 1943
- Areas liberated by Allies to June 1944
- Areas liberated by Allies to Dec. 1944
- Areas liberated by Allies to May 1945
- Areas still held by German forces at end of war
- Neutral
- Boundary of 'Greater Germany' 1942
- Allied advances
- German cities bombed
- International boundary 1 Sept 1939

```
0 km        400
0 mls     300
```

NORWAY

FINLAND
Allied with German

SWEDEN

Oslo

Stockholm

Gulf of Finland

Tal

ESTO

NORTH SEA

Edinburgh

UNITED KINGDOM

DENMARK

Copenhagen

BALTIC SEA

Riga

LA

LITHU

Kaun

Danzig

EAST PRUSSIA

Dublin

IRELAND

Liverpool

London

NETHERLANDS
Amsterdam

Bremen

Hamburg

Hanover

Elbe

Berlin

Vistula

Warsaw

POLAND

Lvov

Bug

Arnhem

Brunswick

Antwerp

Brussels

BELGIUM

Essen

Cologne

GERMANY

Leipzig

Dresden

Prague

Oder

Krakow

English Channel

Allied landings in Normandy, D-Day June 1944

NORMANDY

Falaise

Paris

Meuse

LUX.

Rhine

Schweinfurt

Nuremberg

Danube

SLOVAKIA

ATLANTIC OCEAN

Loire

FRANCE

Munich

Vienna

AUSTRIA

Budapest

HUNGARY

ROMAN

Bay of Biscay

Bordeaux

Vichy

SWITZERLAND
Ps

Brenner Pass

A

Milan

Po

Zagreb

Belgrade

Buc

Marseille

Rhone

Ravenna

ITALY

ADRIATIC SEA

Yugoslav partisans Oct 1944-May 1945

Danube

Sofia

BULGA

PORTUGAL

Madrid

SPAIN

Corsica

Rome

Anzio

Monte Cassino

Naples

Salerno

ALBANIA

Lisbon

Sardinia

Ae

GREECE
German forces evacuated Nov 1944

At

Tangier

Gibraltar (Br.)

SPANISH MOROCCO

Algiers

Palermo

Sicily

Casablanca

Rabat

Oran

Constantine

Tunis

Allied advance Nov 1942

Allied landing in Sicily July 1943

Malta (Br.)

Cre

MOROCCO

MEDITERRANEAN SEA

ALGERIA

TUNISIA

Tripoli

Benghazi

LIBYA

80

The turning point of the war for the Allies came in 1942. By the end of that year Hitler's forces had suffered severe set-backs in Russia and North Africa. In December 1941 the Russians were holding out in Leningrad, Moscow and Sevastopol.

In 1942 Hitler resumed his offensive after a break during the winter. The Germans captured Sevastopol, advanced into the Caucasus and captured most of Stalingrad. However, in November the Soviets launched a counter-offensive at Stalingrad, isolating General von Paulus and his Sixth Army inside the city. The most vicious fighting of the war took place in Stalingrad before von Paulus surrendered on 2 February 1943. The Germans next attempted a counter-offensive against the Red Army in the Kursk salient, but the Germans were defeated and they began to retreat along the entire front from the Baltic to the Black Sea. A Russian offensive in December 1943 relieved Leningrad and brought Russian troops into the Balkans and Poland. By early 1945 the Red Army had reached Berlin.

In the west the Russians pressed the British and Americans to mount a cross-Channel invasion of the continent in 1942 or 1943 to relieve pressure on the Red Army. The British refused: their army was not ready and was short of equipment. Instead an Allied landing in North Africa was agreed upon to coincide with an advance of General Montgomery's Eighth Army from Egypt. In October 1942 Montgomery destroyed Rommel's Afrika Korps at the battle of El Alamein and advanced on Tunisia, while Anglo–American forces landed in Morocco and Algeria in November. Hard fighting ensued before the Axis forces surrendered in Tunisia on 12 May. In July 1943 the Allies invaded southern Italy, causing the Italians to make peace. German occupation of northern and central Italy slowed down Allied progress and so the Allies did not reach northern Italy until April 1945.

On 6 June 1944 an Allied force landed successfully in Normandy, and after heavy fighting the Allies destroyed the German armies at the Falaise Gap. By December 1944 France and Belgium had been liberated and the Allies had reached Germany.

In the autumn of 1944 the Allied armies suffered two major setbacks: the failure of an airborne assault on Arnhem to seize a Rhine bridgehead and a surprise German counter-offensive through the Ardennes which was brought to a halt by Allied resistance in January 1945. On 12 January 1945 a Soviet offensive carried the Red Army to Berlin by mid-April. In March the Allies stormed into the heart of Germany, linking up with the Red Army on the Elbe on 25 April. Hitler committed suicide on 30 April, and the German armed services surrendered unconditionally to the Allies on 7 May.

The Defeat of Japan

USSR

Russian advances in Manchuria
and Sakhalin from 9 Aug 1945

MONGOLIA

Sakhalin

Amur

Kuril Is.

MANCHUKUO
(MANCHURIA)

Mukden

Vladivostok

TIBET

Beijing

KOREA

JAPAN

INDIA

CHINA

Hiroshima

Tokyo

Calcutta

Chongqing

Yangzi

Nanjing

1st atomic bomb dropped
6 Aug 1945

Hankou

Shanghai

Nagasaki

2nd atomic bomb dropped
9 Aug 1945

BURMA

Area retaken by Chinese
forces Aug 1945

Formosa
(Taiwan)

Ryukyu Is.

Rangoon

Hanoi

Guangzhou

Okinawa

Bonin Is.

THAILAND

Hong Kong

Marc

Andaman Is.

Bangkok

Hainan

Iwo Jima

FRENCH
INDO-
CHINA

P A C I F I C

Mekong

Luzon

Marianas Is.

MALAYA

Manila

PHILIPPINE
ISLANDS (US)

Mindoro

SOUTH CHINA SEA

Saipan

Sumatra

Singapore
Recaptured
5 Sept 1945

BRUNEI

Leyte

Battle of Leyte Gulf
24-25 Oct 1944

Mindanao

Guam (US)

BR.
N. BORNEO

Davao

Yap

INDIAN
OCEAN

SARAWAK

Tarakan

Palau I.

Truk

BORNEO

C a r o l i n e

I s l a n d s

Batavia

Celebes

Java

Makassar

Bali

DUTCH EAST INDIES

Hollandia

Manus

St. Matthias

NORTH-EAST
NEW GUINEA

Timor

New Guinea

New Britain

Rabaul

PAPUA

Bougainville

Darwin

AUSTRALIA

Guadalc

CORAL SEA

	Limit of Japanese expansion 6 Aug 1942
	Area reoccupied by Allied forces to Aug 1944
	Area reoccupied by Allied forces to Aug 1945
	Japanese advance in China June 1944-Apr 1945
	Japanese Empire and occupied territory at surrender Aug 1945
	Allied advance
	International boundary 7 Dec 1941

0   km   800

0   mls   600

Aleutian Is.

Attu   Kiska

Midway Is. (US)

Wake I. (US)

C E A N

Eniwetok

Kwajalein

Marshall Is.

Gilbert Is. (Br)

Nauru
(Br)

non Is. (Br)

In May 1942 the Japanese sent a carrier fleet to capture the islands of Midway, which they hoped to use as a base to threaten Pearl Harbor and America's Pacific coast. American intelligence had, however, detected their movements, and between 4–6 June, in a major action fought between aircraft from the two carrier fleets, a United States task force with three carriers sank four Japanese aircraft carriers and a heavy cruiser. The United States lost one carrier, the *Yorktown* on 7 June. This was a major defeat for the Japanese, who could ill afford to sustain losses on this scale. Thereafter the Japanese were gradually pushed back to their home islands by a combination of MacArthur's land forces and Admiral Nimitz's Pacific Fleet, while the Japanese merchant marine was destroyed by American submarines, effectively ending Japan's hopes of using the oil and raw materials of the conquered territories to sustain its war effort.

In June 1944 the Americans occupied the island of Saipan, 1,350 miles south of Tokyo. On 20 October 1944 MacArthur invaded the Philippines, and at the Battle of Leyte Gulf a superior Japanese naval force retired before a much smaller American fleet. Gradually, during the first six months of 1945 the Japanese hold on the Philippines was loosened. During 1945 the Americans also captured Iwo Jima and Okinawa, 500 miles south-west of Tokyo. The Japanese put up suicidal resistance – 100,000 died – and took a heavy toll in Americans killed and wounded before Okinawa fell on 21 June. This suggested to the Allies that a further six months or more of bitter fighting and heavy casualties lay ahead before the Japanese home islands would finally be subdued. However, Japan's economic life had already been brought to a virtual standstill by a continuous American bombing offensive after March 1945. By the early summer Japanese politicians were anxious to end the war, but Japan's reluctance to endorse unconditional surrender, and fears of a coup by Japanese military extremists, led to its approaches for negotiations (through the Soviet Union) to be dismissed by the United States as ambiguous and unsatisfactory. On 6 and 9 August the United States Air Force dropped two atomic bombs on Hiroshima and Nagasaki, totally destroying the two cities and killing 100,000 people. At the same time the Soviet Union declared war on Japan and soon advanced into Manchuria (Manchukuo). As a result of this devastation the Japanese emperor ordered the unconditional surrender of Japan, which took place on 2 September 1945. Although the Americans agreed to allow Emperor Hirohito to remain on his throne, the real ruler of Japan was General MacArthur, the Supreme Commander of the Allied forces.

The End of the War

NORWAY
Oslo
SWEDEN
Stockholm
FINLAND
Helsinki
L. Ladoga
Leningrad
Gulf of Finland
Tallinn
ESTONIAN
60
S.S.R.
NORTH SEA
DENMARK
BALTIC SEA
Copenhagen
Riga
125
LATVIAN S.S.R.
LITHUANIAN
80
S.S.R.
Kaunas
Kaliningrad (Königsberg)
2000 (Russia)
Minsk
BYELORUSSIAN S.S.R.
2400
Gdansk (Danzig)
350
POMERANIA
1800
Hamburg
NETHERLANDS
Amsterdam
Elbe
Berlin
2000
Vistula
Bug
U S S R
Warsaw
WEST
1500
650
Oder
POLAND
500
Kiev
Dnieper
to Siberia
EAST
Bonn
200
SILESIA
2900
3800
3200
Frankfurt
Rhine
GERMANY
Prague
1800
Krakow
1500
Lvov
UKRAINIAN S.S.R.
Ukrainians
Crimean Tartars
Kalmuks
Caucasians
500
CZECHOSLOVAKIA
110
CARPATHO-UKRAINE
Dniester
1800
FRANCE
400
Danube
Munich
100
Vienna
100
MOLDAVIAN S.S.R.
Kishinev
Odessa
SWITZERLAND
AUSTRIA
200
Budapest
Tisza
50
Cluj
ROMANIA
Milan
Trieste
220
HUNGARY
40
60
BLACK SEA
ISTRIA
to Yugoslavia
40
300
200
YUGOSLAVIA
Belgrade
Bucharest
DOBRUJA
Danube
130
ITALY
Sofia
BULGARIA
Tiranë
ALBANIA
90
Salonika
Istanbul
from Libya
from Ethiopia and Eritrea
from Dodecanese
GREECE
TURKEY
95
120
15
Athens

Movement of peoples, 1945–52
(figures in thousands)

- Baltic peoples
- Czechs and Slovaks
- Germans
- Greeks
- Hungarians
- Italians
- Poles
- Romanians
- Russians, White Russians and Ukrainians
- Turks
- Old pre-war boundary
- Post-war international boundary

0   km   500
0   mls   400

With the end of the war imminent in Europe, the 'Big Three' leaders, Winston Churchill, Franklin Roosevelt and Josef Stalin met at Yalta, in the Crimea, in February 1945 to determine the future of Europe. Roosevelt had put forward no concrete American peace aims during the war, hoping that by forging personal links with Stalin their two countries would continue their war-time alliance to maintain world peace through the United Nations Organization. American ambiguity about its post-war policy resulted in vague and unsatisfactory compromises being reached at Yalta. The three powers plus France were to occupy the zones in Germany on which they had agreed in 1944 and to partition the city of Berlin between them, but the future of Germany itself was left for a later peace conference. A Soviet demand for German reparations was referred to a Reparation Commission. The Soviet Union's control of Eastern Europe was confirmed, and was promised territorial and economic compensation in the Far East when it entered the war against Japan. The results of the next 'Big Three' Conference at Potsdam in July and August were even less satisfactory, since in order to preserve the facade of Great Power unity, most substantive issues were referred to future meetings of their Foreign Ministers.

The Europe the three powers were discussing was in chaos. Most of the continent had been heavily fought over and boundaries had changed several times. Under German occupation, large population movements had taken place, while towards the end of the war, many Ukrainians and Byelorussians fled from the advancing Red Army, afraid that they would be suspected of collaborating with the Germans. In 1944–5 Germans were expelled from Czechoslovakia and Poland. Some peoples had to move several times, and many fled to the west.

The problems facing the occupying powers in Germany in 1945 were formidable. Former concentration camp prisoners had to be cared for and re-settled. Many prisoners of war were unable to return to their homes, which were under foreign rule. There were millions of displaced persons and refugees all over war-ravaged Europe, where roads, railways and water supplies had been destroyed. The food supply was also extremely limited because of the destruction of farms and transport systems.

Checkpoints between East and West

1 Büchen
2 Schwanheide
3 Lauenburg
4 Horst
5 Schnackenburg
6 Cumlosen
7 Rühen
8 Buchorst
9 Vorsfelde
10 Obisfelde
11 Helmstedt
12 Marienborn
13 Bebra
14 Herleshausen
15 Warta
16 Probstzella
17 Juchhöh
18 Ludwigstadt
19 Töpen

Occupation zones
  Soviet
  British
  US
  French
✛ Airport
Inter-zonal routes
  Air corridor
  Railway
  Road
⊕ City under 4-power occupation
● Checkpoint

Soviet Expansionism

NORWAY
Oslo

FINLAND
Porkkala
Soviet base
1947-55

Helsinki
1944-56

Leningrad

SWEDEN
Gothenburg

Stockholm

Tallinn

ESTONIA
Soviet republic 1940

Moscow

NORTH
SEA

Copenhagen

BALTIC SEA

Riga

LATVIA
Soviet republic 1940

Smolensk

DENMARK

LITHUANIA
Soviet republic 1940

Kaunas

Vilnius

Minsk

Kaliningrad
(Königsberg)

from Germany

Hamburg

Gdansk
(Danzig)

EAST
PRUSSIA

Gomel

NETHERLANDS

Szczecin

EAST
Berlin

Poznan

Vistula

Warsaw

from Poland

Kiev

WEST
Potsdam

GERMANY
Soviet occupation zone 1945-9,
communist 1949

Lodz

Oder

Cologne

GERMANY

Dresden

Niesse

Wroclaw

POLAND
1947

Krakow

Lvov

Dnieper

Frankfurt

FRANCE

Prague

Nuremberg

Rhine

Danube

CZECHOSLOVAKIA
1948

Brno

Dniester

Chernovtsy

Munich

Vienna
Soviet occupation zone
1945-55

Uzhgorod

from
Czecho-
slovakia

MOLDAVIA

Odessa

from Romania

SWITZERLAND

AUSTRIA

Budapest

HUNGARY
1947

Cluj

Jassy

Milan

Trieste

Zagreb

ROMANIA
1947

Turin

Belgrade

Bucharest

Constanta

ITALY

ADRIATIC
SEA

YUGOSLAVIA
1945
left Soviet bloc 1948

Danube

Varna

BLACK
SEA

Corsica

Sofia

BULGARIA
1946

Rome

Skopje

Bosporus

Sardinia

Tirana

ALBANIA
1946
left Soviet bloc 1961

Istanbul

TURKEY

Dardenelles

GREECE

MEDITERRANEAN
SEA

ICELAND

NORWAY

SWEDEN

FINL

POLAND

Kiev

Kha

Dneprope

BLACK
SEA

Yalta

TURKEY

Ardahan

Kars

SYRIA

194

IRAQ

SAUDI ARABIA

Tb

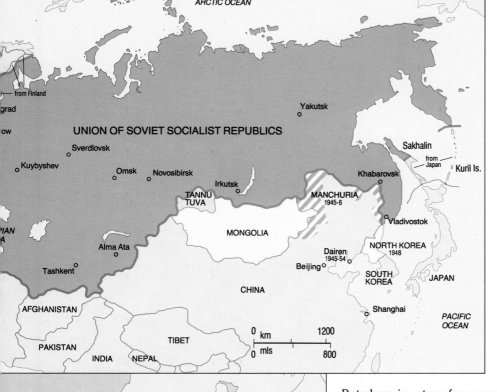

By 1945 the Red Army had occupied Central and Eastern Europe and it was clear that the Soviet Union would insist on retaining close control over those countries after the war to prevent them ever again being used as a base for aggression against Russia. Roosevelt hoped that Stalin would allow these states at least a facade of independence. At the Yalta Conference in February 1945 Stalin signed the Declaration on Liberated Europe, a vague statement which promised democratic elections in areas freed from Axis occupation. Stalin agreed that free elections would be held in Poland. However, the setting up of an all-communist Provisional government in Poland in July 1944 had already led to Anglo–American protests and at the Potsdam Conference in 1945 a compromise was reached whereby non-communists were admitted to the Polish cabinet while Stalin repeated his promise of free elections. At Yalta, Stalin had secured Allied agreement to the Soviet annexation of Eastern Poland, and also the former German port of Königsberg (renamed Kaliningrad) in East Prussia: Poland was compensated by acquiring German territory east of the Oder and Western Neisse rivers.

After 1946 the Soviet grip on Central and Eastern Europe became total as non-communist parties were dissolved and rigid Stalinist governments installed. At Potsdam, in return for a promise that the Soviet Union would enter the war against Japan in the summer of 1945, the Allies agreed that the Soviet Union should annex the Japanese Kuril islands and southern Sakhalin, and be granted concessions in Manchuria.

The Soviets also demanded that their shipping be allowed free passage through the Dardanelles Straits, the return of Kars and Ardahan in the Caucasus, from Turkey, and a naval base on the Straits. Anglo–American suspicions of Soviet ambitions were heightened when the Soviet Union refused, until 1946, to withdraw troops from northern Iran, occupied during the war.

Chronology 1939–1945

EUROPE

Sept	• Germany invades Poland and annexes Danzig: within 10 days controls western Poland
Sept	• (3rd) Britain and France declare war on Germany
Sept	• USSR invades Poland from east
Sept	• Poland partitioned between Germany and USSR
Oct	• British troops sent to France
Nov	• USSR invades Finland

Mar	• Peace treaty between USSR and Finland signed
Apr	• Germany invades Denmark and Norway
Apr	• Allies land in Norway
May	• Neville Chamberlain resigns, Winston Churchill becomes Prime Minister
May	• Germany invades Belgium and Holland: they surrender
May	• Britain occupies Iceland and the Faroe islands
May	• British army evacuated at Dunkirk (May to June)
June	• Norway surrenders
June	• Italy declares war on Britain and France
June	• German army enters Paris
June	• Henri Pétain, Prime Minister of France, requests armistice with Germany
June	• General de Gaulle founds Free French movement
June	• Armistice between France and Germany
July	• Estonia, Latvia and Lithuania vote to become Soviet republics
July	• German troops occupy Channel Islands
July	• Pro-Nazi French government of unoccupied France installed at Vichy, with Pétain as Head of State: Vichy government breaks off relations with Britain
Aug	• Churchill signs alliance with General de Gaulle
Aug	• Battle of Britain – RAF defeats German Air Force (to Oct)
Sept	• Germans bomb London: the 'Blitz' (to Oct)
Oct	• Romania allies with Germany
Nov	• Italy attacks Greece: British troops land in Greece to repel invasion

Feb	• German troops enter Bulgaria
Mar	• Yugoslavia joins tripartite pact of Germany, Italy and Japan
Mar	• Peter II overthrows pro-Axis government in Yugoslavia
Apr	• German troops enter Yugoslavia, and subsequently occupy Albania, Macedonia and Greece
Apr	• Germans crush Yugoslavia and Greece: British Expeditionary Force evacuated from Greece
May	• British forces withdraw from Crete
June	• Hitler invades USSR
June	• Battle of Bialystok–Minsk: Germans take 300,000 Russians prisoner
June	• Germans take Smolensk
July	• Anglo–Russian alliance
Sept	• Siege of Leningrad begins (lifted Jan 1944)
Sept	• (to Oct) 600,000 Russians taken prisoner after battles of Kiev and Viazma–Briansk: Orel, Kharkov and Odessa fall to Germans
Nov	• Battle for Moscow results in German stand-off (Dec)
Dec	• Russo–German front stabilized during winter months
Dec	• Germany and Italy declare war on USA
Dec	• Britain declares war on Finland, Hungary and Romania

AMERICAS

Sept	• Canadian Parliament votes to join war against Germany
Sept	• President Roosevelt declares US neutrality
Sept	• Stocks soar on Wall Street as investors predict war boom
Dec	• Battle of the River Plate: *Graf Spee* scuttled off Montevideo

June	• General Election in Canada: Mackenzie King's Liberal government confirmed in office
Sept	• USA introduces compulsory military service
Oct	• USA leases bases in Brazil and Chile
Nov	• F D Roosevelt re-elected for 3rd term

Mar	• USA introduces lease-lend system of aid to Britain and China
Mar	• USA seizes Italian, German and Danish ships in 16 ports
Apr	• US troops occupy Greenland
July	• Peru and Ecuador reach accord on border conflict
Aug	• USA extends lease-lend to USSR
Aug	• Churchill and Roosevelt meet in mid-Atlantic and issue Atlantic Charter
Dec	• Japan bombs Pearl Harbor, in effort to destroy US Pacific fleet
Dec	• USA declares war on Japan, Germany and Italy

AFRICA, ASIA, AUSTRALASIA

Sept	• Jan Smuts becomes premier of South Africa on J B Hertzog's resignation

Feb	• New five-year-old Dalai Lama enthroned in Tibet
May	• Following preaching of pacifism by Mohandas Gandhi, 40,000 Indian National Congress members imprisoned
June	• Spain occupies Tangier
July	• Italians invade Sudan
July	• British cripple French fleets at Oran and Mers el-Kebir
Aug	• Italians invade British Somaliland
Sept	• Small British force working with Ethiopian guerrillas
Sept	• Tripartite pact between Germany, Italy and Japan
Sept	• Japan invades Tonkin, northern French Indo-China
Dec	• General Wavell's British Offensive in Libya gets as far as El Agheila, expelling all Italians

Jan	• British offensive begins in East Africa: Emperor Haile Selassie re-enters Ethiopia
Feb	• Riot in Johannesburg following pro-Nazi meeting
Feb	• British take Benghazi, Libya
Feb	• German troops cross to North Africa under Field Marshal Erwin Rommel
Feb	• British take Mogadishu in Italian Somaliland
Mar	• German counter-offensive in North Africa begins
Apr	• British take Asmara, Addis Ababa and Massawa in Ethiopia
May	• Ethiopia gains independence from Italian control
June	• British and Free French invade Syria
July	• Japan occupies all French Indo-China
Aug	• Britain and USSR occupy Iran
Sept	• End of Italian operations in Libya
Nov	• British renew offensive in Libya
Dec	• Rommel begins withdrawal from Libya
Dec	• Japan attacks Pearl Harbor, Hawaii
Dec	• Japan occupies Hong Kong and Philippines

SCIENCE & CULTURE

• See page 69

• Penicillin is developed by Howard Florey as an antibiotic
• Discovery in France of Lascaux caves, famous for prehistoric wall paintings
• Glen Seaborg in California obtains plutonium by bombarding uranium with deuterons
• Sergei Prokofiev's ballet *Romeo and Juliet* played at Leningrad
• Charlie Chaplin performs in the film *The Great Dictator*
• Ernest Hemingway *For Whom the Bell Tolls*
• Graham Greene *The Power and the Glory*

• Hans Haas begins subaquatic photography
• First flight by Paul Sayer of Gloster jet fighter, Britain's first jet aircraft, based on work of Frank Whittle
• Orson Welles directs *Citizen Kane*
• Dmitri Shostakovich 7th Symphony (Leningrad)
• Michael Tippett *A Child of Our Time*
• Stanley Spencer *Shipbuilding in the Clyde*

EUROPE	AMERICAS

1942

EUROPE

Mar	● RAF 'saturation bombing' of German targets begins
May	● German offensive in Crimea
June	● In USSR, Germans smash through wide front from Kursk to Kharkhov
July	● Germans enter Sebastopol
Aug	● Allied raid on Dieppe
Aug	● Portugal and Spain form neutral 'Iberian Bloc'
Sept	● Siege of Stalingrad begins (to Jan 1943)
Nov	● Russians recover Kiev
Nov	● Vichy France occupied by Germans and Italians
Nov	● French navy scuttled in Toulon harbour

AMERICAS

Jan	● All American republics except Argentina sever diplomatic relations with Axis powers
May	● Negro recruits allowed in US navy for first time
May	● Japan invades Aleutian Islands
June	● Mexico declares war on Axis powers
June	● General Eisenhower appointed Commander-in-Chief of US forces in Europe
Aug	● Brazil declares war on Axis after sinking of several Brazilian ships
Nov	● USA breaks off diplomatic relations with Vichy France

1943

EUROPE

Jan	● First daylight bombing of Berlin
July	● Allies land on Sicily and take Syracuse and Palermo
July	● Benito Mussolini falls: anti-fascist Marshal Badoglio forms Italian government
July	● Russians defeat German offensive at Kursk
Aug	● Russians retake Orel and Messina taken
Sept	● Donetz basin liberated
Sept	● Italy surrenders unconditionally to the Allies
Sept	● Germany occupies northern Italy and Rome: Allies invade Italian mainland at Salerno
Oct	● Free French troops liberate Corsica
Oct	● Italy declares war on Germany
Dec	● Communist government formed by Josip Broz (Tito) in Yugoslavia

AMERICAS

May	● US forces land on Attu in Aleutian Islands, held by Japanese
June	● Military coup d'état in Argentina – fascist-type government instituted

1944

EUROPE

Jan	● Battle of Monte Cassino (to May)
May	● Crimea liberated
May	● Stalin tells Bulgaria, Romania and Hungary to declare war on Germany
June	● Allies enter Rome
June	● (6th) D-Day: Allies land in Normandy and begin invasion of German-held Western Europe
June	● Germans start to use V1 and V2 rockets to bombard Britain
June	● New Russian offensive against Finland
July	● Abortive attempt on Hitler's life
Aug	● General de Gaulle enters liberated Paris
Sept	● Battle of Arnhem: Allied progress checked
Nov	● Russian forces cross the Danube

AMERICAS

Jan	● Argentina breaks with Axis powers
Feb	● More than 100 German agents captured in Chile
July	● British and US ambassadors recalled from Argentina
Nov	● F D Roosevelt re-elected US President for unprecedented 4th term

1945

EUROPE

Jan	● Stalin, Roosevelt and Churchill meet at Yalta conference
Mar	● Allies reach Rhine and take Cologne
Apr	● Russians take Vienna and Berlin (23rd)
Apr	● Mussolini and mistress lynched by Italian partisans
Apr	● Hitler commits suicide
May	● Germans' unconditional surrender to Allies: end of War in Europe
June	● Germany partitioned into occupation zones between Britain, France, USA and USSR
July	● General Election in Britain: Labour Party takes office under Clement Attlee
July	● Potsdam Conference: Japan warned to make peace or suffer 'prompt and utter destruction'
Nov	● Nuremberg trials of principal Nazi leaders begin
Nov	● De Gaulle appointed head of French provisional government

AMERICAS

Mar	● Argentina declares war on Germany
Apr	● President Roosevelt dies, succeeded by Vice President Harry Truman (to 1952)
Oct	● Military coup d'état by young officers in Venezuela: attempt at democratic government under Romulo Betancourt and Gallegos (until 1948)

AFRICA, ASIA, AUSTRALASIA

Feb	• Japanese invade Burma, Malaysia and Singapore
Mar	• Java surrenders to the Japanese
Mar	• Australia becomes Allied base in Pacific
Mar	• Sir Stafford Cripps sent by British government to India with promise of dominion status for India after war
May	• Japanese take Mandalay
June	• Battle of Midway: Japanese fleet crippled by US forces in the Pacific
June	• British lose Tobruk to Germans
Aug	• All-India Congress Committee rejects 'Cripps Offer'
Oct	• British Eighth Army defeats Germans at El Alamein
Nov	• First battle of Tunisia (to Dec)

Jan	• Eighth Army enters Tripoli, joined by Free French forces from Chad
Jan	• Casablanca Conference: Allies demand unconditional surrender from Germany, Italy and Japan
Mar	• Japanese defeated in Battle of Bismarck Sea
May	• Axis forces surrender in Tunisia
Aug	• Louis Mountbatten appointed Supreme Allied Commander, South-East Asia
Oct	• Japanese declare Burma independent
Oct	• Japanese declare Philippines independent
Nov	• Churchill, Roosevelt and Stalin meet in Tehran to plan defeat of Hitler
Dec	• Tehran Conference: second meeting of Churchill, Roosevelt and Stalin: Stalin promises to declare war on Japan after Germany's defeat
Dec	• Syria and Lebanon given independence by France

Jan	• Moroccan nationalists demand independence, riots follow
Jan	• Americans take Marshall Islands and Solomon Islands
Apr	• Allies begin to retake New Guinea
July	• US forces occupy Guam
July	• US forces seize Saipan in the Mariana Islands from Japan, 1,300 miles from Tokyo, enabling US to begin bombing Japan
Oct	• Japanese fleet heavily defeated as US forces land on Leyte in the Philippines

Feb	• Ahmed Pasha, Egyptian prime minister, assassinated after declaring war on Germany
Mar	• Arab League inaugurated in Cairo
Mar	• USA takes Iwo Jima Island, 750 miles from Tokyo
Mar	• France grants autonomy to Indo-China
Apr	• Japanese fleet destroyed in Battle of Okinawa
May	• Burma liberated by British troops
June	• British occupy Syria and Lebanon
Aug	• First atomic bomb destroys Hiroshima, second atomic bomb destroys Nagasaki
Aug	• Russia declares war on Japan: immediate advance into Manchuria
Aug	• Japan surrenders unconditionally to Allies
Sept	• Ho Chi Minh forms government in part of Indo-China (later North Vietnam)

SCIENCE & CULTURE

- Construction of world's first nuclear reactor at Chicago University led by Enrico Fermi
- Albert Camus *The Outsider* and *The Myth of Sisyphus*
- Richard Strauss *Capriccio*
- Bing Crosby sings *White Christmas*
- T S Eliot completes *The Four Quartets*
- C S Lewis *The Screwtape Letters*
- Magnetic recording tape is invented

- Chubb Crater, largest known meteorite crater, discovered at northern Ungava, Canada
- Rolls-Royce 'Welland' jet engine developed
- Humphrey Bogart and Ingrid Bergman star in *Casablanca*
- J P Sartre *Being and Nothingness*
- Rodgers and Hammerstein musical *Oklahoma!*

- Invention of the kidney machine
- Aaron Copland *Appalachian Spring*
- Jean Anouilh *Antigone*
- Tennessee Williams *The Glass Menagerie*
- Jackson Pollock Abstract Expressionist painting

- Karl Popper *The Open Society and its Enemies*
- George Orwell *Animal Farm*
- Evelyn Waugh *Brideshead Revisited*
- Benjamin Britten *Peter Grimes*
- Henry Moore *Family Group*
- Richard Strauss *Metamorphoses*
- David Lean directs *Brief Encounter*

THE END OF EMPIRE

Decolonization after the war was a haphazard, laborious and often bitter process.

Nationalist fervour in the Asian Empires of the European powers, Britain, France and the Netherlands, was running at fever pitch in 1945. Their European rulers had been humiliated by Japan, which had invaded South-East Asia in 1941–2 and had then promised the European colonies in the region their independence after the war. Furthermore, President Roosevelt was hostile to European colonialism and did not want to see the Europeans recover their empires in 1945. In 1941 he had tried to persuade Britain to sign and the other Allies to agree to the Atlantic Charter, which guaranteed world-wide democratic self-government after the war, and he believed that indigenous democratic regimes in Asia would be pro-American. Britain, France and the Netherlands, however, had as little intention in 1945 of applying the general principle of national self-determination to their empires as they had had in 1919. Although Britain granted independence to India and Pakistan in 1947 and to Burma and Ceylon in 1948 this was based as much on necessity as on conviction. Britain could no longer bear the burden of governing a huge subcontinent in which the mass of the people were in favour of independence and where the continued loyalty of the Indian Army could not be relied upon. As far as Britain was concerned, this was the end of the independence process for the foreseeable future.

▼ On 'Black Saturday' (26 January) 1952 serious rioting against the British military presence in Egypt broke out and many British nationals were killed.

▼ Princess Alexandra in Lagos for Nigeria's independence. Nigeria was one of the first British colonies in Africa to be granted independence.

▲ General Salan urges demonstrators in Algeria, in May 1958, to remain loyal to the French government.

With the defeat of the Japanese in 1945, British forces had re-occupied Malaya, Singapore and Hong Kong and had connived at the re-establishment of French and Dutch rule in Indo-China and the Dutch East Indies. The French and Dutch immediately found themselves faced with powerful nationalist movements. After sustained and bloody battles with Indonesian guerrillas, the Dutch abandoned Indonesia to the nationalists in 1949. The French, however, fought on in Indo-China against the Vietminh (Vietnamese nationalist) guerrillas, dominated by the communists and led by Ho Chi Minh, a veteran nationalist. In 1954, after a series of reverses in northern Vietnam, culminating in the capitulation of an entire French army corps at Dien Bien Phu to the Vietminh, France agreed to grant full independence to Laos and Cambodia, while Vietnam was split in two pending proposed all-Vietnam elections in 1956.

Britain escaped the worst manifestations of the nationalist turmoil, although its efforts to forge a zone of influence in the Middle East collapsed as a result of strenuous Egyptian resistance to continued British tutelage. At the end of 1956 Britain's position in the region was seriously undermined when an Anglo–French military expedition, which had invaded Egypt in protest against the nationalization of the Suez Canal, was forced to withdraw in humiliating circumstances after the United States imposed financial sanctions on Britain. During the 1960s Britain granted independence to most of its colonies but continued to maintain a naval presence east of Suez until 1970, and was burdened with the problem of Rhodesia (Zimbabwe) until 1980.

With the onset of the Cold War in the 1950s, the attitude of the United States towards colonialism became more ambiguous. The victory of Mao Zedong's (Mao Tse-Tung) communists in China in October 1949 convinced Washington that communism was a threat to world peace, and that nationalist movements in Indo–China, the Middle East and Africa were in danger of becoming dominated by Moscow- or Beijing-backed communists. After 1950 France began to receive substantial United States aid for its struggle in Indo–China, while Britain began to lobby for United States assistance in its conflicts with nationalists in Iran and elsewhere. However, the United States insisted that France and Britain should give their colonies real independence while also offering help to suppress communism, hoping that as a result stable, non-communist, democratic governments, would emerge. However, where the United States perceived the rise of left-wing regimes as threatening its interests, it frequently brought about their demise. Given that their successors were often military or right-wing regimes, the United States became identified with reactionary anti-democratic governments in Africa, South America and Asia. For its part the Soviet Union, after 1953, began to support nationalist anti-American leaders in the Third World who might bring their countries into the Soviet bloc.

Decolonization was a haphazard, laborious and often bitter process. France struggled for eight years to crush the nationalists in Algeria, and the outcome brought France to the brink of civil war in 1958. However, by 1955 a recognizable bloc of so-called non-aligned nations had emerged, consisting of left-wing countries like Yugoslavia and China, which had resisted Soviet domination, and newly independent countries like India, all of which wished to avoid involvement in superpower rivalries.

The British Empire after 1945

USSR

CHINA

AFGHANISTAN

KASHMIR

Ceasefire line 1949

Peshawar

Srinagar

Rawalpindi

TIBET

N-W FRONTIER PROVINCES

Lahore

Amritsar

Simla

Lhasa

PUNJAB

Quetta

WEST PAKISTAN

Delhi

NEPAL

UNITED

Katmandu

SIKKIM

Thimpu

BHUTAN

Brahmaputra

ASSAM

BALUCHISTAN

Indus

RAJPUTANA

Jaipur

Agra

Lucknow

Ganges

PROVINCES

Patna

Imphal

Gwadar

Hyderabad

Allahabad

Benares

BIHAR

BENGAL

Dacca

BURMA
independent 1948

Karachi

SIND

Ahmadabad

Jabalpur

Chandernagore

Calcutta

EAST
PAKISTAN

Mandalay

Baroda

CENTRAL
PROVINCES

Nagpur

ORISSA

Cuttak

ARABIAN SEA

INDIA

Bay of Bengal

Bombay

Pune

HYDERABAD
annexed by India Sept 1948

Vishakhapatnam

BOMBAY

Hyderabad

Yanaon

GOA
to India 1961

MADRAS

MYSORE

Madras

Bangalore

Pondicherry

Calicut

G. of Mannar

CEYLON
independent 1948

Colombo

— Boundary of British India to 1937–1947

Province of British India before Aug 1947

Dependent state ruled by a prince

Main concentration of Sikhs before 1947

International boundary 15 Aug 1947

Hindu refugees

Muslim refugees

0 kms 600
0 mls 400

PACIFIC OCEAN

CANADA

UNIT
KING

Bermuda

Gibr

Bahama Is.

ATLANTIC OCEA

Jamaica

St. Lucia

Barbados

Trinidad and
Tobago

GAM

SIERRA
LEONE

BR. GUIANA

Ascensio

St. He

British Commonwealth, 1950

Independent member

Dependent member

Tristan da

Falkland Is.

Area of guerrilla activity 1948
Major concentration of Chinese
State boundary

0 km 150
0 mls 100

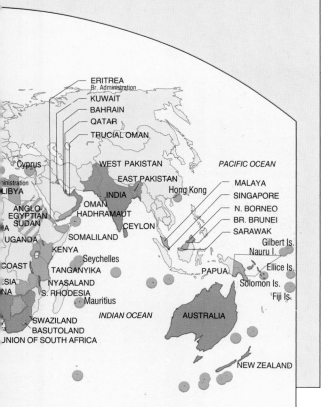

In 1939 the Viceroy of India, without consulting Indian opinion, declared war on Germany. The Indian National Congress Party campaigned against India's involvement in the war and against Britain's continued presence in India. In 1942 India was offered dominion status at the end of the war if the Congress Party would support the war effort. The Congress rejected this proposal and continued its anti-British campaign. Since Muslim opinion favoured the war, the British cultivated the Muslim League, led by Mohammed Ali Jinnah, which increased tensions between Muslims and Hindus in India.

In 1945 the British Labour government, committed to independence, sent a Cabinet delegation to India to try to resolve the differences between the Congress and the League. This effort failed and Jinnah embarked on 'Direct Action' to secure a separate Muslim state, which resulted in considerable communal violence during 1946 and 1947. In desperation the government sent Lord Louis Mountbatten to India as Viceroy, with a mandate to secure Indian independence in June 1948. Finding that the communal violence was intensifying, he advanced the independence date to 15 August 1947 and a mixed Hindu–Muslim boundary commission was set up to determine the borders between the two prospective states.

The commission's difficulties were increased by the fact that the new state of Pakistan would consist of two areas, East and West Pakistan, separated by 1,100 miles of Indian territory. Many Hindus would remain in Pakistan, while India would contain a substantial Muslim minority. Independence therefore resulted in an exodus of 13 million Sikhs and Hindus fleeing from Pakistan into India, and Muslim refugees moving in the other direction. Appalling atrocities ensued as Hindus and Muslims clashed along the borders. The rulers of the 562 princely states, were left to determine whether they wanted to join India or Pakistan. Although the majority of his people were Muslims the Hindu ruler of Kashmir opted for India and this led to clashes between India and Pakistan.

With the independence of India and Pakistan, the British Commonwealth and Empire became known more simply as the British Commonwealth and aimed to unite all of Britain's former colonies and promote economic and cultural ties.

Malayan independence followed from a long guerrilla war conducted by the Malayan Communist party, which consisted mainly of ethnic Chinese. Britain sent troops to crush the guerrillas in 1948 and its efforts were assisted by the lack of support from ethnic Malays for the uprising. In 1957 the communists were defeated and Britain granted independence to Malaya.

The French Empire after 1945

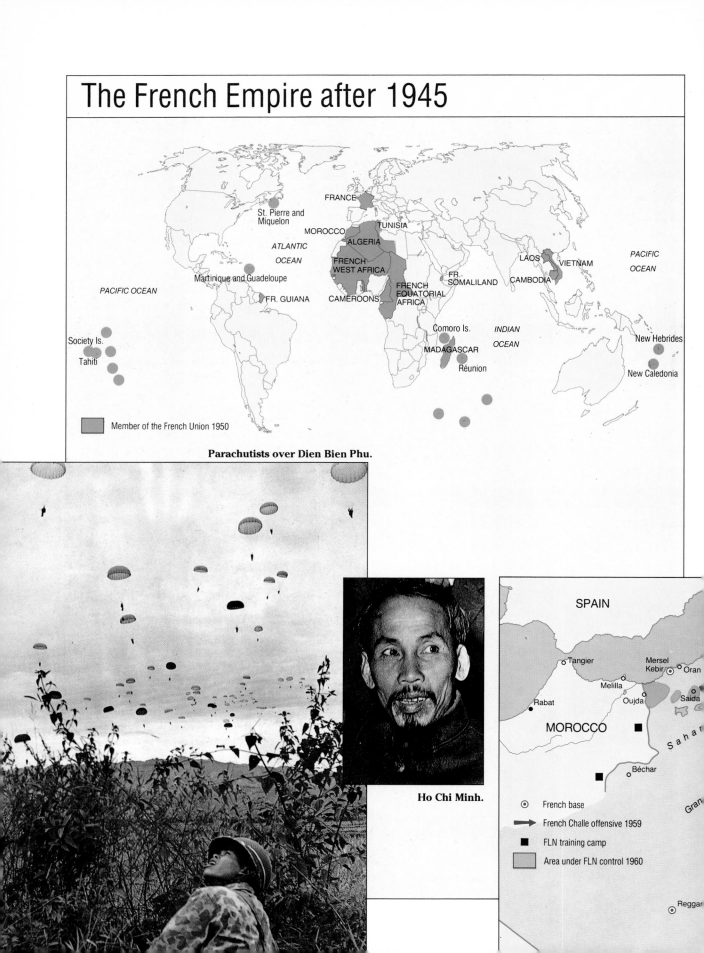

St. Pierre and Miquelon

FRANCE

MOROCCO TUNISIA

ALGERIA

ATLANTIC
OCEAN

FRENCH
WEST AFRICA

LAOS VIETNAM

PACIFIC
OCEAN

PACIFIC OCEAN

Martinique and Guadeloupe

FR. GUIANA

CAMEROONS

FR.
SOMALILAND

CAMBODIA

FRENCH
EQUATORIAL
AFRICA

Comoro Is.

INDIAN

OCEAN

New Hebrides

Society Is.

MADAGASCAR

Tahiti

Réunion

New Caledonia

Member of the French Union 1950

Parachutists over Dien Bien Phu.

Ho Chi Minh.

SPAIN

Tangier

Mersel
Kebir Oran

Melilla

Rabat

Oujda

Saida

MOROCCO

Sahar

Béchar

⊙ French base

➤ French Challe offensive 1959

■ FLN training camp

Area under FLN control 1960

Reggar

In September 1945, Ho Chi Minh, founder of the Vietnam nationalist movement, the Vietminh, set up a communist-dominated coalition government in Vietnam and declared the country independent. When French forces returned after the defeat of Japan, they discovered that Ho's government controlled most of northern Vietnam. After negotiations with the Vietminh broke down at the end of 1946, full-scale conflict broke out between the two sides, with the Vietminh initially employing guerrilla tactics, but later engaging in conventional warfare as their strength grew. The Vietminh secured military equipment and supplies from communist China after 1949 and in the following year the United States provided the French with aid.

In 1953 the French established a large garrison at Dien Bien Phu in northern Vietnam, hoping to lure the Vietminh into the open and then destroy them. The Vietminh, however, besieged the base and forced the French to surrender Dien Bien Phu in May 1954. By this time the French had wearied of the costly Indo-China imbroglio and at an international conference at Geneva in May–July 1954 agreed to grant complete independence to Laos and Cambodia, and to divide Vietnam along the 17th parallel, with the French policing the south and the Vietminh remaining in control of the north until all-Vietnamese elections could be held in 1956.

After the Second World War France was largely incapable of enforcing its rule throughout the colonies of the French Empire. Full independence was given to Morocco and Tunisia in 1956. Algeria, however, was regarded as an integral part of metropolitan France since it contained two million

French settlers. War broke out in Algeria in 1954 when Ben Bella's National Liberation Front (the FLN) began a guerrilla campaign against the French presence. This led to savage French reprisals, in which torture was used against captured communists. By May 1958 the French army in Algeria had gained the upper hand. However, on 1 June General de Gaulle was appointed Prime Minister with a mandate to prevent civil war in France. When, in 1960, he offered to negotiate with the FLN, the French army in Algeria mutinied, but this rebellion was soon crushed. While he had initially hoped that the Algerians would accept some form of autonomy, he soon realized that they would never accept this and after negotiations with the FLN at Evian in France in 1962 he agreed to Algeria's complete independence.

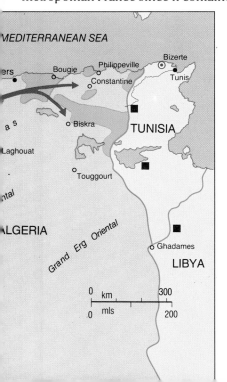

Boundary of French Indo-China to July 1954

ANNAM   Ancient kingdom of Vietnam

→   Vietminh offensive 1951

Area of communist control by

1950

1954

✷   Battle

Britain and the Middle East 1945–1960

GREECE

USSR

CASPIAN

TURKEY

Ankara

Athens

Izmir

Kayseri

Tabriz

Antalya

Adana

Halab

Mosul

Hamadan

Crete

CYPRUS
1960

Nicosia

Dhekelia

SYRIA
1943

Euphrates

Tigris

Zagros

Akrotiri

LEBANON
1943

Beirut

Damascus

IRAQ

Baghdad

Habbaniya

MEDITERRANEAN SEA

Haifa

LIBYA
1943–51

Alexandria

ISRAEL
1948

Amman

Jerusalem

Basra
Shuayba

Abadan

Port Said

Suez Canal

Sinai

TRANSJORDAN
1946

Neutral
Zone

KUWAIT
1961

Kuwait

Cairo

Suez

Neutral Zone

BAHRAIN
1971

Asyut

An Nafud

Persian

EGYPT

Nile

Libyan
Desert

Aswan

L Nasser

RED
SEA

Medina

Riyadh

SAUDI   ARABIA

Jidda

Mecca

Nubian Desert

Port Sudan

SUDAN
1956

Rub al Khal

Atbara

British possession or mandated
territory independent by

	1960
	1970
	1980
	British administration with dates
	British occupation during Second World War
	British military zone to 1956
⊙	British base after independence
1961	Year of independence
	Member of Baghdad Pact 1955
→	Anglo-French/Israeli attacks 1956

ERITREA
1941–52

Massawa

YEMEN

ADEN
(SOUTH YEMEN)
1967

Khartoum

Asmera

Sana

Mukalla

Wad Medani

Al Hudaydah

0 km   400

0 mls   300

White Nile

Blue Nile

ETHIOPIA

Aden

Gulf of Aden

In 1945 Britain was determined to re-establish itself as the dominant power in the Middle East. The British-garrisoned Suez Canal base was to be at the centre of this sphere of influence while Britain sought alliances with the Arab states to enable its forces to remain on their soil. The first challenge to Britain's ambitions took place in the Palestine mandate, where Zionist resentment against British restrictions on Jewish immigration led, after 1944, to increasing Jewish terrorist activities against both British forces and the Palestinian Arabs. In 1947 the United Nations proposed the partition of Palestine into an Arab and a Jewish state, but the Arabs rejected this plan. The United States supported the Jewish cause and in 1947–8 Britain, exasperated by the seemingly endless violence, withdrew its forces from the mandate. The Jews then proclaimed the new state of Israel, whereupon the neighbouring states sent troops to assist the Arabs. They were defeated by the Israelis.

Britain could not persuade Egypt to agree to the continued presence of British troops in the Suez Canal Zone, and in 1954 they agreed to evacuate the Zone, with the proviso that in the event of war they could return. Britain then moved its main base to Cyprus, but in 1955 was faced with a campaign of violence by the Greek Cypriots, who demanded *enosis* or union with Greece, rather than permanent British rule.

In Egypt a nationalist army colonel, Abdul Nasser, seized power in 1954 and began a propaganda campaign to appeal to all Arabs to unite against western imperialism and Israel. The British, alarmed by this threat to their Middle Eastern interests, joined forces with France and Israel to crush Nasser in 1956, after the Egyptian ruler nationalized the Anglo–French owned Suez Canal. An Anglo–French military expedition which landed in Egypt during the late autumn was forced to withdraw after the United States, angered by this display of Anglo–French imperialism, imposed financial sanctions on Britain. This was a major setback, but Britain did not entirely abandon the Middle East. When it gave independence to Cyprus in 1960 it retained bases on the island. Britain had also persuaded Turkey, Iraq, Iran and Pakistan to join it in the Baghdad Pact, a defensive alliance system against the Soviet Union. In 1958 Nasserite and nationalist agitation led to the downfall of the pro-British regime in Iraq, which was followed shortly by the withdrawal of that country from the Pact. In 1958 Britain and the United States sent troops to Jordan and Lebanon respectively to defend them from an alleged Nasserite coup. However, by this time, the United States was taking over Britain's role in the Middle East.

Decolonization in Africa

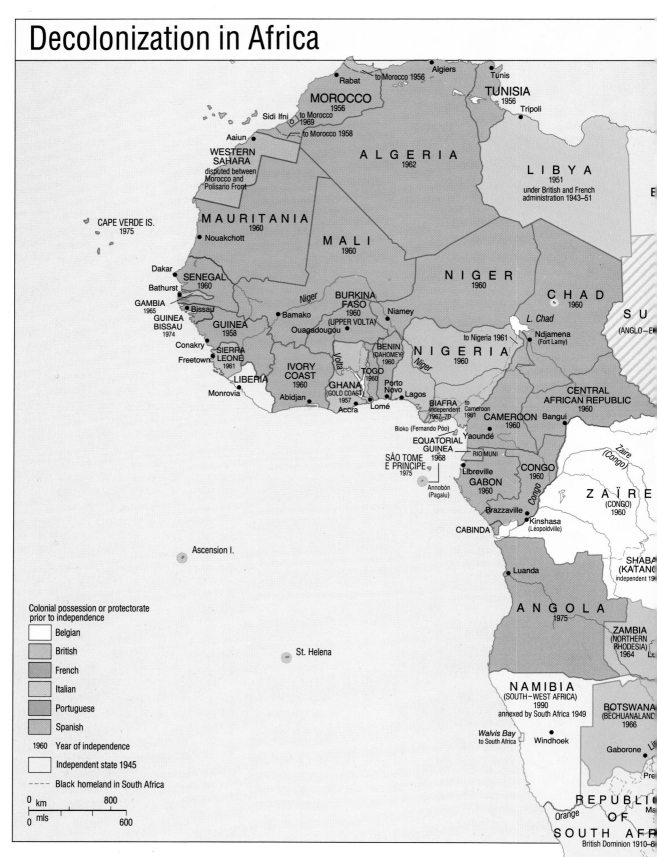

Algiers
Tunis
Rabat
to Morocco 1956
TUNISIA
1956
MOROCCO
1956
Tripoli
Sidi Ifni
to Morocco
1969
to Morocco 1958
Aaiun
A L G E R I A
1962
L I B Y A
1951
under British and French
administration 1943–51
WESTERN
SAHARA
disputed between
Morocco and
Polisario Front

CAPE VERDE IS.
1975

M A U R I T A N I A
1960
Nouakchott

M A L I
1960

N I G E R
1960

C H A D
1960

S U
(ANGLO–E

Dakar
SENEGAL
1960
Bathurst
GAMBIA
1965
Bissau
GUINEA
BISSAU
1974
Niger
BURKINA
FASO
1960
(UPPER VOLTA)
Niamey
Bamako
Ouagadougou
L. Chad
to Nigeria 1961
Ndjamena
(Fort Lamy)
Conakry
GUINEA
1958
SIERRA
LEONE
1961
Freetown
LIBERIA
Monrovia
IVORY
COAST
1960
Abidjan
Volta
GHANA
(GOLD COAST)
1957
Accra
TOGO
1960
Lomé
BENIN
(DAHOMEY)
1960
Porto
Novo
Lagos
N I G E R I A
1960
Niger
BIAFRA
Independent
1967–70
to
Cameroon
1961
CENTRAL
AFRICAN REPUBLIC
1960
Bangui
Bioko (Fernando Póo)
CAMEROON
1960
Yaoundé
EQUATORIAL
GUINEA   1968
SÃO TOME
E PRINCIPE
1975
RIO MUNI
Libreville
GABON
1960
CONGO
1960
Z A Ï R E
(CONGO)
1960
Annobón
(Pagalu)
Brazzaville
Kinshasa
(Léopoldville)
CABINDA
Congo
Zaïre
(Congo)

Ascension I.

SHABA
(KATAN
independent 19

Luanda

A N G O L A
1975

St. Helena

ZAMBIA
(NORTHERN
RHODESIA)
1964

NAMIBIA
(SOUTH–WEST AFRICA)
1990
annexed by South Africa 1949
Walvis Bay
to South Africa
Windhoek

BOTSWANA
(BECHUANALAND
1966
Gaborone

Colonial possession or protectorate
prior to independence

Belgian
British
French
Italian
Portuguese
Spanish

1960   Year of independence

Independent state 1945

- - - -   Black homeland in South Africa

0   km   800
0   mls   600

REPUBLI
O F
SOUTH AFR
British Dominion 1910–6
Orange
Pre
Cape Town

In the late 1950s and 1960s Britain, France and Belgium rapidly divested themselves of their African colonies. Britain began the process in 1957 when Ghana was given its independence, followed by Nigeria in 1960. France granted independence to Equatorial and West Africa between 1958 and 1960. The independence process in West Africa was relatively smooth because white settlers were few in number and the new ruling elites tended to be reformist and pro-Western. In East Africa, after the British crushed the Mau Mau uprising, Kenya achieved independence in December 1963 under Jomo Kenyatta, who sought to modernize Kenya and encouraged white settlers and businessmen to remain in the country. In Rhodesia, however, the situation was far more complicated. The British had established the Central African Federation in 1953, but it was unpopular with the black majority, which viewed it as a device for maintaining white supremacy. In 1963 Northern Rhodesia and Nyasaland seceded and were later granted their independence as Zambia and Malawi respectively. However, Southern Rhodesia had a substantial white settler minority which was determined not to allow black majority rule. Under Ian Smith it declared its independence of Britain in 1965 and despite economic sanctions it survived until 1979, when after prolonged guerrilla activity, the whites agreed to a constitution in which the black Africans were given overall control of the independent Zimbabwe, as Rhodesia was renamed.

Belgium suddenly abandoned the Congo in June 1960 but a few weeks after independence the Congolese army mutinied and Belgian troops returned to restore order. Thereafter, the situation became confused as Katanga, a mineral-rich province, threatened to secede and United Nations forces were sent in to replace the Belgians. Conflict between rival political leaders threatened to lead to civil war with the superpowers being drawn in on opposite sides, but the UN force managed to restore unity and was withdrawn in 1964.

Portugal retained its colonial possessions until 1974 when a change of regime in Lisbon resulted in the granting of independence to Guinea Bissau, Mozambique and Angola, although the process in Angola and Mozambique was complicated when civil war broke out. In Angola, South Africa supported the right-wing nationalists while Cuba sent troops to assist the left (see pages 116–17).

Namibia, the former German colony of South-West Africa which had been governed under mandate by South Africa since 1919, became the last colonial territory in Africa to achieve independence when its flag was finally raised in 1990.

THE POLITICS OF INDEPENDENCE

The struggle remained primarily between the United States and the Soviet Union.

During the Cold War both the United States and the Soviet Union tried to attract the newly independent and developing nations into their respective orbits. The first Third World country to be involved in conflict during the Cold War was Korea in 1950, with war breaking out between North and South Korea, communist China supporting the North and the United States backing the South. With the death of Stalin in 1953 and the eventual succession of Nikita Khrushchev to the Soviet leadership, the Soviet Union embarked on a vigorous campaign to win over the Third World, with well-publicized visits by Khrushchev to India and elsewhere, and promises of Soviet economic and military aid as an inducement to forge closer ties with the Soviet Union. In the Middle East, where Israel was known by its enemies to be a United States client, Khrushchev calculated that Nasser would respond to offers of Soviet military equipment and technical advisers by eagerly embracing the Soviet side in the Cold War. However, leaders like Nasser were nationalists as much as socialists and had no intention of becoming Soviet satellites. Thus, when Anwar Sadat succeeded Nasser as Egyptian leader, he expelled all Soviet military personnel in 1972 and turned to the United States for support. While many Middle Eastern countries accepted Soviet aid, they also persecuted communists within their borders. Egypt, India and Yugoslavia are notable examples of the many countries which sought to avoid taking sides in the Cold War by espousing the cause of non-alignment as an alternative to close identification with either the United States or Soviet Union.

With the increasing breach between communist China and the Soviet Union in the late 1950s, Moscow found itself challenged in the Third World by a Beijing-supported brand of communism which emphasised the revolutionary potential of the peasantry against the Marxist-Leninist emphasis on the proletariat. While communist China was able to provide some assistance to Third World countries, and its emissaries had the advantage of not possessing a white skin, it could not in the last resort compete with the far greater wealth of the Soviet Union in this field. The struggle remained primarily between the United States and the Soviet Union.

The United States dwarfed both the Soviet Union and communist China in the scale of its military and economic influence world-wide after 1950. However, there was no clear victory for either side in the competition for the hearts and minds of the Third World. Most of the new states managed to preserve a precarious independence during the period, and the acceptance of aid from the East or the West did not necessarily entail complete conformity with the policies of either. While Castro was totally dependent on Soviet aid for Cuba, his country was too insignificant to be of much account in the global balance, and his cause did not prosper elsewhere in Latin America. Nor did the communist takeover of South Vietnam result in the spread of communism throughout the rest of South-East Asia, as so many Americans had feared. The influx of newly independent African countries to the United Nations after 1960 significantly altered voting patterns in the United Nations Assembly, but neither the United States nor the Soviet Union could rely on these nations supporting their respective policies. After the trauma of its defeat in Vietnam and the political turmoil of the Watergate affair the United States receded to some extent from the 'Imperial Presidency' during the 1970s as Congress showed itself disinclined to vote funds which might lead to further American involvement in Third World conflicts.

▼ **Castro and Khrushchev at the Lenin mausoleum in May 1964.**

The Growth of Terrorism

Since the 1960s terrorism has become a world-wide phenomenon. Some groups seek to publicize their cause, others to spread fear and confusion within a society so that it will collapse, allowing a new order to take its place. Assassinations, ambushes of security forces, explosions in public places, and guerrilla warfare are just a few of the tactics employed.

The most active terrorist groups in recent years have emerged from the conflict in the Middle East after 1948. Palestinian Arab extremists, deprived of their homeland by Israel's victories in wars with neighbouring Arab states, formed the Popular Front for the Liberation of Palestine (PLO) in 1964 to campaign for the establishment of an independent Arab state in Palestine. Its military wing, Al Fatah, launched commando raids into Israel and in July 1968 hijacked an El Al airliner and forced it to land at Algiers. Thereafter the seizure of airliners and the holding of their passengers as hostages became a regular terrorist activity, providing wide media coverage for various causes. International action to tighten up airport and aircraft security since 1980 has made this activity less prevalent, although in December 1988 terrorists placed a bomb on an American airliner which blew up over Scotland, killing its passengers and crew.

The revolution in Iran and the rise of Islamic fundamentalism during the 1980s gave rise to numerous terrorist groups, notably in the Lebanon, which are closely identified with the Tehran regime and are probably financed by it. The Islamic Jihad (Islamic Holy War) is one such fundamentalist organization and was responsible for the October 1983 bomb attack on the United States Marine barracks in Beirut. The Abu Nidal organization, a band of revolutionary socialist Muslims has been responsible for bomb attacks in the Lebanon, Italy and Greece, and for hijacking planes and ships. Western journalists, diplomats and businessmen in Beirut have been kidnapped and held hostage, including the special envoy of the Archbishop of Canterbury, Terry Waite, in 1987, who was in Beirut negotiating for the release of hostages.

In Europe revolutionary groups ranging from the left-wing Red Army faction or Baader-Meinhof gang in West Germany to the neo-fascist Avanguardia Nationale in Italy have been responsible for bombing and other attacks; a host of revolutionary activists and separatists across Asia and Latin America have often provoked savage reprisals by the authorities.

► In 1979 the Soviet Union sent troops to Afghanistan to defend a pro-Soviet, Marxist regime in Kabul. The Red Army found itself involved in a long guerrilla war with the Afghan Mujaheddin. In 1989, the Soviet Union finally announced the withdrawal of its troops.

American Influence Abroad 1945–60

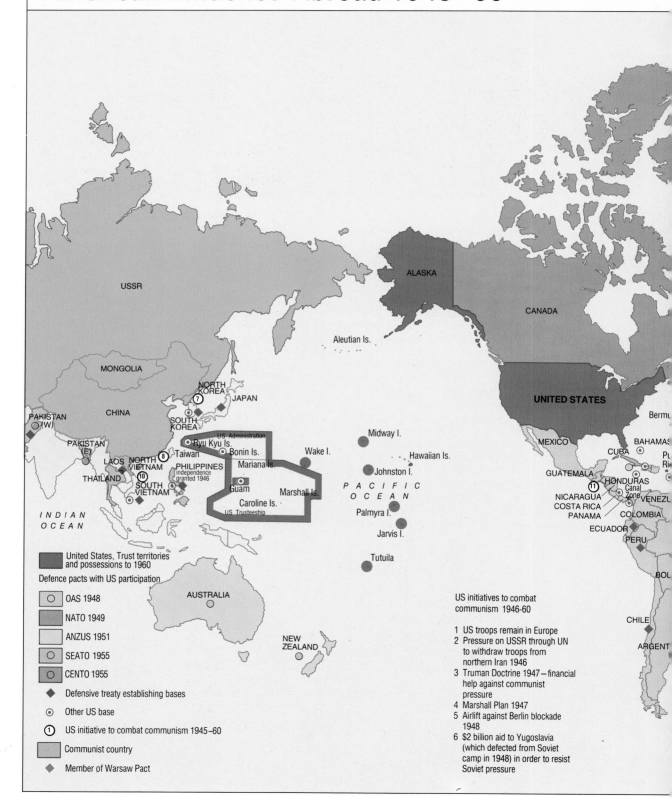

USSR

MONGOLIA

PAKISTAN (W)

PAKISTAN (E)

CHINA

NORTH KOREA ⑦

JAPAN

SOUTH KOREA

Taiwan ⑧

NORTH VIETNAM

LAOS

THAILAND ⑩

SOUTH VIETNAM

PHILIPPINES
independence granted 1946

Ryu Kyu Is. US Administration

Bonin Is.

Mariana Is.

Guam

Caroline Is.
US Trusteeship

INDIAN OCEAN

Wake I.

Marshall Is.

Midway I.

Hawaiian Is.

Johnston I.

PACIFIC OCEAN

Palmyra I.

Jarvis I.

Tutuila

Aleutian Is.

ALASKA

CANADA

UNITED STATES

Bermu

MEXICO

GUATEMALA

NICARAGUA
COSTA RICA
PANAMA

HONDURAS
Canal Zone ⑪

ECUADOR

PERU

COLOMBIA

BAHAMAS

CUBA

Pu
Ri

VENEZU

CHILE

ARGENT

BOL

AUSTRALIA

NEW ZEALAND

United States, Trust territories and possessions to 1960

Defence pacts with US participation

○ OAS 1948

NATO 1949

ANZUS 1951

○ SEATO 1955

○ CENTO 1955

◆ Defensive treaty establishing bases

⊙ Other US base

① US initiative to combat communism 1945–60

Communist country

◆ Member of Warsaw Pact

US initiatives to combat communism 1946–60

1 US troops remain in Europe
2 Pressure on USSR through UN to withdraw troops from northern Iran 1946
3 Truman Doctrine 1947 – financial help against communist pressure
4 Marshall Plan 1947
5 Airlift against Berlin blockade 1948
6 $2 billion aid to Yugoslavia (which defected from Soviet camp in 1948) in order to resist Soviet pressure

7 US troops fight for UN in Korea
  to defend it from invasion 1950
8 Taiwan protected against
  communist Chinese threat 1950s
9 Mossadeq, left-wing Prime
  Minister of Iran deposed by CIA
  plot 1953
10 Takeover of France's
   responsibilities in Indo-China
   after 1954
11 Right-wing Guatemalans
   assisted to overthrow Marxist
   regime 1954
12 Eisenhower Doctrine
   1957 – military assistance
   against communist pressure;
   granted to Lebanon 1958

The United States emerged from the Second World War as the richest and most powerful country in the world. Its troops were stationed across Western Europe, it dominated Japan, and it had acquired a string of bases in the Caribbean and in the Atlantic and the Pacific Oceans. Although they intended to play an active part in the United Nations, America's leaders did not plan to keep American troops in Europe for more than two years after the end of the war, which caused Britain and the other Western European powers to fear that America might return to its pre-war isolationism. Nor would it cooperate with Britain against the Soviet Union. However, when Britain planned the withdrawal of its military aid to the Greek government in March 1947, the United States, alarmed by the prospect of a communist victory in a strategically crucial country, agreed to take over Britain's financial responsibilities in both Greece and Turkey. In order to persuade a reluctant Congress to vote the money, President Truman played on its increasing fears of world communism and, on 12 March, enunciated the doctrine that the United States would "support free peoples who are resisting subjugation by armed minorities or outside pressures". This suggested that the United States had embarked on a crusade to combat communism all over the world.

In 1948, alarmed by the possibility that Europe, whose economies had not recovered from the effects of the war, might succumb to communism, the United States offered, under the Marshall Plan, financial aid to Europe, although the offer was couched in such terms as to discourage the participation of the Soviet Union and its satellites. During the Berlin blockade it showed its resistance to the Soviet Union and then, in 1949, the United States signed the North Atlantic Treaty with the Western European states, Greece, Turkey, Canada and Iceland, a radical departure from the traditional American refusal to become involved in entanglements outside its own hemisphere. The United States was now firmly committed to the containment of communism, as was demonstrated by its intervention in the Korean War in 1950.

The United States continued to support decolonization, in the expectation that this would lead to the emergence of moderate pro-American governments in the former colonies willing to encourage trade and American investment. Nevertheless anti-communism led the United States to conspire with Britain to overthrow the nationalist government of Iran in 1953 which had nationalized the British-controlled Anglo–Iranian Oil Company in 1950. Thereafter American rather than British influence prevailed in Iran.

The Korean War

CHINA

NORTH KOREA

SOUTH KOREA

Najin
Chongjin
Tonghua
Benxi
Hyesanjin
Manpojin
Kilchu
Chosan
Pungsan
Songjin
Antung
Iwon
Sinuiju
Huichon
Chongju
Hungnam
Anju
Sinanju
Sunchon
Wonsan
Pyongyang
Tongchon
Sariwon
Ichon
Haeju
Kumchon
Kaesong
Chunchon
38th Parallel
Kangnung
Munsan
Seoul
Samchok
Inchon
Wonju
Amphibious attack
by US troops
15 Sept 1950
Suwon
Chungju
Ulchin
Chonan
Chongju
Andong
Hamchang
Yongdok
Taejon
Pohang
Kumchon
Yongchon
Kunsan
Taegu
Chonju
Kochang
Namwon
Chinju
Masan
Pusan
Kwangju
Sunchon
Mokpo
Yosu

Yalu
Chongchon
Nam
Imjin
Han
Kum
Naktong

Korea Bay
SEA OF JAPAN
YELLOW SEA

US and UN troops
arrive from Japan
July 1950

Korea Strait

Tsushima (Japan)

North Korean attacks June 1950
Pusan perimeter 10 –15 Sept 1950
UN attacks Sept-Nov 1950
Front line 24 Nov 1950
North Korea
South Korea

0 km 100
0 mls 80

An M-41 tank manned by US army personnel in Korea.

Front line 24 Nov 1950
Front line 24 Jan 1951
Cease-fire line 27 Nov 1951
Chinese attacks
UN attacks
North Korea
South Korea

When Japanese forces in Korea surrendered in 1945, the Russian Red Army occupied North Korea down to the 38th Parallel and the United States Army moved into South Korea. However, subsequent attempts to unify the country foundered on increasing Cold War suspicions, and in 1948 a United Nations Commission supervised elections in the South but was not allowed into the North. After the elections Syngman Rhee, a conservative nationalist, became head of the South Korean government, while in the North the Soviets set up a People's Republic under the Korean communist leader, Kim Il-Sung. Both the Soviet Union and the United States thereupon withdrew their troops. On 25 June 1950 North Korea, having obtained Stalin's agreement, and convinced that the United States would not intervene, invaded South Korea and drove the South Korean army back to Pusan in the far south. President Truman committed American naval and air support and later troops to South Korea, and the United Nations called on its members to send troops to South Korea. Truman believed that with the recent loss of China to communism, he could not allow South Korea to fall, especially given its close proximity to Japan. General Douglas MacArthur – Commander of the US occupation forces in Japan – was appointed Supreme Commander of the United Nations forces and, after a daring amphibious landing at Inchon, near South Korea's capital, Seoul, in September, the UN completely overwhelmed the North Koreans, forcing them to retreat across the 38th Parallel. Truman thereupon ordered MacArthur to unify Korea and United Nations forces advanced into the North and towards the Chinese border on the Yalu river. MacArthur ignored Chinese warnings that they would intervene to prevent the establishment of American positions on the Yalu. In October, under the guise of 'volunteers', the (Chinese) Peoples' Liberation Army crossed the Yalu in force and by December had driven the United Nations forces back to the South. In 1951, after heavy fighting, the United Nations forces fought their way back to the 38th Parallel, where the front stabilized for the rest of the war. MacArthur was relieved of all his commands in April after calling on Truman to extend the war into Manchuria. Truman feared that this would lead to Soviet intervention. Armistice talks began in 1951 and dragged on until 1953, when a truce was arranged.

The death toll was considerable. The UN lost 94,000 troops, while about a million civilians were killed by ground forces and by American air attacks on North Korean cities. The Chinese communists and North Koreans lost 1.5 million, a result of the Chinese employment of 'human wave' tactics to make up for their inferiority in arms and equipment.

The Arab-Israeli Conflict

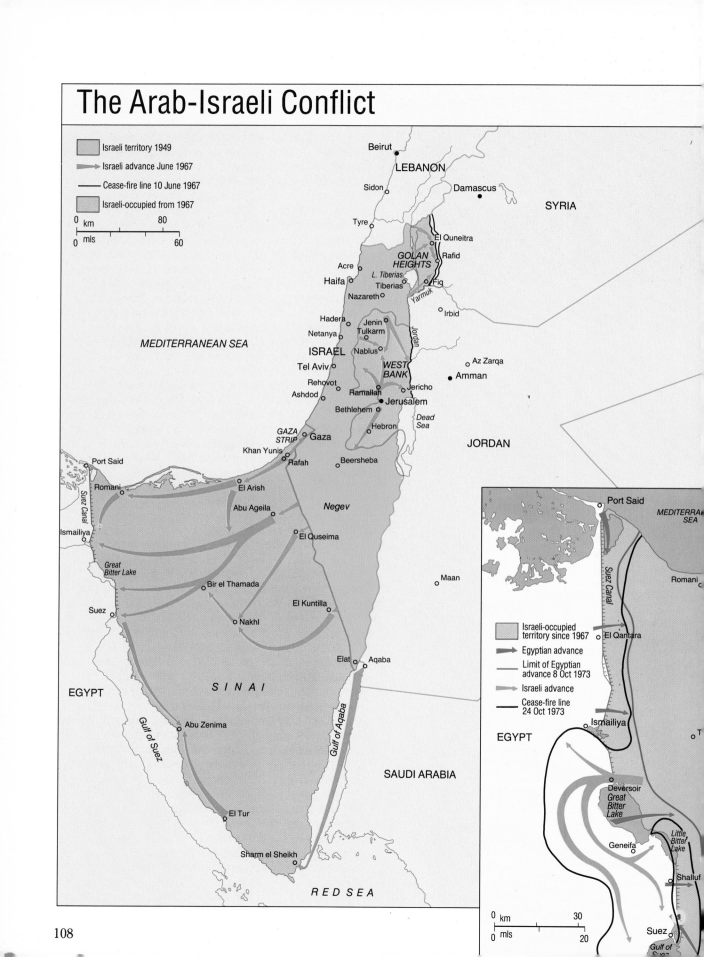

Israeli territory 1949

Israeli advance June 1967

Cease-fire line 10 June 1967

Israeli-occupied from 1967

0 km 80
0 mls 60

Beirut

LEBANON

Sidon

Damascus

SYRIA

Tyre

El Quneitra

GOLAN
HEIGHTS

Rafid

Acre

Haifa

L. Tiberias

Fiq

Tiberias

Nazareth

Yarmuk

Irbid

Hadera

Jenin

Jordan

Netanya

Tulkarm

MEDITERRANEAN SEA

ISRAEL

Nablus

Tel Aviv

WEST
BANK

Az Zarqa

Rehovot

Amman

Ashdod

Ramallah

Jericho

Jerusalem

Bethlehem

Dead
Sea

JORDAN

Hebron

GAZA
STRIP

Gaza

Khan Yunis

Beersheba

Rafah

Port Said

Romani

El Arish

Suez Canal

Negev

Abu Ageila

Ismailiya

El Quseima

Maan

Great
Bitter Lake

Bir el Thamada

Suez

El Kuntilla

Nakhl

Elat

Aqaba

EGYPT

SINAI

Gulf of Suez

Abu Zenima

Gulf of Aqaba

SAUDI ARABIA

El Tur

Sharm el Sheikh

RED SEA

108

Inset map

Port Said

MEDITERRA
SEA

Suez Canal

Israeli-occupied
territory since 1967

El Qantara

Romani

Egyptian advance

Limit of Egyptian
advance 8 Oct 1973

Israeli advance

Cease-fire line
24 Oct 1973

EGYPT

Ismailiya

Deversoir
Great
Bitter
Lake

Little
Bitter
Lake

Geneifa

Shalluf

Suez

Gulf of
Suez

0 km 30
0 mls 20

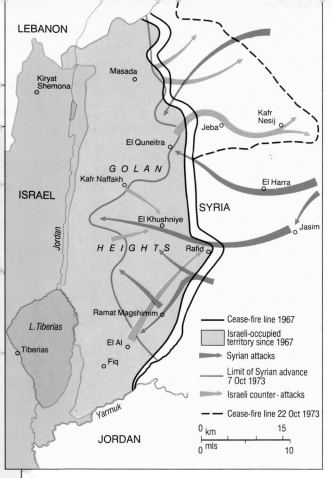

Map 1 (Golan Heights):

LEBANON
Kiryat Shemona
Masada
Kafr Nesij
Jeba
El Quneitra
GOLAN
Kafr Naffakh
El Harra
ISRAEL
SYRIA
El Khushniye
Jasim
HEIGHTS
Rafid
Jordan
Ramat Magshimim
L. Tiberias
Tiberias
El Al
Fiq
Yarmuk
JORDAN

Cease-fire line 1967
Israeli-occupied territory since 1967
Syrian attacks
Limit of Syrian advance 7 Oct 1973
Israeli counter-attacks
Cease-fire line 22 Oct 1973

0 km 15
0 mls 10

Map 2 (Lebanon):

MEDITERRANEAN SEA
Halba
Tripoli
Zgharta
Hermel
Bcharre
Asi (Orontes)
Batrun
Labwah
Jubayl (Byblos)
Qartaba
LEBANON
Baalbek
Beirut
Anti-Lebanon Mts
Hammana
Zahle
Alayh
Biqaa Valley
Damur
SYRIA
NAI
Jezzine
Sidon
Litani
Nabatea
Hasbaya
Marjayun
Tyre
Qiryat Shemona
Golan Heights under Israeli occupation since 1967
ISRAEL
Zefat
L. Tiberias

Religious areas
Shia Muslim
Sunni Muslim
Druze
Christian
Northern limit of Israeli occupation June 1982

0 km 40
0 mls 30

In1956 Israel, colluding with Britain and France, invaded Egypt with the object of destroying Egyptian-backed Arab guerrilla bands in the Sinai Desert. Although Israel achieved its objectives, the humiliating evacuation of the Anglo–French expedition from Egypt enhanced Nasser's prestige in the Arab world and he set about trying to organize a new anti-Israeli coalition of Arab states.

The immediate occasion for renewed conflict was an Israeli attack on Jordan in early 1967 in retaliation for Jordanian-based Palestinian Arab terrorist raids into Israel. Egypt, Jordan, Syria and Iraq prepared a major offensive against Israel, which was heralded in May 1967 by Nasser's expulsion from Egyptian territory of the United Nations Emergency Force, which had been stationed in the Sinai since the Suez war. However, Israel struck first, in what became known as the 'Six Day War'. Israeli forces destroyed the Egyptian Air Force on the ground, defeated the advancing Egyptian and Jordanian forces and occupied Jerusalem, the West Bank of the River Jordan and the Sinai. They also defeated Syria and seized the Golan Heights. A Security Council resolution in November 1967 called on both sides to end the fighting. A cease-fire was arranged in 1970, but Anwar Sadat, the new Egyptian leader, organized another coalition of the front line Arab states in October 1973, launched a surprise attack on the Israeli army in the Sinai and achieved initial successes in what became known as the Yom Kippur War. The Israelis rallied, pushed back the Egyptian forces and surrounded a complete Egyptian army corps near the Canal. They also defeated a Syrian attack on the Golan Heights. The United States Secretary of State, Henry Kissinger, fearing a Soviet–American confrontation in support of their respective Middle East clients, persuaded the Soviet Union to join the United States in imposing a cease-fire and in freeing the Egyptian army corps. In September 1978 President Carter persuaded Sadat and Prime Minister Menachem Begin of Israel to sign a peace treaty whereby the Sinai was to be returned to Egypt in two stages between 1980 and 1982 and Egypt was to recognize Israel. As a result Egypt was alienated from other Arab states, which accused it of betrayal.

Lebanon became involved in the Arab–Israeli conflict in 1970 as Arab extremists launched repeated terrorist attacks into Israel from south Lebanon. In 1982, determined to destroy the Palestinian bases, Israeli troops invaded south Lebanon and reached the outskirts of Beirut. The Israelis were persuaded to withdraw in 1983, but thereafter Lebanon relapsed into anarchy as militia from factions within the various communities fought each other on the streets of Beirut.

Vietnam and Cambodia

CHINA

Ha Giang

Nanning

CHINA

Lao Cai

N O R T H

Lang Son

Phong Saiy

Song Hong

V I E T N A M

Mon Cai

BURMA

Nam Tha

Hanoi

Haiphong

Gulf of Tonkin

Mekong

Thanh Hoa

Luang
Prabang

Xieng
Khouang

Hainan

Chiang Mai

Vinh

L
A
O
S

Lampang

Vientiane

Dong Hoi

Udon Thani

Thakhek

Demilitarized zone 1954

Nakhon
Phanom

Khe Sanh

Quang Tri

Calu

Hue

Savannakhet

Lang Vei

A Shau

Da Nang

Kon Kaen

HO CHI MINH TRAIL

Hoi An
Duy Xuyen

Kham Duc

T H A I L A N D

Quang Ngai

Pakse

Dak To

Nakhon Sawan

Ubon
Ratchathani

Kontum

Nakhon
Ratchasima

Pleiku

An Khe

Qui Nhon

Chao Phraya

Bangkok

Ban Me Thuot

Battambang

Siem Reap

Nha Trang

Tonle Sap

C A M B O D I A

Kratie

Dalat

Cam Ranh

Phan Rang

Gulf of Thailand

Kompong
Chhnang

Kompong
Cham

Mekong

S O U T H

An Loc

Bao Loc

V I E T N A M

Phnom Penh
Falls to communist
forces 17 April 1975

Bien Hoa

Kampot

Saigon
Falls to communist
forces 30 April 1975

Phan Thiet

Chau Dac

My Tho

Vung Tau

Long Xuyen

Ben Tre

Rach Gia

Vinh
Long

Mekong
Delta

SOUTH CHINA
SEA

Can Tho

Ca Mau

Vin Loi

Areas of communist control

◼ 1961

☐ 1967

⊙ US base

✸ Tet offensive assault, Jan-Feb 1968

North Vietnamese supply route

| 0 | km | 200 |
| 0 | mls | 150 |

After the 1954 Geneva Conference the United States backed Ngo Dinh Diem as prime minister of South Vietnam and the French withdrew their forces. Diem's regime, however, became increasingly repressive and corrupt. In November 1963 the United States supported a military coup, which resulted in the murder of Diem, but led to increasing political instability in Saigon. By this time the Vietcong (communist guerrillas) had begun a sustained terrorist campaign in the South, and inflicted several defeats on the demoralized South Vietnamese army. The Americans believed that if South Vietnam fell to communism the rest of South-East Asia would soon follow. President Kennedy refused to send combat troops to South Vietnam but increased the number of military advisers from 600 in 1961 to 15,000 by 1963. His successor, Lyndon Johnson, gained almost unlimited powers from Congress in 1964 to deal with the situation, and following a Vietcong attack on an American base at Pleiku on 7 February 1965, the US Air Force began a bombing campaign on the North while US combat troops were despatched to the South, increasing in number from 23,000 in 1965 to 550,000 in 1969.

The Vietnam War soon became a grinding campaign of attrition. By 1968 American public opinion was turning against the war, largely because of the rising American death toll and the initial success of the Tet Offensive, a major campaign launched from the North in early 1968 which succeeded in capturing numerous provincial towns in the South. American confidence in any prospect of victory ebbed away, opposition grew in the United States to military conscription – the Draft – and demonstrations against the war spread across American college campuses. Americans were also shaken by revelations of atrocities committed by US soldiers, such as the My Lai massacre of Vietnamese civilians which took place in 1968.

After 1969, President Richard Nixon began to wind down American involvement and forced North Vietnam to the negotiating table by stepping up the bombing campaign. In 1973 a truce was agreed: the United States was to withdraw its remaining forces while elections were to be held to unify the country. However, fighting continued until 1975 when the South was conquered by the North Vietnamese and the country was reunited.

The final agony of the Vietnam War was fought out in neighbouring Cambodia. Although supposedly neutral, Cambodia had been sucked into the war and by April 1975 was in the hands of the communist Khmer Rouge, led by Pol Pot. The Khmer Rouge evacuated the population of the cities into the countryside by force and by 1978 had killed or starved to death perhaps three million people (nearly half the population). In December 1978 frontier disputes with Kampuchea (as the country had been renamed) led Vietnam to invade Kampuchea and drive the Khmer Rouge into the jungle, replacing them with a more sympathetic government. China, which had supported the Khmer Rouge and whose relations with Vietnam had deteriorated since 1975, in turn invaded Vietnam in 1979 but its forces were driven back across the border. Faced with a failing economy at home, Vietnam withdrew its forces from Kampuchea in 1989, leaving the country precariously balanced between rival factions.

The Caribbean and South America

UNITED STATES

Tampa
Florida

ATLANTIC OCEAN

GULF OF MEXICO

Miami

Nassau

Key West

BAHAMAS
1973

Havana
Matanzas

Tur
Caic

CUBA

Mérida

Camagüey

Holguin

Bay of Pigs
✹ 1961

Veracruz

Campeche

Cayman Is.
(Br)

Santiago
de Cuba

Cap-Haitien

HAIT

MEXICO

JAMAICA
1962

Port-au-Prince

Belmopan
BELIZE
(BRITISH HONDURAS)
1981

Kingston

*C A R I B B E A N
S E A*

GUATEMALA

Guatemala
City

Tegucigalpa

HONDURAS

San Salvador
EL SALVADOR

*PACIFIC
OCEAN*

Matagalpa

NICARAGUA

Managua

L.Nicaragua

Cartagena

Barranquilla

COSTA
Limón
Puntarenas
San José
RICA

CANAL ZONE
to Panama 1979
(Panama Canal to Panama 1999)

COLOMBIA

Colón

Tampa

David
PANAMA
✹1989
Panama

UNITED STAT

M

Key West

Candelaria
San Cristobal

Ha

Gua

Bay of Pigs
US-backed
Cuban exiles
land 12 April 1961

MEXICO

BR. HONDURAS

GUATEMALA

HONDURAS

EL SALVADOR

NICARAGUA

Current or former colonial possessions

- � US
- British
- Dutch
- French

1962   Year of independence

✹   US military intervention, with date

⊙   US base

⊙   Sandinista base, 1979

Contra base area, 1979-1989

Area of Contra activity

Area of guerrilla activity since 1979

0 km   400

0 mls   300

AIR PATROL

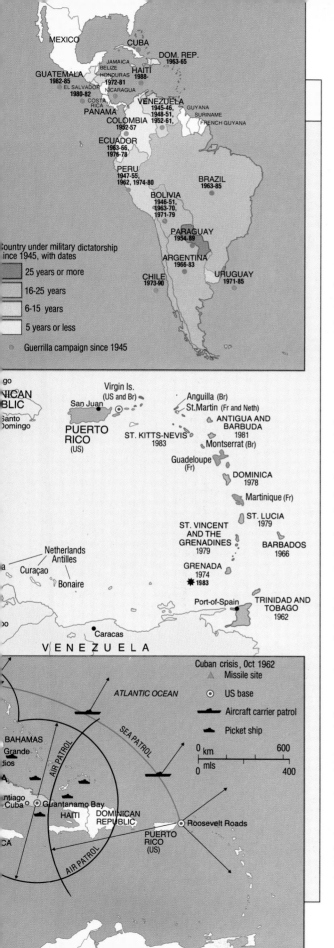

MEXICO

CUBA

DOM. REP.
1963-65

GUATEMALA
1982-85
1980-82

JAMAICA
BELIZE
HONDURAS
HAITI
1988-

HAITI
1972-81

EL SALVADOR
NICARAGUA

COSTA
RICA

VENEZUELA
1945-46,
1948-51,
1952-61,

GUYANA
SURINAME
FRENCH GUYANA

PANAMA

COLOMBIA
1952-57

ECUADOR
1963-66,
1976-78

PERU
1947-55,
1962, 1974-80

BRAZIL
1963-85

BOLIVIA
1946-51,
1963-70,
1971-79

PARAGUAY
1954-89

ARGENTINA
1966-83

CHILE
1973-90

URUGUAY
1971-85

Country under military dictatorship
since 1945, with dates

25 years or more

16-25 years

6-15 years

5 years or less

Guerrilla campaign since 1945

Throughout Latin America the armed forces, traditionally conservative, have frequently intervened in politics, especially where reformers, who have sought to reduce the grip of the United States on their countries' economies and governments, threatened the status quo. In Guatemala, for example, when President Arbenz began to expropriate large holdings and moved against the United Fruit Company's monopoly, the United States in 1954 accused him of being a communist and financed an invasion by right-wing extremists, who deposed Arbenz. Thereafter, the country was ruled by military dictators.

In 1959, after a prolonged guerrilla campaign, the Cuban nationalist Fidel Castro overthrew the corrupt Batista regime. Castro's nationalization of American assets led to an American embargo on trade with Cuba, and Castro turned to the Soviet Union for aid. Soviet influence increased after the failure of an American-backed Cuban refugee invasion of Cuba at the Bay of Pigs in 1961, and in 1962 the Soviets began to build medium range inter-continental ballistic missile sites in Cuba. This escalation of the conflict led to a confrontation with the United States, but Khrushchev backed down and agreed to dismantle the missile sites.

Under President Nixon the United States had thrown its weight behind the right-wing anti-communist regimes in Latin America. After a Marxist, Salvador Allende, was elected President of Chile in 1970 and began to nationalize American companies, the United States supported a military revolt, which overthrew him in 1973 and set up a repressive military dictatorship under Augusto Pinochet. However, in the late 1970s, President Carter adopted a policy of supporting reform movements in Latin America and withdrew support from the corrupt Nicaraguan dictator, Anastasio Somoza, whose family had ruled the country for 40 years. He was overthrown by the left-wing National Liberation Front, which was dominated by the radical Sandinista guerrillas. During the 1980s President Reagan reversed Carter's Latin American policy, denounced the Sandinistas as communists, and armed anti-Sandinista guerrillas, the Contras, operating from Honduras and Costa Rica. Their efforts were not successful and Nicaragua remained under the Sandinista's control until they were defeated by a pro-American coalition in a general election held in 1990.

Elsewhere in the Caribbean, the Americans invaded Grenada and overthrew the government, suspecting it to be aligned with Cuba. Six years later, American forces invaded Panama, overthrowing a military dictator, Manuel Noriega, whom they suspected of drug trafficking.

Virgin Is.
(US and Br)

San Juan

Anguilla (Br)
St.Martin (Fr and Neth)

ANTIGUA AND
BARBUDA
1981

PUERTO
RICO
(US)

ST. KITTS-NEVIS
1983

Montserrat (Br)

Guadeloupe
(Fr)

DOMINICA
1978

Martinique (Fr)

ST. LUCIA
1979

ST. VINCENT
AND THE
GRENADINES
1979

BARBADOS
1966

Netherlands
Antilles

Curaçao

Bonaire

GRENADA
1974
1983

Port-of-Spain

TRINIDAD AND
TOBAGO
1962

Caracas

V E N E Z U E L A

Cuban crisis, Oct 1962
Missile site

ATLANTIC OCEAN
US base

Aircraft carrier patrol

Picket ship

SEA PATROL

BAHAMAS
Grande
dios

0 km   600

0 mls   400

AIR PATROL

ntiago
Cuba
Guantanamo Bay

HAITI
DOMINICAN
REPUBLIC

Roosevelt Roads

PUERTO
RICO
(US)

AIR PATROL

War in the Gulf

TURKEY

Diyarbakir

Adana
Incirlik

KURDIS

L. Ur

Mosul
Arbil

Kirkuk

Nicosia

CYPRUS

Akrotiri

SYRIA

Baija

Tigris

Samarra

Balad

MEDITERRANEAN SEA

Beirut
LEBANON
Damascus

Euphrates

Saddam

Al Fallujah
Habbaniyah
Al Iskandariyah

Bag

F
S

Haifa

Ar Rutbah

Karbala

Numan

Tel Aviv

West
Bank

Jerusalem

Amman

Syrian   Desert

IRAQ

Al H

ISRAEL

JORDAN

Nejef

Radif

Cairo

Suez
Canal

Arar

As S

EGYPT

Aqaba

Rafha

Range of Al-Hussein Scud missiles fired from Western Iraq

Tabuk

SAUDI ARABIA

Range of Al-Hussein Scud missiles fired from South

0 km		300
0 mls		200

Nasiriyah

Euphrates

IRAN

As Salman

Forward base

Basra

IRAQ

Umm Qasr

Bubiyan I.

US and
French forces

Wadi al Batin

KUWAIT

Failaka I.

Nisab

Jahra

Kuwait City

US forces

US and
UK forces

Arab forces

THE GULF

Ground offensive Feb 24-28 1991

SAUDI ARABIA

US forces

Iraqi infantry divisions

Iraqi armoured reserve

Allied advances

Allied battleships

Road

Saudi forces

0 km	50
0 mls	40

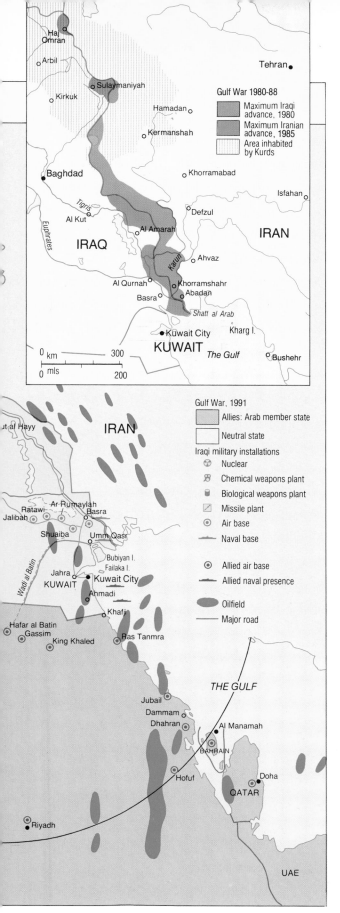

Gulf War 1980-88

- Maximum Iraqi advance, 1980
- Maximum Iranian advance, 1985
- Area inhabited by Kurds

Haj Omran
Arbil
Sulaymaniyah
Kirkuk
Hamadan
Tehran
Kermanshah
Baghdad
Khorramabad
Isfahan
Defzul
Tigris
Al Kut
Euphrates
Al Amarah
Ahvaz
IRAQ
IRAN
Al Qurnah
Khorramshahr
Abadan
Basra
Karun
Shatt al Arab
Kuwait City
Kharg I.
KUWAIT
The Gulf
Bushehr

0 km 300
0 mls 200

Gulf War, 1991

- Allies: Arab member state
- Neutral state

Iraqi military installations
- ☢ Nuclear
- ☣ Chemical weapons plant
- ⬛ Biological weapons plant
- ◪ Missile plant
- ⊙ Air base
- ⎯ Naval base

- ◉ Allied air base
- ⎯ Allied naval presence

- ⬤ Oilfield
- ⎯ Major road

ut al Hayy
IRAN
Ratawi
Jalibah
Ar Rumaylah
Basra
Shuaiba
Umm Qasr
Bubiyan I.
Failaka I.
Jahra
KUWAIT
Kuwait City
Ahmadi
Khafji
Wadi al Batin
Hafar al Batin
Gassim
King Khaled
Ras Tanmra
THE GULF
Jubail
Dammam
Dhahran
Al Manamah
BAHRAIN
Hofuf
Doha
QATAR
Riyadh
UAE

In December 1980 the Iraqi dictator, Saddam Hussein, ordered his army to attack Iran in pursuit of long-standing Iraqi territorial claims in the Shatt al Arab region. The Iranians launched vigorous counter-offensives and war dragged on for eight years before the United Nations could arrange a cease-fire in July 1987.

On 2 August 1990 Iraq invaded Kuwait in order to secure Kuwait's valuable oilfields and thus sustain Iraq's war-torn economy. On the same day, the Security Council passed a unanimous resolution, demanding the immediate and unconditional withdrawal of Iraq's forces. On 6 August the United Nations imposed a blockade on Iraq. In Operation 'Desert Shield' the United States, Britain, France, Egypt, Syria, Morocco and twenty-two other countries sent land, sea and air forces to Saudi Arabia and the Gulf to defend Saudi Arabia against an anticipated Iraqi invasion. The blockade and frequent diplomatic efforts failed to persuade Saddam to evacuate Kuwait. On 15 January 1991, in accordance with a United Nations resolution authorizing the use of force to drive Iraq from Kuwait, the multinational coalition's air forces began a sustained air campaign against strategic targets in Iraq. Operation 'Desert Storm' succeeded in destroying Iraq's air force and severely undermined the morale of Saddam's frontline troops. In a desperate but unsuccessful effort to involve Israel in the war and to split the Arabs from the Western allies in the coalition, the Iraqis launched Scud missile attacks on Tel Aviv, and tried to link Iraq's withdrawal from Kuwait with an Israeli withdrawal from the Palestinian West Bank. Last-minute Soviet efforts to mediate an Iraqi withdrawal from Kuwait were unsuccessful and the coalition launched a land offensive against Iraqi forces on 24 February. The Iraqis were taken completely by surprise as allied deception had convinced them their attack would be from the east, but in fact their assault was launched from the west. In a lightning attack with heavy armour, the allies occupied south-east Iraq and were within 150 miles of Baghdad in a few hours, completely encircling the Iraqi armies. In a series of battles, the allies defeated the élite Iraqi Republican Guard, and on 26 February Saddam ordered his forces to withdraw from Kuwait. As they fled towards Basra, Iraqi troops suffered further losses from allied bombing. The allies liberated Kuwait City on 27 February and President Bush suspended the campaign on 28 February.

The war had serious consequences for both Iraq and Kuwait. The bulk of Kuwait's oilfields had been set on fire by the retreating Iraqi forces and Kuwait City was badly damaged. Civil war soon erupted in Iraq and hundreds of thousands of Kurdish refugees fled to the borders of Turkey and Iran.

Wars in Africa

LIBYA

Aozou

AOZOU STRIP
Occupied by Libya
from 1975

CHAD

Faya Larg

Approximate division between
rebel-held north and governmen
held south.

Abéché

Ndjamena

Sarh

MOROCCO

ALGERIA
1954-62

WESTERN
SAHARA
1957

war with Polisario
front 1976-

MAURITANIA

CAPE VERDE
IS.
1963-74

GUINEA
BISSAU
1959-74

CHAD
1968-

SUDAN
1952-73
1983-

ETHIOPIA
1962-

1963-
SOMALIA

NIGERIA
1967-69
1977

LIBERIA
1990

GHANA
1981

CAMEROON
1955-60

CENTRAL
AFRICAN REPUBLIC
1979

UGANDA
1980
1985-86

KENYA
1952-60

1982

ZAÏRE
1960-71
1978

RWANDA
1962-65

1978-79

BURUNDI
1962-65

TANZANIA

ANGOLA
1961-75
1975-89

ZIMBABWE
1964-80

MOZAMBIQUE
1964-75
1981-

NAMIBIA
1966-89

SOUTH AFRICA
Armed struggle against
white rule. 1964-

Inset (lower left)

ZAÏRE

Uige

Luanda

Malanje

A N G O L A

Lobito
Benguela

Huambo

Menongue

ZAMBIA

Lubango

Mocamedes

Ondjiva

Quedas
do
Raucana

Ondangua

Tsumeb
Grootfontein

BOTSWANA

N A M I B I A

Windhoek

Walvis
Bay
(S.Afr.)

Keetsmanshoop

Lüderitz

	Area held by MPLA, Feb 1976
	Area held by UNITA, late 1980s
	Main area of Euro pean occupation
●	South African army base
→	South African incursions into Angola

0 km — 500
0 mls — 400

SOUTH AFRICA

Legend

- ● Colonial war
- ✳ Interstate war
- ○ Civil war
- ✳ Guerrilla activity, late 1980s

0 km — 1000
0 mls — 750

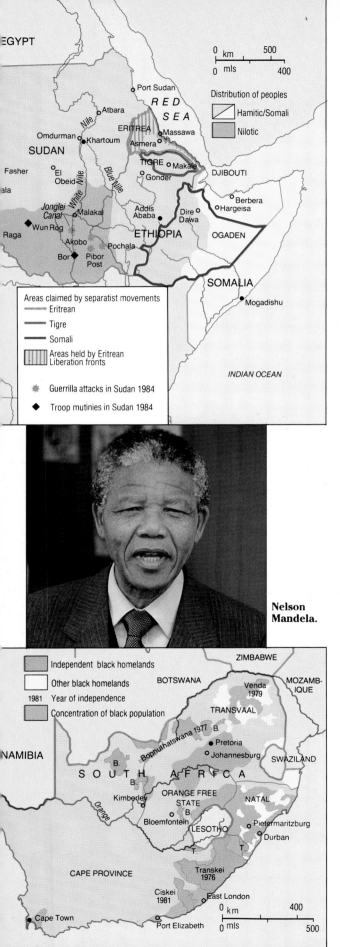

Nelson Mandela.

Since the withdrawal of the European colonial powers from Africa and the granting of independence to their former colonies in the 1960s, civil wars have raged in various parts of the continent. A common feature of nearly all the wars has been the troubled inheritance of colonial boundaries that do not correspond to the loyalties of the peoples.

In 1967 the Ibos of eastern Nigeria seceded to create their own state of Biafra. Civil war ensued leading to the defeat of Biafra in 1970 by General Gowan and Muslim forces from northern Nigeria. In 1974 the Emperor of Ethiopia, Haile Selassie, was overthrown by a military coup which brought a Marxist-Leninist military regime to power. In 1977 Somalia took advantage of the confusion in Ethiopia to invade the country in order to seize the disputed Ogaden province. Ethiopia secured military aid from the Soviet Union and troops from Cuba, and defeated Somalia in 1978. Civil war also raged in Sudan and in Chad, where conflict arose between nomadic Arabs and black African Christians. After independence in 1974 both Angola and Mozambique lapsed into civil war. In Angola, the Marxist People's Movement for the Liberation of Angola (MPLA), backed by Soviet aid and 17,000 Cuban troops, fought two competing nationalist organizations, the National Union for the Total Independence of Angola (UNITA) and the National Front for the Liberation of Angola (FNLA), supported by the United States and South Africa. Although the FNLA was destroyed in 1976, the struggle between the MPLA and UNITA continued. However, under the 1989 United Nations sponsored agreement granting independence to Namibia the South Africans promised to withdraw from Namibia if Cuban troops evacuated Angola.

The situation in both Angola and Mozambique was complicated by South Africa which intervened in both countries in order to destabilize their governments and prevent them from being used as bases for black nationalist forces seeking the overthrow of apartheid in South Africa itself. For while the rest of Africa had already gained black majority rule, South Africa remained governed by its white minority population. Black 'homelands', all due to become independent, had been created within South Africa's borders, but they were still economically dependent on South Africa, and failed to receive recognition by any other country. In the late 1980s, violence broke out in the black townships against the apartheid system and it was met by repressive measures by the white government. In 1990, however, President F.W. de Klerk released the veteran African National Congress leader Nelson Mandela from prison after 26 years of captivity and began moves towards the dismantling of apartheid.

A NEW BALANCE OF POWER

The United States used its nuclear superiority to threaten 'massive retaliation'.

President Roosevelt's vision of 'One World' after the Second World War was shattered by the unwillingness of the Soviet Union to accept American perceptions about how the post-war order should be organized. Historians have argued endlessly about which of the two superpowers was responsible for causing the 'Cold War', but certainly Stalin's ingrained suspicions of the aims and ambitions of the United States resulted in a series of confrontations with the West which antagonized moderate opinion while convincing Western leaders that Moscow was seeking world hegemony. By 1949 the world was divided into two hostile blocs which nevertheless shrank from all-out war with its attendant risk of nuclear annihilation. The American strategy of containing the further expansion of the Soviet bloc encouraged the United States to rebuild Western Europe economically and militarily and to embark on a massive rearmament programme. The struggle between the two blocs became more intense during the 1950s. The United States adopted a rigid doctrinaire posture, which assumed that the entire communist world was centrally controlled from Moscow and even regarded nations like India, which sought to avoid taking sides, as Soviet fellow travellers. The United States used its nuclear superiority to threaten 'massive retaliation' and deter communist expansionism worldwide.

However, during the late 1950s cracks were beginning to appear on both sides. Yugoslavia had already broken away from the Soviet bloc, while the rift between the Soviet Union and communist China widened until by 1960 the two powers had become deadly rivals. France under General de Gaulle was challenging United States domination of Western Europe. New African and Asian Third World nations resisted involvement in the Cold War.

During the 1960s these divergences became more pronounced as Soviet and Chinese troops fought along their disputed borders, while in Western Europe President de Gaulle pulled French forces out of NATO's military command structure when the United States refused his demand for a greater French voice in the alliance. De Gaulle's grand design for a French-led Western Europe which could negotiate on equal terms with both superpowers did not prevail, but it demonstrated increasing French dissatisfaction with the existing configuration of power.

The Europeans were also critical of American involvement in Vietnam, and, as the Soviet Union began to catch up with the United States during the 1960s in nuclear capability, they became concerned that the United States, fearing nuclear annihilation, might not intervene in the event of a threat to Western Europe by the Soviet Union. The bi-polar system became even more fragmented during the 1970s as the United States receded from its global role after its

Revolution in Eastern Europe

In just one year, 1989, the communist regimes which had ruled Eastern Europe since the late 1940s were swept away by a tide of revolution. Poland gained its freedom when the anti-communist Solidarity movement won control of both houses of parliament in elections held in June. In Hungary the Communist party split over political reform opening the way for free elections in April 1990 in which the conservative anti-communist parties secured a majority. In East Germany the Communist government attempted to placate mounting unrest by promising reforms but it was swept away by street demonstrations in November. The opening of the Berlin Wall and the victory of the Christian Democrats in elections held the following March resulted in overwhelming pressure for re-unification with West Germany. In Czechoslovakia Communist party rule was brought to an end by street demonstrations in November and the dissident playwright Vaclav Havel became President of a parliamentary democracy. In Bulgaria a reformist communist took power and promised free elections.

Only in Romania in the days leading up to the Christmas of 1989 was there major bloodshed when huge popular demonstrations overthrew Nicolae Ceausescu's tyrannical regime. Elections were held in May 1990 which led to a massive majority for Iliescu's National Salvation Front.

◀ **In China, April 1989, Beijing University students gathered in Tiananmen Square in support of freedom of speech and the end of corruption in the Communist Party. Martial law was declared and on 3–4 June detachments of the People's Liberation Army cleared the area by firing on unarmed crowds killing many.**

Vietnam experience, as communist China emerged as an independent nuclear power, and as France, now also a nuclear power, and the European NATO allies sought to improve their relations with the Soviet Union. West Germany recognized the 1945 territorial status quo and normalized its relations with East Germany and other Eastern European countries. The United States and communist China became reconciled while the United States also signed Strategic Arms Limitation Agreements with the Soviet Union, thus inaugurating a period of détente and friendlier East–West relations. The American Secretary of State Henry Kissinger talked of a 'pentagonal multipolar world' in which five new power centres – the United States, the Soviet Union, Western Europe, China and Japan – would form a new global balance of power.

By 1980 Soviet–American tension re-surfaced as Washington complained that the Soviet Union had used détente as a smoke-screen behind which to overtake the United States in military capability, while Moscow had taken advantage of American post-Vietnam passivity to extend its influence into Africa and the Indian Ocean. The Reagan administration revived Cold War animosities by denouncing the Soviet Union as an 'evil empire' and adopted a massive rearmament programme. By 1987, with the advent of Mikhail Gorbachev as Soviet leader, promising political and economic liberalization at home and a relaxation of tensions abroad, the dialogue between the superpowers over arms reductions was resumed and there was a revival of Western optimism about the prospects for a new détente. Gorbachev has introduced a number of reforms into the Soviet system of government, which have given the Russian people more electoral freedom than they have ever enjoyed before, but the Communist Party remains supreme. The relaxation of Party controls has, however, led to a measure of freedom of speech, but more ominously for the stability of the country it has also encouraged the re-emergence of provincial nationalism. The Red Army has been withdrawn from Afghanistan and there has also been an increasing measure of liberalization in Central and Eastern Europe.

The same has not been true of China, where the process of reform was abruptly halted in 1989. Nor, despite the increasing fragmentation of the world in the late 1980s and early in 1990, has there been any substantial change in the relative power positions of the United States and the Soviet Union. Despite the economic strains of the arms race, and the increasing economic strength of Japan and the European Community, notably West Germany, the joint military might of the two superpowers remains overwhelming and they continue to wield immense influence throughout the world.

The United Nations

GREENLAND
(Den)

ICELAND

USSR

CANADA

See inset

TURKEY

SYRIA IRAQ
LEBANON
ISRAEL
JORDAN
KUWAIT

AFGHANIS

IRAN

PAK

UNITED STATES

MOROCCO

TUNISIA

ALGERIA

LIBYA

EGYPT

SAUDI
ARABIA

QATAR

U.A.E.

OMAN

MEXICO

WESTERN
SAHARA

MAURITANIA

CUBA

HAITI

DOMINICAN REPUBLIC

BELIZE

GUATEMALA
EL SALVADOR

HONDURAS

NICARAGUA

COSTA RICA

PANAMA

VENEZUELA

GUYANA
SURINAME
FRENCH GUIANA

COLOMBIA

ECUADOR

MALI

NIGER

CHAD

SUDAN

YEMEN

S.
YEMEN

DJIBOUTI

SENEGAL
GAMBIA
GUINEA-BISSAU
GUINEA
SIERRA LEONE

BURKINA

BENIN
NIGERIA

IVORY
COAST

LIBERIA

GHANA

TOGO
CAMEROON

EQ. GUINEA

GABON

CENT.
AFR. REP.

ETHIOPIA

SOMALIA

UGANDA

CONGO

ZAÏRE

RWANDA

KENYA

BURUNDI

TANZANIA

IND

ATLANTIC
OCEAN

PERU

BRAZIL

PACIFIC
OCEAN

BOLIVIA

ANGOLA

ZAMBIA

MALAWI

MADAGASCAR

NAMIBIA

ZIMBABWE

MOZAMBIQUE

BOTSWANA

SWAZILAND

LESOTHO

PARAGUAY

CHILE

URUGUAY

ARGENTINA

SOUTH AFRICA
Suspended 1974

**States admitted to the
United Nations**

Founder member 1945

1946–55

1956–65

Since 1966

◆ Permanent member of
the Security Council

UN Trusteeship in 1946

Non-members

The Atlantic Charter of August 1941 made only a vague reference to the need for a permanent system of international security. Roosevelt preferred to avoid specific recommendations, fearing that to propose a new international organization to replace the League of Nations would arouse similar opposition in the United States to that which Woodrow Wilson encountered in 1919. Instead he put forward the notion of the 'Four Policemen' – the United States, the Soviet Union, Britain and China – who would act together against would-be aggressors. However, he soon discovered that this concept failed to satisfy the need for a more far-reaching and democratic body to preserve world peace. His eventual concept of a United Nations Organization retained the 'Four Policemen' in that the four powers (and later France) would have permanent seats in the Security Council, the executive organ of the United Nations. There would also be a General Assembly of all those powers who had fought against the Axis. In 1943 the Soviet Union announced its support for the proposed organization and the American Congress voted in its favour, which was crucial to its success. Detailed discussions took place at conferences at Dumbarton Oaks (near Washington DC) and San Francisco in 1944 and 1945, at which it was agreed that the five permanent members of the Security Council should each have a veto on substantive issues. The US Senate approved the United Nations Charter in July 1945 and the first meeting of the new organization took place in London in January 1946, although its permanent site was to be in New York, thus assuring continued United States membership. Other international bodies were incorporated into the United Nations, including the World Health Organization (WHO), the International Labour Organization (ILO) and the United Nations Relief and Rehabilitation Administration (UNRRA), which distributed some $4 billion worth of relief aid to Europe after the war.

Alongside the United Nations and its various affiliated bodies, a further group of organizations arose, designed to regulate the world economic order. The United States government, convinced that pre-war aggression had been caused by the collapse of world trade and financial dislocation after the depression, was the prime mover in this direction, instigating the setting up of the International Monetary Fund (IMF) and the International Bank for Reconstruction and Development (the World Bank). The task of these organizations was to provide loans and cheap credit for reconstruction purposes and help to stabilize currencies, in the expectation that this would encourage the growth of world trade.

Military and Regional Groupings

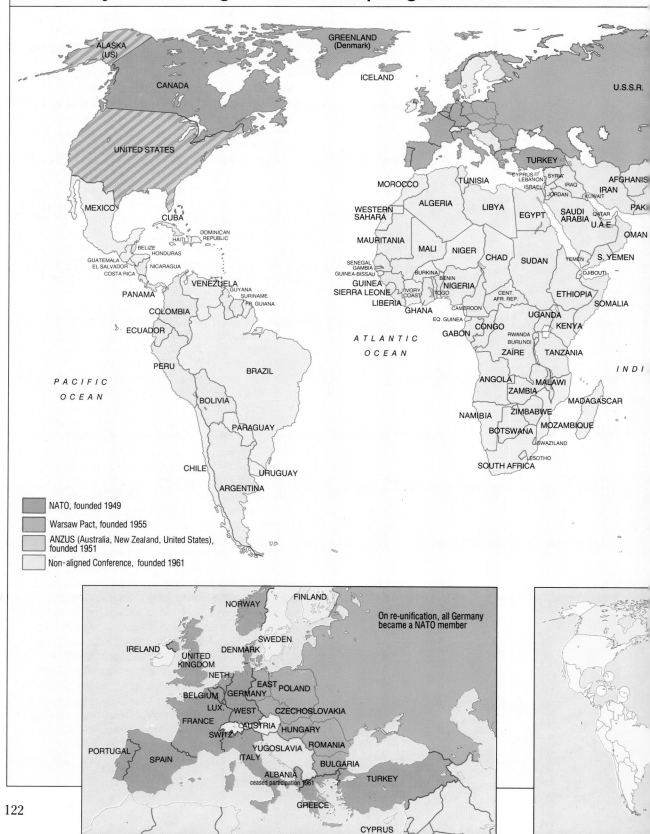

ALASKA (US)

GREENLAND (Denmark)

U.S.S.R.

CANADA

ICELAND

UNITED STATES

TURKEY

MEXICO

CUBA

DOMINICAN REPUBLIC

HAITI

BELIZE
HONDURAS

GUATEMALA
EL SALVADOR
COSTA RICA   NICARAGUA

PANAMA

VENEZUELA

GUYANA
SURINAME
FR. GUIANA

COLOMBIA

ECUADOR

PACIFIC OCEAN

PERU

BRAZIL

BOLIVIA

PARAGUAY

CHILE

URUGUAY

ARGENTINA

MOROCCO

WESTERN SAHARA

MAURITANIA

SENEGAL
GAMBIA
GUINEA-BISSAU

GUINEA
SIERRA LEONE

LIBERIA

TUNISIA

ALGERIA

LIBYA

MALI   NIGER

BURKINA

IVORY
COAST

GHANA

BENIN
TOGO

NIGERIA

EQ. GUINEA

CAMEROON

GABON

CONGO

ZAÏRE

CYPRUS
LEBANON
ISRAEL

SYRIA
IRAQ
JORDAN

KUWAIT

EGYPT

SAUDI
ARABIA

QATAR
U.A.E.

AFGHANIS

IRAN

PAK

OMAN

YEMEN   S. YEMEN

DJIBOUTI

SUDAN

CHAD

CENT.
AFR. REP.

ETHIOPIA

SOMALIA

UGANDA

KENYA

RWANDA
BURUNDI

TANZANIA

ATLANTIC OCEAN

INDI

ANGOLA   MALAWI

ZAMBIA

MADAGASCAR

NAMIBIA

ZIMBABWE

BOTSWANA

MOZAMBIQUE

SWAZILAND

LESOTHO

SOUTH AFRICA

NATO, founded 1949

Warsaw Pact, founded 1955

ANZUS (Australia, New Zealand, United States), founded 1951

Non-aligned Conference, founded 1961

NORWAY   FINLAND

IRELAND

UNITED
KINGDOM

DENMARK

SWEDEN

NETH.

BELGIUM

LUX.

FRANCE

EAST
GERMANY

WEST
GERMANY

POLAND

CZECHOSLOVAKIA

AUSTRIA   HUNGARY

SWITZ.

PORTUGAL

SPAIN

ITALY

YUGOSLAVIA

ROMANIA

ALBANIA
ceased participation 1961

BULGARIA

TURKEY

GREECE

CYPRUS

On re-unification, all Germany became a NATO member

OAS (Organization of American States), founded 1948

Arab League, founded 1945

In March 1948 Britain, France, Belgium, the Netherlands and Luxembourg signed the Treaty of Brussels, pledging that if any of them was attacked by an outside power, the others would come to its assistance. This was plainly directed against the Soviet Union, but clearly United States membership would be essential if the alliance was to possess any credibility. The United States, while increasingly suspicious of Soviet intentions after 1947, concentrated on assisting Western Europe to re-build its economic strength, and it was not until April 1949, during the Berlin blockade, that Washington agreed to the signature of the North Atlantic Treaty Organization between the United States, the Brussels Pact countries, and Canada, Iceland, Norway, Italy, and Portugal. Each signatory was obliged to assist any member which was the victim of an armed attack. United States participation in this alliance was not intended to lead to any increase in the number of US troops in Europe beyond the two divisions occupying West Germany. Its motivation was psychological: to help restore European morale and to encourage the re-building of armies and defence industries. However, the Korean War in 1950 led the United States to offer the Europeans the despatch of American reinforcements to Europe, to increase its military aid, and to appoint General Dwight D. Eisenhower as NATO Supreme Commander in return for European acceptance of West German military contribution to NATO. The French rejected the re-militarization of West Germany and it was not until 1954 that West Germany and Italy were admitted to the Brussels Pact (re-named the Western European Union) and West Germany admitted to NATO. To reassure the French, Britain promised to maintain four divisions and an air force in Europe. West Germany's admission to NATO resulted in the Soviet Union setting up the Warsaw Pact in 1955, involving Soviet and satellite armies, on the same lines as NATO and with its headquarters in Moscow.

Outside Europe, similar defence arrangements were negotiated in the 1950s between the USA and its allies in Asia and Australasia to prevent Soviet and Chinese expansion in that region. Many nations preferred, however, to remain non-aligned and joined in a grouping of nations led by Yugoslavia and India, which resisted all blandishments to support either the Soviet Union or the United States. Many of these non-aligned nations are also members of regional groupings, such as the Arab League, set up in 1945 in the Egyptian capital of Cairo to promote Arab unity, or the Organization of American States, set up in Bogotá in Colombia in 1948 to promote cooperation throughout the American continent.

Communist China

UNION OF SOVIET SOCIALIST REPUBLICS

Amur

1969

Blagoveshchensk

Khab

Hailaer

Qiqihaer

Songhu

1969

Ulaan Baatar

MONGOLIA

Urumqi

INNER
MONGOLIA

Ulanhot

Haerbin

Changchun

Vlad

Shenyang

1969

NORTH
KOREA

SE
JA

Kashgar

XINJIANG-UIGHUR

Huhehot

Baotou

Beijing

Tianjin

Lüda

Intervention in
Korean war, 1950

SOUTH
KOREA

ceded to China
by Pakistan

Yumen

Ningxia

Taiyuan

Qingdao

YELLOW SEA

KASHMIR

Oct–Nov
1962

under Chinese administration
since Nov 1962

Lanzhou

NINGXIA-
HUI

Ji'nan

Huang

Kaifeng

CHINESE PEOPLE'S REPUBLIC

Xi'an

Nanjing

Shanghai

TIBET
Invasion, 1950

Lhasa

Chengdu

Yangzi

Wuhan

Hangzhou

EAST CHINA SEA

NEPAL

Chongqing

BHUTAN

Oct–Nov 1962

Changsha

INDIA

ASSAM

Guiyang

Fuzhou

Matsu

BURMA

Kunming

GUANGXI
ZHUANG

Xi

Nanning

Quemoy

TAIWAN
(NATIONALIST CHINA

Mekong

Feb–Apr 1979

Guangzhou

Hong Kong (Br.) to be returned to China, 1997
Macau (Port.)
to be returned to China, 1999

Hanoi

LAOS

Hainan

VIETNAM

SOUTH CHINA SEA

PHILIPPINES

THAILAND

Boundaries of
Autonomous Regions

Territory claimed by China

Border clash

Ethno-linguistic areas

Han Chinese majority

Ethnic minorities

Hui Chinese		Turkic
Tibeto-Burman	Sino-Tibetan	Mongolian
Thai		Korean
Others		Uninhabited

Altaic

0 km ———— 750
0 mls ———— 500

Communist revolution

Communist base, 1945

Areas subsequently occupied by communist forces

1945–June 1946

July 1946–June 1948

July 1948–June 1949

July–Sept 1949

Seat of Nationalist government

USSR

MONGOLIA

Haerbin

Shenyang

NORTH KOREA

Baotou

Beijing
Capital after 1949

Port Arthur
to USSR 1945-55

Tianjin

SOUTH KOREA

Yan'an

Qingdao

Lanzhou

Huang

Xi'an

Kaifeng

Nanjing
Capital before 1949

C H I N A

During 1949 Nationalist government moves to Chongqing, then Chengdu

Chengdu

Hankou

Shanghai

Chongqing

Yangzi

INDIA

Changsha

Guiyang

Fuzhou

Taipei

Kunming

Taiwan
End 1949. Nationalist government flees to Taiwan

Xi

Guangzhou

Nanning

BURMA

FRENCH INDO-CHINA

Hong Kong (Br.)

THAILAND

Hainan

Modern China

Birth rates (per thousand)

over 26

21–25

19–20

18

under 18

Industrial area

USSR

MONGOLIA

Haerbin

Shenyang

NORTH KOREA

Beijing

Tianjin

Lüda

SOUTH KOREA

Lanzhou

Huang

Xi'an

Kaifeng

C H I N A

Nanjing

Chengdu

Wuhan

Shanghai

Chongqing

Yangzi

INDIA

Changsha

Fuzhou

Kunming

Xi

Guangzhou

TAIWAN

BURMA

VIETNAM

0 km 500

LAOS

THAILAND

Hainan

0 mls 500

After the defeat of Japan at the end of the Second World War, the conflict between the Guomindang (nationalists) led by Jiang Jieshi (Chiang Kai-shek) and the communists under Mao Zedong (Mao Tse-tung) flared into open warfare. By October 1949 the communists had defeated the Guomindang and Jiang had fled to Taiwan.

The new Beijing government concentrated on the reconstruction of China's devastated economy. Agricultural production had risen, but the population increased even more rapidly; in the 1970s the government embarked on a birth control programme promoting one-child families.

In pursuit of a centralized China, the new regime tried to assimilate the various ethnic groups. The dominant Han ethnic group, concentrated in central, southern and eastern China, made up 90 per cent of China's population. The minority ethnic groups, many of whom were Muslims, lived mainly in the 'Autonomous Regions' of the far north and north-west. The persecution of these peoples and the seizure of their land led to frequent revolts in the 1950s and 1960s. In 1950 Tibetan autonomy was suppressed and a Tibetan uprising in 1959 was ruthlessly crushed. After 1978 Beijing adopted a more tolerant policy towards the cultural and religious life of the minorities.

In 1958 Mao embarked on 'The Great Leap Forward' designed to promote agricultural and industrial expansion in China, but disastrous harvests led to the failure of the programme. In 1966 Mao launched 'The Cultural Revolution', hoping to revive communist principles in Chinese society and to restore Communist party control. The ensuing violence against bourgeois and intellectual elements led by student Red Guards was only brought under control after it had done untold damage to the Chinese economy. When Mao died in 1976 political power was taken by a reformer who had been arrested during the Cultural Revolution, Deng Xiaoping. Deng purged the radical Maoists and embarked on a modernization programme, based on a limited capitalist revival and private ownership of land. However, restrictions on personal freedom were not relaxed, leading to an uprising against the regime in 1989 (see pages 118–19).

The Chinese communist regime has reacted forcibly to threats along its borders. The Chinese intervened in the Korean War (1951–3) when United Nations troops approached the Yalu frontier, defeated India during a dispute on the northern Indo-Chinese frontier in 1962, engaged in savage fighting with the Soviet Union over territory on the Usurri river boundary in 1969 and invaded North Vietnam in 1979 after the Hanoi regime occupied Kampuchea.

The Nuclear Threat

UNITED STATES

U.S.S.R.

U.K., FRANCE

Washington

Moscow

CHILE

ARGENTINA

BRAZIL

IRAN

IRAQ

ISRAEL

EGYPT

LIBYA

SOUTH
AFRICA

Nuclear capability, 1985

Known

Suspected

Potential

NATO

Warsaw Pact

Nuclear arsenals, 1985

· Missile site

🚀 100 intercontinental ballistic missiles

╱ 100 intermediate and medium range ballistic missiles

⬟ 100 ballistic missile launching submarines

✈ 100 strategic bomber aircraft

▲ 1000 strategic nuclear warheads

▭ Sea area within 11,500 km of Moscow (range of submarine-launched Trident D-5)

CHINA

The Test Ban Treaty, signed in 1963, was the first post-war nuclear agreement. During the 1960s the Soviet Union caught up with the United States in Inter-Continental Ballistic Missiles (ICBMs). This parity between the two superpowers enabled the Soviet Union and the United States to enter into Strategic Arms Limitation Talks (SALT) in 1969. The SALT I agreement was signed in Moscow in 1972, freezing the number of ICBMs and Submarine-Launched Ballistic Missiles (SLBMs). Further Soviet–American negotiations led to the signing of SALT II in Vienna in 1979 which limited the number of Multiple Independently Targeted Re-entry Vehicles (MIRVs). The United States Senate failed to ratify this treaty, claiming that the Soviet Union had cheated on the agreement. In the 1970s the Soviet Union also replaced its short-range missiles in Eastern Europe with new medium-range ones capable of hitting any Western European target. This led the Reagan administration in 1981 to deploy Cruise and Pershing intermediate-range missiles (IRBMs) in Western Europe and to increase defence expenditure by five per cent per annum. In 1983 Reagan announced the so-called Strategic Defence Initiative (SDI) or Star Wars Programme, intended to provide space-based defences against a Soviet missile attack by the year 2000. However, with the advent of Mikhail Gorbachev as Soviet leader in 1985 and his offer of nuclear weapon reduction negotiations, there was a successful conclusion to the Intermediate Range Nuclear Force (INF) talks, which had begun at Geneva in November 1981. The INF Treaty of 1988 provided for the elimination of all land-based medium-range ballistic missiles in Europe.

In November 1990 the East and West signed a Conventional Forces Europe Agreement which halved the number of tanks on both sides in Europe and evened out the imbalance between Soviet and Western forces in Europe. By this time Russian troops had already begun to withdraw from Eastern Europe.

May Day military parade in Moscow, 1961.

Modern USSR

Franz
Josef Land

BARENTS
SEA

Murmansk

Novaya
Zemlya

Kara Sea

Karelian
A.S.S.R.

White
Sea

LATVIAN
S.S.R. ESTONIAN
S.S.R.

Kaliningrad

LITHUANIAN
R.S.F.S.R. S.S.R.

Tallinn

Riga

L.
Ladoga

Vilnius

Leningrad

L. Onega

Petrozavodsk

Arkhangelsk

Naryan
Mar Nenets
N.O.

Yamal Nenet
N.O.

Vorkuta

N. Dvina

Komi
A.S.S.R.

SOVIET

Salekhard

FEDERA

Gulf of Ob

BYELORUSSIAN

Minsk

S.S.R.

Lvov

Smolensk

Kalinin

Syktyvkar

RUSSIAN

Komi Permyak
N.O.

Ob

Khanty Mansi
N.O.

Khanty Mansiysk

UKRAINIAN
S.S.R.

Dnieper

Kiev

Moscow

Nizhniy Novgorod
(Gorkiy)

Kirov

MOLDAVIAN
S.S.R.

Kishinev

Kharkov

1

2
Kazan

3

Tatar
A.S.S.R.

4

Ustinov

Perm

Sverdlovsk

Tobolsk

Odessa

Voronezh

Tyumen

Dnepropetrovsk

Donetsk

Don

Saratov

Ufa

Bashkir
A.S.S.R.

Chelyabinsk

Magnitogorsk

Kuybyshev

Sevastopol

Rostov

Volga

Volgograd

Orenburg

Omsk

BLACK
SEA

Krasnodar

Adygey
A.O.

Maykop

Kalmyk
A.S.S.R.

Astrakhan

Novosibirsk

5

GEORGIAN
S.S.R.

6

7

10

8

9

11

Dagestan
A.S.S.R.

Irtysh

Karaganda

Semipalatinsk

Ordzhonikidze

Makhachkala

Tbilisi

ARMENIAN S.S.R.

Yerevan

12

13

AZERBAIJAN
S.S.R.

Baku

Aral
Sea
Karakalpak
A.S.S.R.

Nukus

KAZAKH

S.S.R.

Kzyl Orda

L. Balkhash

CASPIAN
SEA

Krasnovodsk

Syr Darya

TURKMEN
S.S.R.

UZBEK
S.S.R.

Ashkhabad

Samarkand

Amu Darya

Tashkent

Frunze

KIRGIZ
Issyk Kul
S.S.R.

Alma Ata

Dushanbe

TAJIK
S.S.R.

Gorno-Badakhsan
A.O.

Khorog

Ethno-linguistic areas

- Russian
- Ukrainian
- Byelorussian
- Baltic
- Romance
- Iranian
- Armenian
- Finno-Ugrian
- Turkic
- Mongolian
- Caucasian
- Sparsely populated or uninhabited areas

1. Mordovian A.S.S.R.
2. Chuvash A.S.S.R.
3. Mary A.S.S.R.
4. Udmurt A.S.S.R.
5. Karachay-Cherkess A.O.
6. Abkhaz A.S.S.R.
7. Kabardin-Balkar A.S.S.R.
8. Adzhar A.S.S.R.
9. Yugo-Ossetian A.S.S.R.
10. Severo-Ossetian A.S.S.R.
11. Chechen-Ingush A.S.S.R.
12. Nakhichevan A.S.S.R.
13. Nagorno-Karabakh A.O.

S.S.R. = Soviet Socialist Republic
A.S.S.R. = Autonomous S.S.R.
A.O. = Autonomous Oblast } Autonomous regions
N.O. = National Okrug within Soviet Republics

ARCTIC OCEAN

Wrangel Is.

Severnaya Zemlya

LAPTEV SEA

New Siberian Is.

Anadyr

Chukot N.O.

Nordvik

Taimyr N.O.

Tiksi

Sredne Kolymsk

Kolyma

Koryak N.O.

Indigirka

Verkhoyansk

Magadan

Kamchatka

Norilsk

SOCIALIST

Yakut A.S.S.R.

Lena

Yakutsk

Okhotsk

SEA OF OKHOTSK

Petropavlovsk-Kamchatskiy

Lower Tunguska

Tura

REPUBLIC

Evenk N.O.

Aldan

Kuril Is.

Upper Tunguska

Sakhalin

Lena

Amur

Krasnoyarsk

Komsomolsk

Sovetskaya Gavan

Buryat A.S.S.R.

Skovorodino

Amur

Ust Orda Buryat N.O.

L. Baykal

Aginsk Buryat N.O.

Blagoveshchensk

Birobidzhan

Khabarovsk

Kuznetsk

Abakan

Chita

Jewish A.O.

ass

Irkutsk

Ulan Ude

Aginskoye

Kyzyl

Tuva A.S.S.R.

Vladivostok

ikhail Gorbachev became party leader on 11 March 1985 and the parlous economic state of the Soviet Union presented him with a major challenge. He introduced the twin processes of *glasnost* – the opening up of a dialogue inside the country and with the outside world – and *perestroika* – the complete restructuring of party, society and the economy. Centralized controls over the economy were relaxed and the Soviet Union sought greater access to Western capital and technology. At the same time, the Soviet people were promised greater political and press freedoms.

The relaxation of party and state controls had the effect of encouraging the revival of nationalism in some constituent republics of the Union. Demonstrations in Georgia resulted in clashes between troops and nationalists; there was increasing unrest in the Ukraine and amongst the Romanians in Soviet Moldavia. In the Baltic republics of Latvia and Estonia the Communist party lost its monopoly of power, while early in 1990 Lithuania declared its independence from the Soviet Union. After failing to quell nationalism in the Baltic republics, Gorbachev held a referendum in March 1991. This gave qualified support for a 'renewed federation of equal sovereign republics'.

Revolution in Eastern Europe 1989–90

WEST

G E R M

Munich

Po

Trieste

ITALIANS Ljubljana

Rijeka

A U S T R I A

SLOVENIA

Danube

Vienna

Pragu

⑫ ①

BOHE

Bratislava

CZECHOSL

⑭

⑤

SLOVAKS

SLOV

Zagreb

CROATIA

SERBS

Pécs

Budapest

⑥

H U N G A R Y

Knin

SERBS

Split

Banja Luka

BOSNIANS

Sava

Drava

Tisza

Miskolc

ITALY

BOSNIA-
HERCEGOVINA

Szeged

Debrecen

ADRIATIC SEA

BOSNIANS Sarajevo

Y U G O S L A V I A

Novi Sad

Vojvodina

ROMANIANS

Timişoara

⑮

Mureş

Cluj

MEDITERRANEAN
SEA

MONTENEGRO

Titograd

Belgrade

SERBIA

ROMANIANS

Şebeş

Tirgu M

Shkodër

Sibiu

⅄

Tiranë ㉓ ㉔

ALBANIA

Peć

Kosovo
Prizren

① Priština

SERBS

Niš

R O M A N

Braşov

0 km   150

0 mls   100

Skopje

MACEDONIA

BULGARIANS

TURKS

⑯ ⑰

Bucharest

Sofia

⑩

GREEKS

Thessaloniki

GREECE

Plovdiv

B U L G A R I A

Danube

Brăila

Galaţi

RUSSIANS

Peoples of Eastern Europe

☐ Poles	☐ Turks	
☐ Czechs	☐ Albanians	
☐ Slovaks	☐ Serbs	
☐ Lithuanians	☐ Croats	
☐ Latvians	☐ Macedonians	
☐ Estonians	☐ Montenegrins	
☐ Germans	☐ Slovenes	
☐ Hungarians		
☐ Romanians	*POLES* Significant minority	
☐ Bulgarians	✸ Site of popular demonstration	

② ⑱

Kŭrdzhali

AEGEAN SEA

Burgas   Varna

Constanţa

TURKEY

BLACK SEA

130

1989

23 Mar **Yugoslavia** Violent protest by ethnic Albanians in Kosovo in opposition to Serbian Assembly's decision to reduce the region's autonomy **1**

20 May **Bulgaria** Ethnic Turkish protests violently suppressed; 300,000 Turks leave country between June and August **2**

18 June **Poland** Landslide win for Solidarity in National Assembly elections; one-party rule formally ended 24 August **3**

28 June **USSR** Ethnic Romanians in Moldavia demonstrate against Soviet rule (Kishinev) **4**

10 Sept **Hungary** Austrian border opened allowing mass exodus of East Germans to West **5**

18 Sept **Hungary** Parties sign accord for new constitution and transition to Western-style democracy **6**

27 Sept **Yugoslavia** Slovene parliament votes for right to secede from Yugoslavia **7**

3 Oct **East Germany** Border with Czechoslovakia closed in an attempt to halt emigration to the West **8**

18 Oct **East Germany** Communist Party leader Erich Honecker retires **9**

3 Nov **Bulgaria** Demonstrators in Sofia demand political reform; Communist Party leader Zhivkov replaced (10 Nov) **10**

10 Nov **East Germany** Opening of Berlin Wall between East and West **11**

17 Nov **Czechoslovakia** Opposition demonstration in Prague broken up with force by authorities **12**

27 Nov **Czechoslovakia** General strike, followed by rally in Wenceslas Square, Prague **13**

3 Dec **Czechoslovakia** New federal government formed with non-communist majority **14**

16 Dec **Romania** Mass demonstrations in protest at deportation order on Protestant pastor in Timisoara; quickly escalates to popular uprising **15**

21 Dec **Romania** Army goes over to uprising; fighting breaks out between pro-Government 'Securitate' forces and demonstrators **16**

25 Dec **Romania** Execution of President Nicolae Ceausescu **17**

1990

1 Jan **Bulgaria** Nationalist protests at restoration of Turkish minority rights (Kurdzhali) **18**

11 Mar **USSR** Lithuania's supreme council passes unilateral act proclaiming independence from USSR **19**

25 Mar **USSR** Estonia's Communist Party votes for independence from Moscow **20**

4 May **USSR** Supreme Soviet of Latvia passes resolution proclaiming Latvia's independence from USSR **21**

5 May **Germany** East and West Germany begin talks with the four war-time allies ('two plus four') on programme for re-unification **22**

8 May **Albania** Wide-ranging liberal reforms announced following outbreaks of popular unrest since December 1989 **23**

13 July **Albania** 4,000 refugees allowed to leave for Italy **24**

3 Oct **Germany** East and West officially re-unified as one state **25**

For commentary see page 119.

Chronology 1946–1990

EUROPE

Feb '46 ● Hungary becomes a republic
June '46● Umberto II abdicates and Italy becomes a republic
May '47 ● Communist ministers excluded from French and Italian cabinets
Dec '47 ● King Michael of Romania abdicates: republic proclaimed
Feb '48 ● Communist rule established in Czechoslovakia
Mar '48 ● Brussels Treaty organization formed: United Kingdom, France and Benelux countries (defensive alliance)
Apr '48 ● Organization for European Economic Cooperation established
June '48● Soviet blockade of West Berlin
Jan '49 ● Council for Mutual Economic Aid (Comecon) established in Moscow
Apr '49 ● North Atlantic Treaty signed by Brussels Treaty powers and USA, Canada, Italy, Denmark, Iceland, Norway and Portugal
May '49 ● Council of Europe founded
May '49 ● Federal German Republic founded: Konrad Adenauer becomes Chancellor (Sept)
Oct '49 ● German Democratic Republic founded

Oct '51 ● Conservative party wins British General Election: Winston Churchill re-elected Prime Minister
Feb '52 ● George VI of Britain dies: accession of Elizabeth II
Aug '52 ● First meeting of European Coal and Steel Community
Jan '53 ● Anti-Jewish campaign in Russia
Feb '53 ● Catholic Church in Poland put under state control and Cardinal Wyszynski, Primate of Poland, arrested
Mar '53 ● Stalin dies, succeeded by Georgy Malenkov as Chairman of Council of Ministers
June '53● Anti-communist riots in East Germany
Nov '54 ● Start of Algerian war of independence

Feb '55 ● Malenkov resigns: collective leadership of Nikita Khrushchev and Nikolai Bulganin
May '55 ● Occupation of Germany ends: Germany joins NATO and Brussels Treaty Organization
Mar '56 ● De-Stalinization begins in Russia: Stalin's 'cult of personality' disowned by Khrushchev at Party Congress
Oct '56 ● Britain, France and Israel invade Egypt after nationalization of Suez Canal
Jan '57 ● Harold Macmillan becomes Prime Minister of Britain
Mar '57 ● Common Market comes into being: Treaty of Rome signed by 'The Six': France, West Germany, Italy, Netherlands, Belgium, Luxembourg
Apr '57 ● Archbishop Makarios released by British government in return for cessation of hostilities by EOKA
Feb '58 ● Benelux Economic Union formed
Mar '58 ● Khrushchev premier of USSR as well as First Secretary of Party
June '58● General de Gaulle Prime Minister of France (elected President Dec)
June '59● Eamon de Valera elected President of Ireland
Nov '59 ● EFTA (European Free Trade Association) convention agreed: Austria, Scandinavian countries, Switzerland, UK and Portugal

AMERICAS

Feb '46 ● Juan Perón elected President of Argentina
July '46 ● Atomic tests at Bikini atoll: US battleship *Arkansas* sunk by blast
Aug '47 ● US Secretary of State General Marshall calls for European Recovery Programme (the Marshall Plan)
July '48 ● Communist leaders arrested in USA
Nov '48 ● Harry Truman elected President of USA
Mar '49 ● Newfoundland becomes 10th Canadian Province
Apr '49 ● NATO founded in Washington

Feb '50 ● Senator Joseph McCarthy denounces American State Department as full of communists
Nov '51 ● Juan Perón re-elected President of Argentina
Mar '52 ● General Batista seizes power as President of Cuba (to 1959)
Nov '52 ● General Dwight D Eisenhower (Republican) elected President of USA
Jan '53 ● New constitution in Venezuela: President Jimenéz given unlimited powers
July '53 ● Abortive revolt in Cuba led by Fidel Castro
June '54● Conservative rebellion in Guatemala: military dictatorship (to 1966)
Nov '54 ● Juan Perón's anti-clerical campaign in Argentina results in uprising
Dec '54 ● Senator McCarthy's anti-communist witch-hunt condemned by US Senate

Sept '55 ● Military and naval revolts in Argentina: Juan Perón resigns and flees
Mar '56 ● Blacks in Alabama led by Martin Luther King boycott public buses on grounds of illegality of segregation
Sept '56 ● General Somoza, President of Nicaragua, assassinated: succeeded by his son, Luis Somoza
Nov '56 ● Dwight D Eisenhower re-elected President of USA
Dec '56 ● Seven different governments in Haiti (to Sept '57)
June '57● Martin Luther King emerges as leader of desegregation campaign in USA
June '57● Overwhelming Conservative victory in Canadian General Election
Aug '57 ● Federation of West Indies established by Britain
Sept '57 ● François Duvalier elected President of Haiti
Apr '58 ● Fidel Castro issues decree for 'total war' against President Batista
Jan '59 ● Fidel Castro's guerrillas take Havana: Batista flees and Castro becomes Prime Minister
Apr '59 ● St Lawrence Seaway opened in Canada
Apr '59 ● Abortive coup attempts in Panama and Dominica with Cuban aid (to June)
Aug '59 ● Haiti repels invasion by Cuban forces

AFRICA, ASIA, AUSTRALASIA

Mar '46 • Britain declares Transjordan independent: renamed Jordan
Dec '46 • Communist Vietminh forces open hostilities against French in Indo-China
Aug '47 • India and Pakistan become independent: Nehru becomes Prime Minister of India, Muhammed Ali Jinnah Governor General of Pakistan: thousands killed in violence between Muslims and Hindus
Sept '47 • Britain announces withdrawal from Palestine
Oct '47 • Maharaja of Kashmir accedes to India
Nov '47 • India and Pakistan at war over Kashmir
May '48 • Jan Christian Smuts defeated in South African general election: Nationalist Afrikaaner Party wins on apartheid platform
May '48 • Israel proclaimed independent state and British mandate in Palestine is terminated
July '48 • Arab League forces attack Jewish positions
Jan '49 • Jiang Jieshi resigns as President of China: Communists gain control under Mao Zedong and proclaim People's Republic (Sept): Chiang retreats to Formosa (Taiwan)
Feb '49 • Armistice between Israel and Arab states
June '49 • USA withdraws from South Korea

June '50 • Korean war begins: North Korean forces invade South Korea: US troops disembark in Korea and take Seoul (in Sept)
Oct '50 • Chinese invade Tibet
Oct '51 • Egypt denounces 1936 treaty with Britain and King Farouk is proclaimed King of Sudan
July '52 • Gamal Abdul Nasser seizes power in Egypt and King Farouk forced to abdicate
Nov '52 • Vietminh offensive begins in Laos
Feb '53 • Anglo–Egyptian agreement on Sudan
July '53 • Armistice in Korea
May '54 • French forces heavily defeated by Vietminh at Dien Bien Phu
July '54 • Anglo–Egyptian agreement: all British forces to leave Egypt by 1956
July '54 • Vietnam split at 17th parallel: north Vietnam under communist control
Nov '54 • Nationalist rising begins in Algeria: civil war follows
Dec '54 • Cambodia becomes independent from France

Apr '55 • Bandung Conference: 29 Afro-Asian non-aligned states gather to condemn colonialism
Oct '55 • South Vietnam proclaimed a republic with Ngo Dinh Diem as president
Jan '56 • Sudan proclaimed independent from Anglo–Egyptian control
Mar '56 •.Morocco and Tunisia become independent from France
Apr '56 • Spanish Morocco made independent and reunited with Morocco
June '56 • Britain evacuates Canal Zone
Aug '56 • Nasser nationalizes Suez Canal
Oct '56 • Israel invades Sinai Desert: Anglo–French expedition lands at Pord Said (Nov)
Nov '56 • Anglo–French ceasefire as UN force arrives
Mar '57 • Gold Coast becomes independent from Britain: renamed Ghana
Mar '57 • Israel withdraws from Sinai and hands over Gaza strip to UN troops
July '58 • King Faisal of Iraq and other members of royal family assassinated
Aug '58 • General de Gaulle announces autonomy within 'French Community' for all French African colonies
May '59 • US reconnaisance aircraft, from base in Turkey, brought down in USSR: crisis follows

SCIENCE & CULTURE

1946 • Electronic Numerical Integrator and Calculator (ENIAC), first completely electronic computer
1947 • First supersonic flight
• Tennessee Williams *A Streetcar Named Desire*
• Discovery of the Dead Sea scrolls
1948 • Invention of long-playing record
• Invention of transistors
• Albert Camus *The Plague*
• Olivier Messiaen *Turangalíla Symphony*
• Richard Strauss *Four Last Songs*
1949 • Cortisone is discovered
• George Orwell *1984*
• Arthur Miller *Death of a Salesman*
• Simone de Beauvoir *The Second Sex*
• Rodgers and Hammerstein *South Pacific*
• T S Eliot *The Cocktail Party*

1950 • Ezra Pound *Seventy Cantos*
• Edith Piaf *La Vie en Rose*
1951 • J D Salinger *Catcher in the Rye*
• Electrical power first produced from atomic energy
• Benjamin Britten *Billy Budd*
• Salvador Dali *Crucifixion*
1952 • First atomic submarine
• USA explodes first hydrogen bomb
1953 • James Watson and Francis Crick identify structure of DNA
• Dmitri Shostakovich Tenth Symphony
• Arthur Miller *The Crucible*
1954 • Arnold Schoenberg *Moses and Aaron*
• William Golding *The Lord of the Flies*

1955 • Vaccine for polio discovered
• Vladimir Nabokov *Lolita*
• Ludwig Wittgenstein *Philosophical Investigations*
• Walter Piston Sixth Symphony
1956 • Elvis Presley *Love Me Tender*
• Transatlantic telephone service inaugurated
• John Osborne *Look Back in Anger*
1957 • Russia launches the unmanned *Sputnik I* and *II*
• Jack Kerouac *On The Road*
• Samuel Beckett *Endgame*
1958 • Hovercraft invented in UK
• USA launches *Vanguard* and *Explorer* satellites
• First US nuclear submarine passes under North Pole
• Boris Pasternak *Dr Zhivago*
• J K Galbraith *The Affluent Society*
• Harold Pinter *The Birthday Party*
1959 • USSR rocket begins orbit round Sun
• Russian satellite photographs back of the Moon
• Billy Wilder produces *Some Like It Hot* starring Marilyn Monroe

EUROPE

Jan '60 ● USSR reduces armed forces by 1.2 million to 2.4 million
Apr '60 ● Completion of collectivization in East Germany
Aug '60 ● Cyprus proclaimed independent republic
Aug '61 ● Berlin Wall erected to separate East and West Berlin
Nov '61 ● Portugal institutes a common market with its overseas territories
Mar '62 ● Evian Agreement ends Algerian War: France grants independence to Algeria
Nov '62 ● Greece joins EEC as associate member
Feb '63 ● Geneva disarmament talks
Feb '64 ● Heavy fighting between Greeks and Turks in Cyprus
Oct '64 ● Harold Wilson leads Labour Party to victory in British General Election
Oct '64 ● Khrushchev falls from power and is succeeded by Alexei Kosygin and Leonid Brezhnev

Jan '65 ● Prime Ministers of Ireland and Northern Ireland meet for first time in 40 years
Nov '65 ● Death penalty for murder abolished in Britain
Jan '66 ● Britain imposes trade sanctions on Rhodesia
Mar '67 ● First French nuclear-powered submarine launched
Apr '67 ● Military coup in Greece: King Constantine goes into exile in December
Jan '68 ● Alexander Dubček begins reforms in Czechoslovakia – the 'Prague Spring'
May '68 ● Student riots in Paris and Nanterre and serious strikes throughout France: French Assembly dissolved in Paris
Aug '68 ● Warsaw Pact troops occupy Czechoslovakia and halt 'Prague Spring'
Oct '68 ● Riots in Londonderry by civil rights demonstrators
Jan '69 ● Martial law proclaimed in Spain following riots and student unrest
Apr '69 ● Riots in Londonderry and Belfast involving Catholics and Protestants: Army ordered to guard key installations
June '69 ● Georges Pompidou elected President of France after resignation of General de Gaulle (Apr)
Oct '69 ● Willy Brandt becomes Chancellor of West Germany

June '70 ● Conservatives win British General Election and Edward Heath becomes Prime Minister (to 1974)
Oct '70 ● Major British oil find in North Sea
Dec '70 ● State of emergency in Spain following demonstrations and strikes by Basque separatists
Feb '72 ● IRA blow up British Embassy in Dublin
Mar '72 ● Parliament of Northern Ireland taken over by British government
Sept '72 ● Beginning of 'Cod War' – Iceland unilaterally extends fishing limits from 12 to 50 miles: resisted by Britain
Oct '72 ● At Munich Olympic Games, Palestinian guerrillas kill two members of Israeli team and take nine hostages
Aug '73 ● Greece proclaimed republic with George Papadopoulos as President
Apr '74 ● Left-wing coup in Portugal
July '74 ● President Makarios of Cyprus overthrown in military coup: Turks invade island
Nov '74 ● End of military dictatorship in Greece: democratic elections lead to Constantine Karamanlis becoming Prime Minister

AMERICAS

Jan '60 ● USA protests at expropriation of American property in Cuba and places embargo on shipments to Cuba (Oct)
Nov '60 ● John F Kennedy (Democrat) elected President of USA
Jan '61 ● USA breaks off diplomatic relations with Cuba
Feb '61 ● Large-scale economic and military aid agreed by USSR for Cuba
Apr '61 ● US-backed Cuban exiles, led by Jose Cardona, attempt unsuccessful invasion of Cuba at Bay of Pigs
Oct '62 ● Cuban missile crisis: US navy blockades Cuba to prevent further imports of Soviet missiles and USSR removes nuclear missiles from Cuba
Aug '63 ● Nuclear Test Ban Treaty signed by USA, USSR and Britain
Nov '63 ● President Kennedy assassinated: Vice-President Lyndon B Johnson takes over
Oct '64 ● Martin Luther King awarded Nobel Peace Prize
Nov '64 ● Lyndon Johnson elected US President in landslide victory: pledges 'Great Society' expansion of social welfare provisions

Feb '65 ● Malcolm X, Black Muslim leader, assassinated
Feb '65 ● Martin Luther King arrested in Dallas
Mar '65 ● Civil Rights march from Selma to Montgomery, Alabama: Ku Klux Klan shootings in Selma
Apr '65 ● Military junta deposes civilian government in Dominican Republic: USA sends marines to prevent establishment of communist government
Oct '65 ● Demonstrations in USA against American involvement in Vietnam War
May '66 ● British Guiana becomes independent as Guyana
June '66 ● Joaquin Balaguer elected President of Dominican Republic
July '66 ● Race riots in Chicago, Cleveland and Brooklyn, USA
Feb '67 ● General Somoza Junior, elected President of Nicaragua
Oct '67 ● 'Che' Guevara killed by Bolivian troops while waging guerrilla campaign in Andes
Apr '68 ● Pierre Trudeau (Liberal) becomes Prime Minister of Canada
Apr '68 ● Martin Luther King assassinated
June '68 ● Senator Robert Kennedy assassinated in Los Angeles
Nov '68 ● Richard Nixon (Republican) elected President of USA
Sept '69 ● President Salinas of Bolivia overthrown by General Ovando

Sept '70 ● Salvador Allende elected President of Chile heading Marxist government
Apr '71 ● President Duvalier of Haiti dies: succeeded by his son Jean-Claude Duvalier
Dec '71 ● USA devalues dollar
May '72 ● SALT I agreements signed in Moscow by Nixon and Brezhnev
June '72 ● Beginning of 'Watergate' affair with arrest of five men inside Democratic National HQ in Washington
Nov '72 ● President Nixon re-elected President of USA
Jan '73 ● USA withdraws remaining combat troops from Vietnam after cease-fire agreement
Jan '73 ● Watergate trial opens in Washington
Apr '73 ● President Nixon's chief advisers resign over Watergate bugging
Sept '73 ● Military coup in Chile: President Allende killed and General Pinochet takes over power with military government
Sept '73 ● Juan Perón re-elected President of Argentina
July '74 ● Juan Perón dies: his wife Isabel Perón succeeds
Aug '74 ● President Nixon resigns over Watergate affair to avoid impeachment: succeeded by Vice-President Ford

AFRICA, ASIA, AUSTRALASIA

Sept '60 ● OPEC (Organization of Petroleum Exporting
Countries) instituted in Baghdad
July '62 ● Algeria becomes independent from France
Oct '62 ● Uganda becomes independent from Britain
Oct '62 ● China attacks India: ceasefire (in Nov)
May '63 ● Organization of African Unity founded at conference
in Addis Ababa
June '63 ● Civil War in Iraq between Arabs and Kurds
Nov '63 ● Military coup in Iraq
Apr '64 ● Ian Smith becomes Prime Minister of Southern
Rhodesia
Apr '64 ● Tanganyika and Zanzibar united (known as Tanzania
from Oct)
June '64 ● Nelson Mandela and seven other black leaders
sentenced to life imprisonment in South Africa
Aug '64 ● North Vietnamese torpedo boats attack US warships
in Gulf of Tonkin
Oct '64 ● Northern Rhodesia becomes independent as Zambia
with Dr Kenneth Kaunda as its first President

Mar '65 ● Escalation of war in Vietnam as US ground forces sent
in to aid South Vietnam
Apr '65 ● Hostilities between Pakistan and India over Kashmir
(to Sept)
Nov '65 ● Ian Smith unilaterally declares Rhodesia independent
Jan '66 ● Mrs Indira Gandhi becomes Prime Minister of India
Jan '66 ● Military coup in Nigeria
Feb '66 ● Milton Obote seizes power in Uganda
Aug '66 ● 'Cultural Revolution' begins in China
Sept '66 ● Dr Verwoerd, South African Prime Minister,
assassinated: John Vorster succeeds
May '67 ● Egypt closes Gulf of Aqaba to Israel
May '67 ● Civil war in Nigeria with proclamation of independent
republic of Biafra
June '67 ● Six-day War between Israel and neighbouring Arab
states
Nov '67 ● People's Republic of South Yemen proclaimed in
Aden
Sept '68 ● Swaziland becomes an independent constitutional
monarchy under King Sobhoza II
Mar '69 ● Golda Meir becomes Prime Minister of Israel (to 1974)
July '69 ● North Vietnam rejects US peace proposal
Sept '69 ● King Idris I of Libya overthrown in military coup led
by Colonel Moamer Gaddafi

Jan '70 ● Biafran civil war ends in Nigeria
July '70 ● Aswan High Dam begins operation
Sept '70 ● General Nasser dies and is succeeded by Anwar Sadat
(Oct)
Oct '70 ● Kingdom of Cambodia becomes the Khmer Republic
Jan '71 ● General Idi Amin leads military coup in Uganda
Mar '71 ● East Pakistan declared independent as Bangladesh
Apr '72 ● 50,000 killed in attempted coup in Burundi
Sept '72 ● General Amin gives 8,000 Asians 48 hours to leave
Uganda: European missionaries expelled from
Uganda
Oct '73 ● Yom Kippur 'Day of Atonement' War between Arabs
and Israel begins: Sinai and Golan Heights invaded
Oct '73 ● Cut in Arab oil production and increased prices cause
oil crisis in USA and Europe
Apr '74 ● Golda Meir resigns as Prime Minister of Israel and is
succeeded by Yitzak Rabin
Sept '74 ● Emperor Haile Selassie deposed in Ethiopia

SCIENCE & CULTURE

1960 ● R D Laing *The Divided Self*
● Heart pacemaker developed
● Harper Lee *To Kill a Mockingbird*
1961 ● Major Yuri Gagarin is the first man to travel in space
round Earth
● Joseph Heller *Catch 22*
● Leonard Bernstein *West Side Story*
1962 ● Second Vatican Council, attended by over 2,000
bishops, opened in Rome
● Benjamin Britten *War Requiem*
● US manned space flights
● Ken Kelsey *One Flew over the Cuckoo's Nest*
● Alexander Solzhenitsyn *One Day in the Life of Ivan
Denisovich*
1963 ● Vaccine for measles perfected
● Roy Lichtenstein *Whaam!*
● The Beatles *She Loves You*
1964 ● China explodes an atom bomb
● Close-up photos of Moon's surface taken by
Ranger VII
● Saul Bellow *Herzog*

1965 ● US spacecraft lands on Moon: Edward White first man
to walk in space
● Mao Zedong (Mao Tse-tung) *The Thoughts of
Chairman Mao*
● Mary Quant introduces the miniskirt
1966 ● Russian and American spacecraft made soft landings
on the Moon
● Michael Tippett *The Vision of St Augustine*
● Metropolitan Opera House opens in New York
1967 ● First public flight of Franco–British supersonic
aircraft, *Concorde*, from Toulouse
● World's first heart-transplant carried out in South
Africa by Christian Barnaard
● Desmond Morris *The Naked Ape*
● Karlheinz Stockhausen *Anthems*
1968 ● Flower power in San Francisco
● Stanley Kubrick *2001, A Space Odyssey*
● Gabriel García Marquez *A Hundred Years of Solitude*
● Mies van der Rohe, National Gallery, Berlin
1969 ● Neil Armstrong is first man to walk on Moon
● Fertilization in a test tube of a human ovum in
Cambridge
● Woodstock pop music festival
● Vladimir Nabokov *Ada*

1970 ● David Hockney *Mr & Mrs Ossie Clark and Percy*
● Germaine Greer *The Female Eunuch*
1971 ● First microprocessor produced in California, USA
● Luchino Visconti directs *Death in Venice*
1972 ● Liza Minnelli stars in *Cabaret*
● Steve Reich *Drumming*
1973 ● Bernardo Bertolucci *Last Tango In Paris*
● Alexander Solzhenitsyn *The Gulag Archipelago*
● Ernst Schumacher *Small is Beautiful*
1974 ● Philip Larkin *High Windows*
● Harrison Birtwistle *Imaginary Landscape*

EUROPE

Feb '75 • Turkish Cypriot federated state proclaimed
Nov '75 • General Franco of Spain dies: inauguration of King Juan Carlos I
Apr '76 • James Callaghan (Labour) becomes British Prime Minister
Apr '77 • Communist party legalized in Spain
June '77 • Leonid Brezhnev becomes President of USSR
Sept '77 • Catalans granted autonomy within Spanish state
Aug '78 • Pope Paul VI dies: John Paul I elected, dies (Sept): John Paul II is elected in October, the first non-Italian Pope for 450 years
May '79 • British Conservative Party wins General Election bringing Margaret Thatcher to power as first woman Prime Minister of Britain
June '79 • First direct elections to European Parliament
Aug '79 • Earl Mountbatten of Burma murdered in Ireland by IRA
Oct '79 • NATO reaffirms decision to deploy long-range nuclear weapons in Europe
Dec '79 • Soviet troops begin invasion of Afghanistan

May '80 • President Tito of Yugoslavia dies
July '80 • Olympic Games in Moscow boycotted by over 30 countries as protest against Soviet invasion of Afghanistan
Sept '80 • Solidarity union founded in Poland under Lech Walesa after two months of strikes
May '81 • François Mitterrand elected President of France
Dec '81 • Martial law declared in Poland
Oct '82 • Solidarity outlawed by Polish government
Oct '82 • Helmut Kohl elected Chancellor of West Germany
Nov '82 • President Brezhnev dies: Yuri Andropov succeeds
July '83 • Poland suspends martial law
Feb '84 • Yuri Andropov dies and is succeeded by Konstantin Chernenko

Mar '85 • Konstantin Chernenko dies and is succeeded by Mikhail Gorbachev as party general secretary
Nov '85 • Anglo-Irish agreement on Northern Ireland
Oct '87 • 'Black Monday' on London Stock Market: worst day for shares this century
Dec '88 • Bomb kills 259 on Pan-Am flight over Lockerbie in Scotland
Aug '89 • Tadeusz Mazowiecki becomes first non-communist Prime Minister of Poland since Second World War
Sept '89 • Mass exodus from East Germany as opening of Hungarian border allows entry to West Germany
Oct '89 • Erich Honecker, East German Communist Party leader forced to resign
Nov '89 • Berlin Wall comes down
Nov '89 • Czechoslovak Communist Party leaders resign
Dec '89 • Nicolae Ceausescu, Romanian dictator, executed
Mar '90 • Lithuania declares its independence from USSR
May '90 • Free elections in Romania
June '90 • Free elections in Czechoslovakia and Bulgaria
Oct '90 • Unification of East and West Germany
Nov '90 • Margaret Thatcher resigns as British prime minister: John Major succeeds
Jan '91 • Soviet troops seize nationalist defence headquarters in Lithuania, killing unarmed civilians
Mar '91 • Gorbachev seeks support for a 'renewed federation of equal sovereign republics' in Soviet referendum

AMERICAS

Nov '75 • Suriname gains independence from the Netherlands
Jan '76 • Military coup in Ecuador
Mar '76 • President Isabel Perón of Argentina overthrown: succeeded by General Videla
Nov '76 • Jimmy Carter (Democrat) elected US President
Nov '78 • Dominica gains independence from Britain
Feb '79 • USA withdraws support from President Somoza in Nicaragua
June '79 • SALT II Treaty signed by Carter and Brezhnev in Geneva
July '79 • President Somoza resigns and goes into exile: Sandinista government in Nicaragua sworn in

Oct '80 • Peace and border treaty between El Salvador and Honduras
Nov '80 • Ronald Reagan (Republican) elected President of USA
Jan '82 • Honduras ends military rule and installs President Cordova
Apr '82 • Argentina invades Falkland Islands
May '82 • British forces land on East Falklands and Argentinian forces surrender (in June)
Oct '83 • Maurice Bishop, prime minister of Grenada, overthrown and murdered: US military intervention follows
Dec '83 • Military junta dissolved in Argentina
Feb '84 • Pierre Trudeau resigns as Canadian Prime Minister
Nov '84 • Sandinistas led by Daniel Ortega win elections in Nicaragua

Jan '85 • Ronald Reagan begins second term as US President
May '85 • US trade embargo against Nicaragua
Feb '86 • Haitians overthrow President Duvalier ('Baby Doc') after years of oppressive rule
Jan '87 • Ecuadorean President and 30 others kidnapped by air force commandos demanding release of rebel leader
July '87 • Colonel Oliver North and Admiral Poindexter give testimonies over sales of arms to Iran and transfer of funds to Nicaraguan Contras
Dec '87 • USA and USSR sign historic INF (Intermediate-range Nuclear Forces) treaty to reduce nuclear arsenals
July '88 • 200,000 march on National Palace in Mexico City to protest against fraudulent elections in which Salinas de Gortari becomes President
Nov '88 • George Bush (Republican) wins US Presidency
Dec '89 • US invasion of Panama
Jan '90 • USA begins to reduce defence budget and withdraw troops from Europe and elsewhere
Feb '90 • Sandinista government in Nicaragua defeated in general elections
July '90 • Attempted coup in Trinidad and Tobago by Muslim extremists

AFRICA, ASIA, AUSTRALASIA

Apr '75 • Vietnam war ends with South falling to communists
Nov '75 • Angola gains its independence from Portugal: civil war breaks out between rival independence movements
Sept '76 • Death of Mao Zedong
Mar '77 • Indira Gandhi resigns and is replaced by Morarji Desai
July '77 • General Zia becomes President of Pakistan after military coup
Sept '77 • Steve Biko dies in South African jail
Apr '78 • President of Afghanistan overthrown: left-wing Democratic Republic established
Sept '78 • Camp David summit between Anwar Sadat of Egypt, Menachem Begin of Israel and Jimmy Carter of the USA
Dec '78 • Vietnamese invade Cambodia and capture Phnom Penh (Jan '79)
Jan '79 • Shah of Iran goes into exile
Feb '79 • Ayatollah Khomeini returns to Iran from exile in Paris and Iran adopts Islamic constitution (Dec)
Mar '79 • Egypt and Israel sign peace treaty ending state of war existing since 1948
July '79 • Former President Bhutto executed in Pakistan
Dec '79 • Soviet troops airlifted into Afghanistan

Apr '80 • Republic of Zimbabwe declared independent
Sept '80 • Conflict escalates between Iran and Iraq
Nov '80 • Trial of 'Gang of Four' in Beijing (to Dec)
Jan '81 • Iran releases American Embassy hostages after 444 days
Oct '81 • President Sadat of Egypt assassinated: Hosni Mubarak succeeds
June '82 • Israeli forces invade Lebanon
Sept '82 • Massacre of Palestinians in Beirut refugee camps
Sept '82 • President Bashir Gemayel of Lebanon assassinated in Beirut
June '83 • Yasser Arafat expelled from Syria
Oct '84 • Indian Prime Minister Indira Gandhi assassinated by Sikh bodyguards

Apr '86 • US planes bomb five sites in Libya in retaliation for Berlin disco bombing
Jan '87 • Truce declared in Afghan war
May '88 • Soviets begin withdrawal from Afghanistan
Aug '88 • Ceasefire agreed to in Iran–Iraq war
Nov '88 • Benazir Bhutto claims victory in Pakistani general elections
Dec '88 • Treaty signed agreeing to withdrawal of Cuban troops from Angola
May '89 • Mass demonstrations for democracy by Chinese students in Tiananmen Square, Beijing, ends in massacre (June)
Sept '89 • Vietnamese troops complete withdrawal from Cambodia after 10-year occupation
Feb '90 • South African President, F W de Klerk lifts ban on ANC and South African Communist party and promises reforms to dismantle apartheid
Feb '90 • Nelson Mandela, deputy leader of the ANC, released after 26 years in prison
Feb '90 • Civil war breaks out in Liberia
Aug '90 • Iraq invades Kuwait; US and allied countries respond by sending forces to the Gulf region
Jan '91 •Operation Desert Storm commences: Arab and Western allied airforces attack strategic targets in Iraq; allied land offensive liberates Kuwait (Feb) and civil war erupts in Iraq

SCIENCE & CULTURE

1975 • Anthony Powell *A Dance to the Music of Time*
• Gabriel García Marquez *Autumn of The Patriarch*
• Stephen Spielberg directs *Jaws*
• US/Soviet astronauts link up in space
1976 • First commercial *Concorde* flight
1977 • Pompidou Centre opens in Paris
• George Lucas directs *Star Wars*
• Woody Allen directs and stars in *Annie Hall*
1978 • World's first 'test-tube baby' is born in Oldham, England
1979 • Nobel Peace Prize awarded to Mother Teresa of Calcutta
• Two Voyager spacecrafts fly past Jupiter sending back close-up views
• James Baldwin *Just Above My Head*
• Francis Ford Coppola directs *Apocalypse Now*

1980 • Scientists at Harvard University synthesize interferon, a natural virus-fighting agent, by genetic engineering
• WHO announces elimination in world of smallpox
1981 • French high-speed train makes record journey from Paris to Lyon in 2 hrs 40 mins
• US Space Shuttle is launched: first spacecraft to be used more than once
1983 • The Compact Disc makes first appearance
• Stephen Spielberg directs *ET*
• Richard Nobel drives *Thrust* at 633.46 mph (1019.46 kmh)
1984 • AIDS virus is discovered
• 15-day-old baby is given baboon's heart in California
• Milan Kundera *The Unbearable Lightness of Being*

1985 • Pierre Boulez *Third Mallarmé Improvisation*
• Live Aid concert at Wembley
1986 • Andrei Sakharov, physicist and Nobel Peace Prize winner, is released from exile in Gorky
• First non-stop around the world flight completed by Dick Rutan's *Voyager*
• Sight of Halley's Comet (last seen in 1910)
• Nobel Prize awarded to African writer, Wole Soyinka
1988 • Russian Orthodox Church celebrates its millennium
• USA revives space programme with successful launch of Shuttle, *Discovery*
• Stephen Hawking *A Brief History of Time*
• Salman Rushdie *The Satanic Verses*
• 'Turin Shroud' pronounced of medieval origin
1989 • 12 years after launch *Voyager 2* spacecraft reaches Neptune
• Michael Tippett *New Year*

AN UNCERTAIN FUTURE

Dramatic reversal in America's fortunes has increased global economic instability.

From 1945 until the late 1960s the United States dominated the world economy. By the early 1970s, however, its economy began to falter. The heavy expenditures on the Vietnam War and President Johnson's programme of reforms, with little corresponding increase in taxation, and the effects of the OPEC oil price rises of the early 1970s resulted in mounting budgetary deficits. Imports began to exceed exports for the first time since the 1890s. Inflation leapt from 3 per cent in 1967 to 12 per cent in 1974 while unemployment doubled to 6 per cent in 1970. Productivity also declined. The United States was experiencing the phenomenon known as 'stagflation' – high levels of inflation coupled with recession. The Nixon Administration raised interest rates in an effort to reduce the supply of money, which triggered a severe fall in stock market prices. In 1971 the US government suspended the convertibility of the dollar into gold, and the dollar fell in value on the world exchanges.

Externally American exporters faced rising competition for their products from new centres of economic strength. West Germany, Japan, Taiwan and South Korea had modernized their economies during the 1950s and 1960s and had achieved astonishing growth rates, especially in such modern industries as electronics, micro-chip and computer technology, motor car and truck manufacturing, shipbuilding and chemicals where formerly the United States had been pre-eminent. Internally many American manufacturers were driven into insolvency by the flood of imports from the newly developed Pacific Rim countries, whose high quality ensured that they found a ready market among American consumers. During the 1980s the Reagan Administration promoted tax cuts as a means of increasing incentives to greater efficiency and because it believed that the growth at the top would have a 'trickle down' effect on all sections of the economy. The deficits, which had been mounting since the 1970s, assumed astronomic proportions as the expansion of the American armed forces placed a further heavy strain on the economy. In 1982 the deficit was $110.6 billion dollars and the level of the national debt had reached $1 trillion. The United States was hit by a further recession in 1982, although after 1984 there was a slight recovery partially attributable to a fall in oil prices. President Bush has made a start in tackling this huge deficit by imposing a one-year freeze in real growth for defence in the 1990 financial year and has cut the defence budget by a further $3,700 million.

This dramatic reversal in America's economic fortunes has resulted in increasing global economic instability. The sudden New York stock market collapse in 1987 precipitated a world-wide panic, although the markets have since managed a slow recovery. Fears have been expressed that the United States might take some dramatic step, such as imposing a wide range of import controls, in an effort to solve its economic problems, which would encourage retaliation by other countries and a dramatic shrinking of international trade in an already volatile situation.

The European Revival

◄ In the 1980s thousands suffered and many died as a result of severe drought and famine in Ethiopia. Civil war in the northern provinces hampered relief work.

▼ Trees dying in Vosges Forest, France. It is believed that acid rain, created by the emission of nitrogen oxides and sulphur dioxide from power stations and factories, may be killing the forests of Europe.

In 1945, after the war, most of the European continent was in ruins. Roads, railways and factories had been damaged or destroyed during the fighting, and agricultural production had virtually ceased. From 1948, however, Western European recovery, which was already slowly underway, was assisted by the Marshall Plan or European Recovery Programme, whereby the United States provided dollar aid to overcome acute balance of payments difficulties in Europe. Under the Plan, the Organization of European Economic Unity (OEEC) assessed each country's needs for loans and credits. The Soviet Union and its satellites refused to participate. By 1952, when the Programme ended, European industrial production had increased by 35 per cent, and agricultural production by 10 per cent, over pre-war levels.

Economic experts recognized that West European recovery depended on the revival of the West German economy. When West Germany emerged as a separate political entity after the setting up of the Federal Republic and the election of Konrad Adenauer's pro-Western Christian Democratic Party in 1949, West Germany received Marshall Aid. Soon West Germany's trade and industry recovered from the effects of the war, and by the end of 1949 productivity had reached 1939 levels. During the 1950s West Germany became one of the world's major industrial powers. However, the European Recovery Programme did not lead to European economic integration as many European federalists like Jean Monnet of France and Paul Henri Spaak of Belgium had anticipated. In May 1950 the French government proposed the pooling of Franco–German iron and steel production and in the following year the European Coal and Steel Community, consisting of France, West Germany, Italy, Belgium, the Netherlands and Luxembourg, came into existence. This supranational body – the precursor of the more far-reaching European Economic Community established in 1957 – supervised coal and iron production and sought the removal of internal customs barriers and quota systems. Britain, anxious not to prejudice its economic independence or its ties with the Commonwealth and the United States, refused to join, convinced that in any case the experiment would fail. During the 1950s Western Europe enjoyed an unprecedented economic boom, centred on the northern French and Ruhr industrial areas and on northern Italy. While the British economy also improved during this period, it slipped behind its European competitors, especially West Germany, and was afflicted with high inflation and frequent balance of payments crises.

American and West European banks have contributed to this problem by lending large sums of money to Third World and Eastern European countries during the 1970s. Much of this money was spent on grandiose and unprofitable projects and by the 1980s many of these debtor countries were finding it impossible to pay even the interest charges on these loans. West European banks had used the inflow of profits from the Middle East oil producers to lend money to Eastern European countries to enable them to purchase Western technology and Western industrial products in order to improve their economic prospects. With the fall in world trade these countries could not finance their growing trade imbalance with the West and had to borrow more money for this purpose: their indebtedness rose from $19 billion in 1975 to $62 billion in 1981. Fears that one of the debtor countries might default on its loans, and so begin a chain reaction, have led the banks to agree to the re-scheduling of their debts and to arrange fresh loans in order to re-pay their existing obligations which, in a decade of high interest rates, increases their predicament and merely postpones any effective solution to the problem.

▲ Hectic trading at the Tokyo stock exchange in 1987, the year of the New York stock market collapse which caused panic in markets world-wide.

The Soviet economy, which since 1945 had largely been insulated from the global economy, also faces many problems. Heavy defence expenditures, shortfalls in agricultural production necessitating large grain imports from the United States, financial aid to overseas countries, the costs of the war in Afghanistan and the bureaucracy, inefficiency and corruption which permeates the entire economic and political system led Mikhail Gorbachev to promise major structural reforms designed to reduce the increasing budget deficit and at the same time to switch resources from heavy industry and the military to consumer production. In 1988 the Soviet economy grew by only 1.5 per cent having also performed poorly in 1987, thus placing Gorbachev's reform programme in jeopardy. In 1989 Gorbachev announced defence cuts of 14.4 per cent over the next two years.

Technological change

Since 1945 the world has been transformed by great technological change. New industries – notably those based on computers – have grown quickly, while old industries, such as car manufacturing, have been revolutionized by the use of automation and robotics. Air travel has almost completely replaced ocean liners as a means of overseas travel, largely as a result of the development of jet-propelled aircraft during the 1950s, while, in the developed world at least, people's lives have been radically altered by a range of new electrical and electronic goods for both domestic and entertainment purposes. Two aspects of technological change since 1945 stand out in particular.

On 4 October 1957 the Soviet Union launched the world's first artificial satellite, *Sputnik 1*. This was the beginning of a space exploration race between the Soviet Union and the United States that resulted in America landing two men on the moon on 20 July 1969, and both countries exploring the outer planets and the rest of the solar system during the 1980s and 1990s. The United States launched its first satellite, *Explorer 1*, in 1958, France its first in 1965, Japan and China in 1970 and Britain in 1971. In total, more than 1,700 satellite and space probes have been launched over the last three decades, designed chiefly for scientific, meterological, photographic and navigational research, reconnaissance purposes, and the provision of world-wide telephone and television links.

Nuclear power has been developed from research on the atomic bomb since 1945, with nuclear energy

▲ **The space shuttle *Columbia* takes off from Kennedy Space Centre.**

▼ **The nuclear reactor at Chernobyl after it exploded in 1986.**

being harnessed to produce electricity. While a number of nuclear power plants have been constructed throughout the world, progress in the generation of cheap electricity has been slow. Disasters like the explosion of a nuclear power plant at Chernobyl in the Soviet Union in 1986, which caused widespread radioactive contamination, and the problem of nuclear waste disposal have alarmed many conservationists about the dangers to people and the environment of continuing nuclear development.

International Economic Groupings

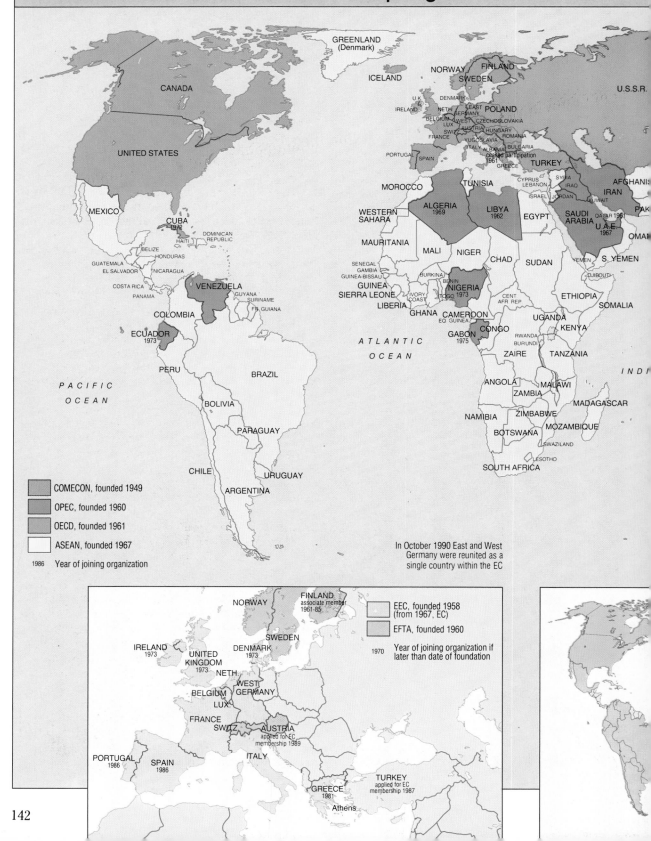

GREENLAND (Denmark)

CANADA

UNITED STATES

MEXICO

CUBA 1972

BELIZE
GUATEMALA
EL SALVADOR
HONDURAS
NICARAGUA
COSTA RICA
PANAMA

DOMINICAN REPUBLIC
HAITI

VENEZUELA

COLOMBIA

ECUADOR 1973

PERU

BRAZIL

BOLIVIA

PARAGUAY

CHILE

URUGUAY

ARGENTINA

GUYANA
SURINAME
FR. GUIANA

PACIFIC OCEAN

ICELAND

NORWAY FINLAND
SWEDEN

U.K
DENMARK
IRELAND
NETH
BELGIUM EAST GERMANY POLAND
LUX WEST CZECHOSLOVAKIA
FRANCE AUSTRIA HUNGARY
SWITZ ROMANIA
ITALY YUGOSLAVIA BULGARIA
ALBANIA
ceased participation 1961
PORTUGAL GREECE
SPAIN

U.S.S.R.

TURKEY

MOROCCO TUNISIA
CYPRUS SYRIA
LEBANON IRAQ
ISRAEL JORDAN

AFGHANIS
IRAN
KUWAIT
PAK

WESTERN SAHARA

ALGERIA 1969

LIBYA 1962

EGYPT

SAUDI ARABIA

QATAR 1961
U.A.E. 1967

OMA

MAURITANIA

MALI NIGER

CHAD SUDAN

YEMEN S. YEMEN

DJIBOUTI

SENEGAL
GAMBIA
GUINEA-BISSAU

GUINEA
SIERRA LEONE
LIBERIA

BURKINA
IVORY COAST
GHANA

BENIN
TOGO
NIGERIA 1973

EQ. GUINEA

CAMEROON
GABON 1975
CONGO

CENT AFR REP

ETHIOPIA

SOMALIA

UGANDA KENYA

RWANDA
BURUNDI

ATLANTIC OCEAN

ZAIRE TANZANIA

INDI

ANGOLA

ZAMBIA

MALAWI

MADAGASCAR

NAMIBIA

ZIMBABWE

BOTSWANA

MOZAMBIQUE

SWAZILAND

LESOTHO

SOUTH AFRICA

COMECON, founded 1949	
OPEC, founded 1960	
OECD, founded 1961	
ASEAN, founded 1967	

1986 Year of joining organization

In October 1990 East and West Germany were reunited as a single country within the EC

NORWAY

FINLAND associate member 1961-85

IRELAND 1973

UNITED KINGDOM 1973

SWEDEN

DENMARK 1973

NETH.
BELGIUM WEST GERMANY
LUX.
FRANCE
SWITZ. AUSTRIA
applied for EC membership 1989

PORTUGAL 1986

SPAIN 1986

ITALY

GREECE 1981

Athens

TURKEY
applied for EC membership 1987

EEC, founded 1958 (from 1967, EC)	
EFTA, founded 1960	

1970 Year of joining organization if later than date of foundation

MONGOLIA 1962

N. KOREA

JAPAN

S. KOREA

CHINA

PACIFIC OCEAN

BHUTAN

BANGLADESH

TAIWAN

BURMA

LAOS

THAILAND

VIETNAM 1978

PHILIPPINES

CAMBODIA

SRI LANKA

BRUNEI 1984

MALAYSIA

SINGAPORE

INDONESIA 1962

PAPUA NEW GUINEA

OCEAN

AUSTRALIA

NEW ZEALAND

Colombo Plan founded 1950

LAFTA (now LAIA), founded 1961

The two most influential economic groupings set up since the Second World War are the European Economic Community (EEC) and the Organization of Petroleum Exporting Countries (OPEC). The EEC (or Common Market) was established under the Treaty of Rome in 1957. The six member countries agreed to abolish their internal tariffs and institute a common external tariff within 15 years. Britain refused to join on the grounds that the common external tariff would destroy her Commonwealth trade. In 1959 Britain formed the European Free Trade Association (EFTA), initially with Norway, Sweden, Denmark, Switzerland, Austria and Portugal, to abolish internal tariffs on industrial goods, but with no common external tariff. During the 1960s, however, the EEC became increasingly successful while the British economy continued to falter. France twice refused to allow Britain to join the EEC (known as the European Community since 1967), but it eventually became a member, along with Denmark and Ireland, in January 1973; Spain, Portugal and Greece joined in the 1980s. A similar regional grouping of Eastern European countries and the Soviet Union – COMECON, later incorporating Vietnam, Mongolia and Cuba – was founded in 1949 and a Latin American Free Trade Association (renamed Latin American Integration Association, LAIA, in 1981) and a Central American Common Market were founded in 1960, all of which attempted to emulate the EEC.

The Organization of Arab Petroleum Exporting Countries, (OAPEC), part of OPEC, first met in 1971 but was strengthened by the Middle East war of 1973 when, in protest against United States and Dutch arms supplies to Israel, it cut off oil supplies to those two countries and raised oil prices generally by 70 per cent. The result was a serious recession in Western economies and a major effort was made to develop alternative sources of energy.

Groupings which exist to further development in the Third World include the Organization for Economic Cooperation and Development (OECD), founded in 1960 by the USA, Canada and 18 European states with the aim of increasing world trade and providing financial security. The Colombo Plan arose out of a desire of the old, white Commonwealth of Britain, Australia, New Zealand and Canada to help the emerging new nations of the Indian subcontinent and elsewhere. It was founded in 1950 and soon attracted American support, evolving into a Marshall Plan for Asia. In 1967, five of its main beneficiaries – Indonesia, Malaysia, Philippines, Singapore and Thailand – grouped together in the Association of South-East Asian Nations (ASEAN), designed to promote regional progress and stability.

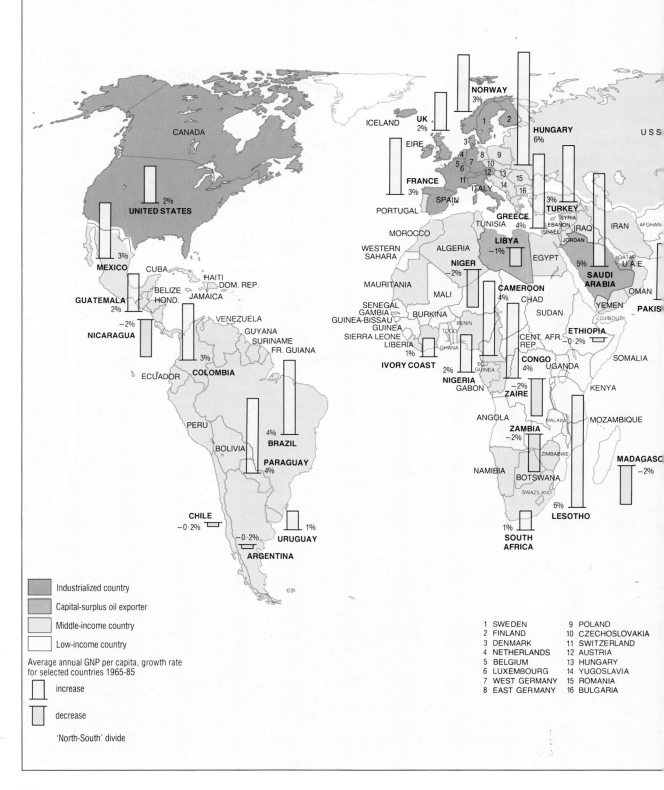

CANADA

NORWAY
3%

ICELAND

UK
2%

HUNGARY
6%

USSR

EIRE

1 SWEDEN
2 FINLAND
3 DENMARK
4 NETHERLANDS
5 BELGIUM
6 LUXEMBOURG
7 WEST GERMANY
8 EAST GERMANY
9 POLAND
10 CZECHOSLOVAKIA
11 SWITZERLAND
12 AUSTRIA
13 HUNGARY
14 YUGOSLAVIA
15 ROMANIA
16 BULGARIA

FRANCE
3%

SPAIN

ITALY

PORTUGAL

GREECE
4%

TURKEY
3%

IRAN

AFGHAN.

UNITED STATES
2%

MEXICO
3%

CUBA

HAITI
DOM. REP.

TUNISIA
SYRIA
LEBANON
ISRAEL
JORDAN
IRAQ

MOROCCO

WESTERN
SAHARA

ALGERIA

LIBYA
−1%

EGYPT

QATAR
U.A.E.

GUATEMALA
2%

BELIZE
HOND.

JAMAICA

NIGER
−2%

SAUDI
ARABIA
5%

OMAN

NICARAGUA
−2%

VENEZUELA

MAURITANIA

MALI

CAMEROON
4%

CHAD

SUDAN

YEMEN

DJIBOUTI

PAKIS

GUYANA
SURINAME
FR. GUIANA

SENEGAL
GAMBIA
GUINEA-BISSAU
GUINEA
SIERRA LEONE
LIBERIA
1%

BURKINA

BENIN
TOGO
GHANA

ETHIOPIA
−0·2%

ECUADOR

COLOMBIA
3%

IVORY COAST

EQ. GUINEA

CENT. AFR.
REP.

CONGO
4%

UGANDA

SOMALIA

NIGERIA
2%

GABON

ZAIRE
−2%

KENYA

PERU

BRAZIL
4%

BOLIVIA

ANGOLA

MALAWI

MOZAMBIQUE

ZAMBIA
−2%

PARAGUAY
4%

ZIMBABWE

MADAGASC
−2%

CHILE
−0·2%

URUGUAY
1%

NAMIBIA

BOTSWANA

SWAZILAND

LESOTHO
6%

ARGENTINA
−0·2%

SOUTH
AFRICA
1%

Industrialized country

Capital-surplus oil exporter

Middle-income country

Low-income country

Average annual GNP per capita, growth rate
for selected countries 1965-85

increase

decrease

'North-South' divide

The Brandt Report (Independent Commission on International Development Issues) of 1980 divided the world economy into two. The 'North', consisting of the dominant economies of Europe, North America, the Soviet Union, Japan and Australasia, constituted 90 per cent of the world's manufacturing capacity and its multinational corporations monopolized world investment, technology and trade. The 'South', on the other hand, made up of the rest of Asia, Africa and Latin America, populated by nearly four billion people, existed on just one-fifth of the world's income. Another analysis divides the World into three: the 'First World' of the advanced capitalist economies, the 'Second World' of centrally planned economies (the Soviet bloc and China), and the 'Third World' of the developing nations. None of these definitions is entirely satisfactory since even within them there are wide variations. The Arab oil-producing countries, Taiwan, South Korea and Singapore have, for example, unlike other Third World economies, been prosperous, while American and British manufacturing output has fallen behind that of West Germany and Japan, particularly in high-technology industries.

The Third World failed to benefit from the economic boom of the 1950s and 1960s which brought the developed countries unparalleled prosperity. Furthermore, when rising prices for oil, wheat, rice and raw materials in the 1970s resulted in an economic downturn, the Third World suffered the most and the gap between the rich and poor nations widened still further. After 1960, the Third World tended to concentrate on industrialization while neglecting agriculture, so that by the 1970s many became totally dependent on food supplies from the West. Their economies were also affected by wide fluctuations in the prices of primary raw materials. In an effort to compensate for falling revenues, Third World countries borrowed heavily from Western banks during the late 1970s and rising interest rates have compounded their repayment difficulties.

In reviewing global economies, changes in gross national product are particularly significant. Middle-income countries with high growth rates are a sign of global economic development. Low-income countries with high growth rates starting from a low base, show a process of catching-up, while negative growth reflects severe problems. Growth in the industrialized countries (except Japan) is low, largely because of their high starting points.

The World Population Explosion

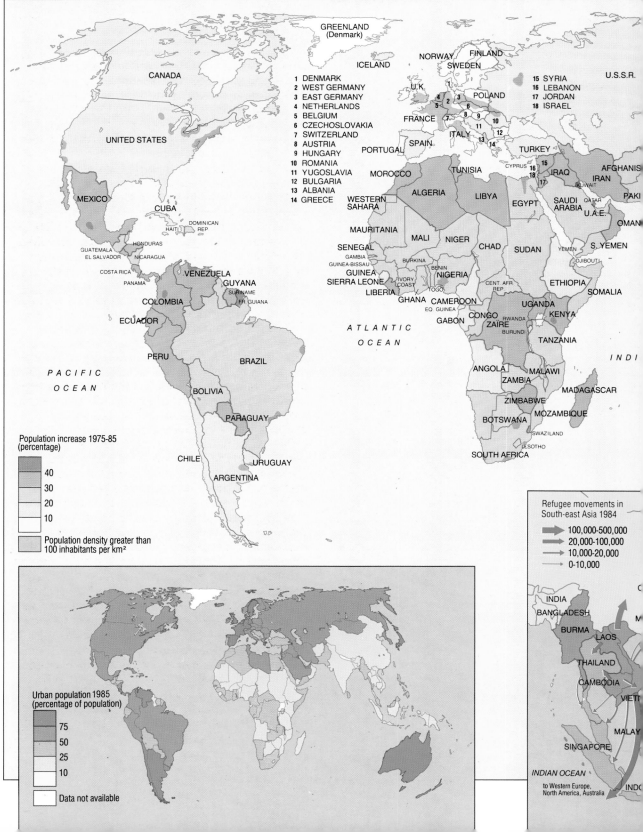

GREENLAND
(Denmark)

NORWAY FINLAND
ICELAND SWEDEN

CANADA

1	DENMARK	15 SYRIA
2	WEST GERMANY	16 LEBANON
3	EAST GERMANY	17 JORDAN
4	NETHERLANDS	18 ISRAEL
5	BELGIUM	
6	CZECHOSLOVAKIA	
7	SWITZERLAND	
8	AUSTRIA	
9	HUNGARY	
10	ROMANIA	
11	YUGOSLAVIA	
12	BULGARIA	
13	ALBANIA	
14	GREECE	

U.S.S.R.

U.K. POLAND
FRANCE
ITALY
PORTUGAL SPAIN TURKEY
CYPRUS IRAQ AFGHANIS
IRAN
MOROCCO TUNISIA KUWAIT PAKI
ALGERIA LIBYA EGYPT SAUDI
ARABIA OMAN
U.A.E.
WESTERN
SAHARA
MAURITANIA
MALI NIGER CHAD SUDAN YEMEN S. YEMEN
SENEGAL DJIBOUTI
GAMBIA BURKINA
GUINEA-BISSAU BENIN
GUINEA NIGERIA
SIERRA LEONE IVORY
COAST CENT. AFR
REP ETHIOPIA
LIBERIA TOGO SOMALIA
GHANA CAMEROON
EQ. GUINEA UGANDA
GABON CONGO RWANDA KENYA
ZAIRE BURUNDI
TANZANIA INDI

UNITED STATES

MEXICO
CUBA
DOMINICAN
REP
HAITI
HONDURAS
GUATEMALA
EL SALVADOR NICARAGUA
COSTA RICA
PANAMA
VENEZUELA
GUYANA
SURINAME
FR. GUIANA
COLOMBIA

ECUADOR

PERU

ATLANTIC
OCEAN

BRAZIL

ANGOLA MALAWI
ZAMBIA
MADAGASCAR
ZIMBABWE
MOZAMBIQUE
BOTSWANA
SWAZILAND
LESOTHO
SOUTH AFRICA

PACIFIC
OCEAN

BOLIVIA

PARAGUAY

CHILE URUGUAY
ARGENTINA

**Population increase 1975-85
(percentage)**

- 40
- 30
- 20
- 10

Population density greater than
100 inhabitants per km²

**Refugee movements in
South-east Asia 1984**

- 100,000-500,000
- 20,000-100,000
- 10,000-20,000
- 0-10,000

INDIA
BANGLADESH M
BURMA
LAOS
THAILAND
CAMBODIA
VIET
MALAY
SINGAPORE

INDIAN OCEAN

to Western Europe,
North America, Australia

INDO

**Urban population 1985
(percentage of population)**

- 75
- 50
- 25
- 10
- Data not available

Between 1960 and 1989 the world's population increased by more than one billion to more than five billion in 1990, largely as a result of improved health facilities and better food supplies. The United Nations has estimated that the life expectancy of individuals has increased by five years in each decade since 1945. Third World population growth has been double that of the developed West since 1950, rising from 70 per cent of the total world population in 1950 to about 75 per cent in 1985. This proportion is expected to increase in the 21st century to about 80 per cent, and world population is expected to more than double to 11.3 billion by the year 3000.

If present trends continue, by the year 2000, 48 per cent of the world's population will live in towns and cities, with the majority in Third World urban areas. Twenty-seven of the world's largest cities will be situated in the Third World against 18 in 1970. Of the world's population today 47 per cent is involved in agriculture but, of course, the proportions vary widely between the developed and developing worlds. In Africa 65 per cent of the population is engaged in agriculture, while in the United States only about 11 per cent are so employed.

There is likely to be little opportunity for emigration as an outlet for surplus populations as there had been in the 19th and early- and mid-20th centuries. During the 1950s and 1960s there was an influx of migrants to the United Kingdom from the West Indian islands and the Indian subcontinent, while Algerians went to France in search of work. During the years of economic growth in the 1960s and 1970s, countries like West Germany welcomed Greek and Turkish labour to perform tasks that the indigenous population was unwilling to perform, but during the 1970s these immigrants became increasingly unpopular in their host countries when unemployment began to rise. Britain has imposed severe restrictions on immigration and other countries have also tightened up entrance requirements. Although Australia has abandoned its 'White Australia' policy, a points system still regulates the inflow of Asian and other immigrants. The United States also operates strict immigration controls but has been unable to stem the flow of Mexican and other Latin American illegal migrants across the long United States–Mexico border. Immigration controls have been tested elsewhere by the arrival of refugees from south-east Asia. After the communist North Vietnamese victory in 1975, thousands of refugees from Vietnam took to sea in small boats making for such countries as Hong Kong and Malaysia, while other refugees fled from communist rule in Laos and Cambodia (renamed Kampuchea).

Food and Health

Infant mortality rate per 1,000 live births

- 200
- 150
- 100
- 60
- 40
- 20

Data not available

Dietary energy supplies per capita
Percentage below requirement

- 15
- 10
- 5

Percentage above requirement

- 30
- 15
- 5

Data not available

NEW ZEALAND

MEXICO
UNITED STATES
CANADA
GUATEMALA
EL SALVADOR
HONDURAS
COSTA RICA
NICARAGUA
PANAMA
JAMAICA
CUBA
ECUADOR
COLOMBIA
HAITI
DOMINICAN REPUBLIC
PERU
NORWAY
ICELAND
FINL
SWEDE
VENEZUELA
CHILE
BOLIVIA
GUYANA
SURINAME
ARGENTINA
PARAGUAY
BRAZIL
URUGUAY

IRELAND
U K
FRANCE
PORT
SPAIN
ITALY
TUNISIA
MOROCCO
WESTERN SAHARA
ALGERIA
LIB
MAURITANIA
GAMBIA
SENEGAL
MALI
NIGER
C
GUINEA-BISSAU
GUINEA
BURKINA
NIGERIA
CAMERO
SIERRA LEONE
LIBERIA
IVORY COAST
EQ GUINEA
GABON

1 DENMARK
2 WEST GERMANY
3 EAST GERMANY
4 NETHERLANDS
5 BELGIUM
6 CZECHOSLOVAKIA
7 SWITZERLAND
8 AUSTRIA
9 HUNGARY
10 ROMANIA
11 YUGOSLAVIA
12 BULGARIA

13 ALBANIA
14 SYRIA
15 LEBANON
16 JORDAN
17 ISRAEL
18 GHANA
19 TOGO

Although the world has sufficient food for its population, many countries are still afflicted by famine, and the United Nations has estimated that 340 million of the world's population remain undernourished. Climatic changes, over-cropping and drought in North Africa have contributed to under-production, and lack of food and endemic poverty have in turn severe health implications. In a rich country such as Japan, infant mortality, at seven deaths per thousand live births, is tiny in comparison with a poor country such as Tanzania, where the rate is 90 deaths per thousand. Life expectancy is similarly different, for the average Japanese person expects to live 75 years, the average Tanzanian lives 51.4 years.

In the past 40 years, considerable advances have been made in medical technology, enabling doctors in the Third World to eliminate or control various diseases. However, the arrival of AIDS – Acquired Immune Deficiency Syndrome – during the 1980s has presented many poor nations with a major health epidemic, for there is as yet no known cure.

Cumulative number of AIDS cases reported to the World Health Organization to August 1988

- More than 1,000
- 100-1,000
- Less than 100
- One figure represents 1,000 cases

UNITED STATES

MEXICO

CANADA

BRAZIL

AUSTRALIA

UNITED KINGDOM
WEST GERMANY
FRANCE
ITALY
SPAIN

KENYA   ZAMBIA
UGANDA   CONGO
TANZANIA   BURUNDI
RWANDA

149

A Global Environment

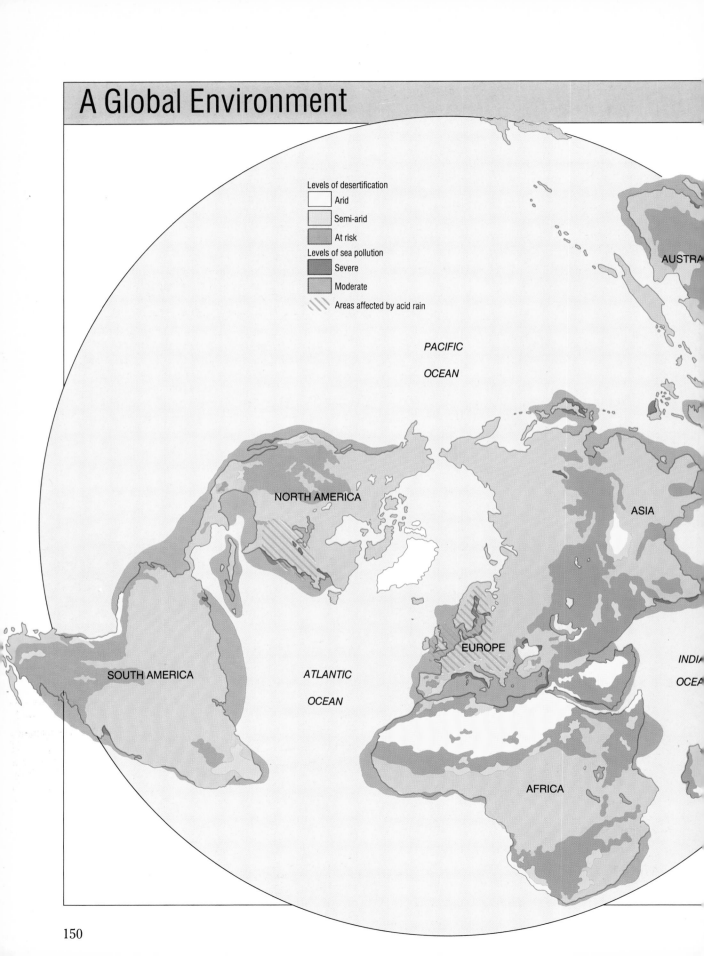

Levels of desertification
- Arid
- Semi-arid
- At risk

Levels of sea pollution
- Severe
- Moderate

Areas affected by acid rain

PACIFIC

OCEAN

AUSTRA

NORTH AMERICA

ASIA

SOUTH AMERICA

ATLANTIC

OCEAN

EUROPE

INDI

OCEA

AFRICA

In the last decade public awareness of the problem of pollution has increased dramatically as people appreciate the effects that industrial and agricultural practices have on the environment. In rural areas land clearance schemes have reduced plant and forest cover, leading to soil erosion and flooding, while the over-use of chemicals has exhausted the soil and contaminated crops. In the rain forests of Brazil and Indonesia, the desire for agricultural growth to meet the needs of an expanding population has entailed soil erosion and the extinction of wild life, but the governments of these countries are reluctant to change their policy. Industrialization and urbanization around the world have led to the release of toxic waste – gas and chemicals – into the atmosphere and these in turn threaten to destroy the ozone layer in the upper atmosphere, leading to fears of a 'greenhouse effect'. Some environmental problems have been tackled successfully. Agreements have been signed to protect endangered species and to limit the pollution of seas such as the Mediterranean. However, the Green Movement faces a long and difficult task.

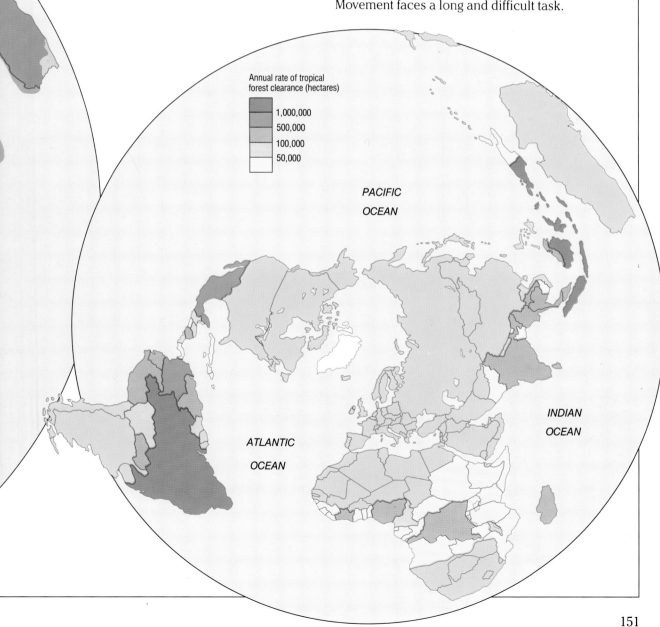

Annual rate of tropical
forest clearance (hectares)

1,000,000
500,000
100,000
50,000

PACIFIC
OCEAN

ATLANTIC
OCEAN

INDIAN
OCEAN

The World in 1990

GREENLAND
(Denmark)
0·05

ALASKA
(US)

CANADA
25

ICELAND
0·2

NORWAY
4

FINLA
5

SWEDEN
8

UNITED KINGDOM
57

DEN.
5

IRELAND
4

NETH.
16

London [7]

BELGIUM 6

Paris [8]

GERMANY
78

POLAND
37

CZECH.16

AUSTRIA

SWITZERLAND

8

HUNG
11

R

FRANCE
55

ITALY
57

YUGOSLAVIA
23

ALBANIA
3

GR

PORTUGAL
10

SPAIN
39

TUNISIA
7

MOROCCO
24

ALGERIA
23

LIBYA
4

UNITED STATES
239

Chicago [7]

New York [9]

Los Angeles [9]

WESTERN
SAHARA
0·2

MAURITANIA
2

MALI
8

NIGER
6

CH

MEXICO
79

CUBA
10

BAHAMAS
0·2

DOMINICAN REPUBLIC
6

SENEGAL
7

GAMBIA 1

GUINEA-BISSAU 1

BURKINA
9

GUINEA
6

BENIN
4

NIGERIA
100

Mexico City [18]

JAMAICA
2

HAITI
7

PUERTO RICO (US)
3

SIERRA LEONE
4

IVORY
COAST
10

TOGO
3

CAMEROON
10

BELIZE
0·2

HONDURAS
4

LIBERIA
2

GHANA
14

GUATEMALA
8

EL SALVADOR
5

NICARAGUA
3

EQ. GUINEA
0·4

CONGO
2

COSTA RICA
3

VENEZUELA
17

GUYANA
1

FR. GUYANA
0·1

GABON
1

PANAMA
2

SURINAME
0·4

COLOMBIA
27

ECUADOR
9

ATLANTIC
OCEAN

PACIFIC
OCEAN

PERU
20

BRAZIL
136

ANGC
9

Lima [5]

BOLIVIA
6

NAMIBI
1

BOTSV

Rio de Janeiro [5]

PARAGUAY
4

São Paulo [8]

SC
AF

CHILE
12

URUGUAY
3

Buenos Aires [10]

ARGENTINA
31

Population of countries
(figures in millions)

500
200
100
50
20
10
5
1

[7] City with 5 million inhabitants or more
(figure indicates millions of inhabitants)

• City with 1 to 5 million inhabitants

USSR
282

PACIFIC OCEAN

MONGOLIA
2

ow

RKEY
44

SYRIA
10

N 3

L 4

IRAQ
16

JORDAN
3

KUWAIT
2

SAUDI
ARABIA
12

QATAR 0·3

U.A.E.
2

OMAN
2

REPUBLIC OF YEMEN
7

DJIBOUTI
0·4

ETHIOPIA
43

SOMALIA
6

GANDA
15

KENYA
20

BURUNDI
5

TANZANIA
22

MALAWI
7

BWE

MOZAMBIQUE
14

SWAZILAND
0·6

HO

MADAGASCAR
11

Tehran 6

AFGHANISTAN
18

IRAN
50

PAKISTAN
96

Delhi 6

NEPAL
18

BHUTAN
1

Karachi 5

BANGLADESH
100

Calcutta 9

Bombay 8

INDIA
751

Beijing 6

Tianjin 5

CHINA
1,080

N. KOREA
20

Seoul 10

S. KOREA
41

JAPAN
122

Tokyo 11

Shanghai 7

TAIWAN
19

BURMA
37

LAOS
4

HONG
KONG (Br)
6

THAILAND
53

VIETNAM
62

PHILIPPINES
57

Bangkok 5

CAMBODIA
7

SRI
LANKA
16

BRUNEI
0·2

MALAYSIA
16

SINGAPORE
3

Jakarta 6

INDONESIA
165

PAPUA NEW
GUINEA
3

INDIAN   OCEAN

New Caledonia (Fr)
0·2

AUSTRALIA
16

NEW
ZEALAND
3

153

Glossary

AIDS Acquired Immune Deficiency Syndrome, disease of potential epidemic scale, identified 1980 and transmitted by sexual contact, shared syringes and transfusion of infected blood.

Allies The Grand Alliance of the USSR, USA and Great Britain in World War II, and later China and France. Also used to refer to the coalition of Britain, France, Russia (until 1917) and Italy against Germany in WW I.

Amnesty International Privately sponsored organization campaigning for release of political prisoners.

ANC African National Congress formed in 1912 to protect interests of black people in South Africa, made illegal by South African government between 1961–90. Nelson Mandela is its most famous leader.

Apartheid System of segregation between blacks and whites in South Africa.

Arab League Formed 1945 to increase political and economic cooperation between Arab states. Formerly, its main concern was to expel French from Arab territory, since 1967 its main activity is coordinating opposition to Israel.

Arms race Continuous competition between USSR and the West in post-war period to establish superiority in armaments.

Axis Term used by Benito Mussolini to describe relationship between Nazi Germany and fascist Italy.

Baader-Meinhof Terrorist anarchist group operating in West Germany after wave of student protests in 1968.

Balfour Declaration Issued by British Foreign Secretary in 1917, it supported Jewish homeland in Palestine, and served as a basis for the British Mandate.

Blitz Massive air attacks by night on London and other British cities between September 1940 and May 1941 by German airforce.

Blitzkrieg German term for 'lightning war' or the use of armoured vehicles supported by air power to penetrate and defeat the enemy quickly.

Boat people Refugees from Vietnam who, after communist North Vietnamese victory in 1975 in the Vietnam War, left in small boats making for Hong Kong, Malaysia and elsewhere.

Bolshevik Radical faction of Russian Social Democratic Party after it split in 1903; it seized power in October revolution of 1917.

Boxer Rebellion Uprising in Beijing in 1900 of secret society opposed to European interests in China.

Central Powers Members of Triple Alliance (Germany, Austria–Hungary and Italy) formed in 1882; on outbreak of WW I Italy remained neutral and subsequently Bulgaria and Turkey joined Germany in the war effort.

CIA US Central Intelligence Agency, established 1947 to coordinate foreign intelligence.

Cold War Political and ideological conflict between the USSR, the USA and their respective allies during the 1950s and 1960s, and saw the formation of *Warsaw Pact* and

NATO. The war occasionally went 'hot', as in Korea and Vietnam, and was gradually superseded by *détente* in the 1970s and 1980s.

Comecon Council for Mutual Economic Assistance, established in 1949 to further trade links between the USSR and *Eastern Bloc* countries.

Communism Social system in which property is communally owned by all people; many states claim such a society, including China and Cuba.

Concentration camp First used by Spanish in Cuba, and British in South Africa to detain the Boers in 1900. In Nazi Germany, camps were established in 1930s for detention of political and 'racial' enemies and many were converted into extermination camps for Jews during WW II.

Contras Nicaraguan exiles in Honduras and USA opposed to *Sandinista* government in Nicaragua during the 1980s. They received military and financial aid from USA.

D-Day landing Largest ever seaborne invasion, June 1944 when Allied troops landed on the Normandy coast.

Détente Improved relations beginning 1969 between *Warsaw Pact* countries (led by USSR) and the West (led by USA) and resulting in SALT I (Strategic Arms Limitation Treaty I).

Disarmament Reduction, limitation or abandonment of armaments (nuclear and conventional) as proposed by USSR and USA since early 1950s.

Eastern Bloc Formerly those nations in Eastern and Central Europe dominated by the USSR and forced to adopt Soviet methods of communist government. Disintegrated 1989–90.

EEC European Economic Community, also known as the Common Market, was incorporated into the European Community in 1967; formed in 1958 for the purpose of free, intra-community trade and sharing common economic and social policies.

ETA Militant Basque separatist movement responsible for violent acts against government authorities in northern Spain.

Famine Widespread food shortage and starvation caused by harvest failure, notably in Russia in 1921 and Ethiopia/ Sudan during the 1980s.

Fascism Nationalist, authoritarian and anti-communist political creed founded by Benito Mussolini in Italy, 1919. Italian fascism served as a model for Spain, Germany and elsewhere.

FBI Federal Bureau of Investigation, founded 1908 as agency of US Department of Justice, responsible for general internal security. J Edgar Hoover was longest-serving director, 1924–72.

Feminism Movement for rights of women, particularly social, economic and political equality with men, which includes the British suffragettes (mainly pre-WW I), militant Women's Lib of USA in the 1960s and such theorists as Simone de Beauvoir and Germaine Greer.

Fundamentalist Christian: one who believes in literal

truth of the Bible, as in southern states of USA, popularly known as the Bible Belt; Muslim: for example Ayatollah Khomeini of Iran, one who insists on strict adherence to Islamic law rejecting non-Islamic Western or communist influences.

Gestapo Secret state police in Germany in 1930s, an instrument of terror to arrest and murder opponents of the *Nazi* regime and an arm of the SS, the Nazi storm troopers.

Global warming The rising temperature of the world's atmosphere said to be caused by an increased amount of carbon dioxide in the atmosphere.

Great Depression World economic slump of 1929–35.

Greens Environmentalists who seek a political platform to further the cause of ecological conservation world-wide; issues include greenhouse effect, nuclear power, rainforest conservation and protection of endangered species.

Guerrilla warfare Irregular forces, often acting independently behind enemy lines and avoiding direct conflict with superior armies. Actions include strikes at enemy supplies, communications and isolated army detachments.

IMF International Monetary Fund, founded 1944, makes foreign exchange resources available to members with balance of payments difficulties.

Indian National Congress Political party in India, led by Mohandas Gandhi from 1915 whose policy of non-violent civil disobedience to the Raj government characterized the party in the 1920s and 1930s.

IRA (Irish Republican Army) organized in 1919 to expel the British and establish a unified republic in Ireland. Split in late 1969, and while the Provisional wing pursued the policy of urban *guerrilla warfare*, the Official wing emphasized political rather than guerrilla activities.

Iron Curtain Armed border between Soviet-dominated eastern Europe and the West denoting strict limits placed on ideology and movement by the communist regimes of the *Eastern Bloc*.

Jihad Holy war of Muslims against infidels.

Khmer Rouge Cambodian communist movement taking its name from the Khmer people of Cambodia. It took power in 1975 and instituted a regime of genocide until removed by the Vietnamese army in 1979.

Ku Klux Klan American anti-Negro secret society. Violently active during 1920s and 1960s in mid-west and south. Attacks were broadened to include Jews, Roman Catholics and foreigners.

League of Nations International organization established in 1919 to preserve international peace through settlement of disputes by arbitration but it collapsed during WW II.

Long March 8000-mile migration in China in 1934–5 of 100,000 communists led by Mao Zedong to establish communist region in Yan'an, north-west China.

Mafia Criminal society originating in Sicily, spread to USA late 19th and early 20th century and became dominant force in organized crime during the *Prohibition* era. By 1950s it

controlled in the USA every aspect of vice, including gambling, prostitution and drugs.

Marshall Plan Arrangements for US financial help given to Europe after WW II devised by US Secretary of State General George Marshall in June 1947. The Plan offered financial aid for recovery and, in all, $17,000 million of Marshall Aid was forthcoming 1948–52.

Mau Mau Secret anti-European terrorist movement in Kenya in 1950s.

McCarthyism Name given to wave of anti-communist hysteria in USA during Cold War of 1950s, deriving from Senator Joseph McCarthy.

Mujaheddin Afghan Muslim resistance groups who fought against the Soviet military invasion of Afghanistan 1979–1989.

NATO North Atlantic Treaty Organization, established 1949 to assist any fellow signatory state suffering aggression. Arose out of western European concern over territorial ambitions of USSR.

Nazis Members of the German National Socialist Workers' Party that came to power under Hitler in 1933, espousing anti-Semitic, racialist doctrines of Aryan superiority.

Nazi–Soviet Pact Non-aggression pact agreed between Hitler and Stalin in August 1939 on eve of WW II.

Nuremberg Rallies Mass rallies staged by *Nazis* at Party Congresses in Nuremberg between 1933 and 1938.

OPEC Organization of Petroleum Exporting Countries, formed 1960 to regulate crude oil prices. By 1973 OPEC was strong enough to force four-fold increase in oil prices.

Pacific Rim Established and emerging industrial giants around edge of Pacific Ocean – notably USA, Japan, Korea, Taiwan – whose economic and trade links are now dominating the world economy.

PLO Palestine Liberation Organization, formed in Jordan 1964 to coordinate Arab efforts (including numerous guerrilla raids) to reclaim Israeli-held territory. Led by Yasser Arafat.

Privatization Policy of selling-off state-run industries to private ownership. Pioneered in Britain in 1980s and adopted by many other nations, including *Eastern Bloc* countries and, tentatively, the Soviet Union.

Prohibition The outlawing of manufacture, sale and distribution of alcoholic liquor in USA between 1920 and 1933.

Raj British rule in India, 1858–1947.

Rastafarianism Movement originating in West Indies taking name from Ras Tafari Makonnen, crowned Emperor of Ethiopia as Haile Selassie in 1930. Ethiopia is regarded as the spiritual homeland of estranged black people in the West Indies or Britain.

Red Brigades Left-wing urban terrorist organizations active in Italy since 1970s.

Resistance movements Groups of underground fighters united against a foreign occupying force. Activities include peaceful non-cooperation, sabotage of industrial and communication targets, ambush of foreign troops and outright conflict.

Sanctions Economic or diplomatic blockades used by the international community, through the *League of Nations* or United Nations *(UN)*, to force aggressor nations to reverse their policies and others to comply with United Nations resolutions. Sanctions aim to isolate a country and cripple its economy.

Sandinista National Liberation Front (FSLN) A group which opposed the Somoza dictatorship in Nicaragua. After a revolution it took over power in July 1979 but lost a majority of seats in the Assembly to anti-Sandinista parties in free elections in 1989.

Shi'ites Members of Islamic sect based in Iran who maintain Ali, son-in-law of prophet Mohammed, was true successor; Ayatollah Khomeini was its charismatic leader 1979–89.

Solidarity The non-communist, Polish trade union organization, headed by Lech Walesa, which, by a series of strikes and demonstrations, forced the resignation of the community hierarchy.

Suez Crisis (1956) Following nationalization of Suez Canal by President Nasser of Egypt, a failed attempt by the British, French and Israelis to repossess the Canal and oust Nasser.

Third World Poorer nations of the world, economically less-developed, located in Latin America, Asia and Africa.

Treaty of Versailles One of four peace settlements ending WW I. Signed June 1919 by victorious powers and reluctantly by Germany who criticized it for its harshness.

UN United Nations, international organization founded 1945 to maintain international peace and security. Member states have to provide armed forces for peace-keeping missions.

Vietminh Vietnam Independence League founded 1941, to resist Japanese occupation of Indo-China and, later, French colonial authorities.

Wall Street Site of New York stock exchange and synonym for US finance and banking.

Warsaw Pact Eastern European equivalent of *NATO*. The command structure controlled from Moscow required combined armed assistance for any member state attacked.

Watergate American political scandal of early 1970s involving bugging of Democrat's campaign HQ at Watergate complex, Washington, which led to the resignation of President Nixon in 1974.

Zionism Militant Jewish movement, launched by Theodor Herzl in 1896, to establish autonomous Jewish homeland in Palestine, named after City of Zion or Jerusalem, capital of biblical Promised Land.

Bibliography

Banks, Arthur, *A Military Atlas of the First World War* (Heinemann, 1975)

Bramwell, Anna, *Ecology in the Twentieth Century: A History* (Yale UP, 1989)

Calvocoressi, P., Wint, G. and Pritchard, J., *The Total War: The Causes and Courses of the Second World War* (Viking, 1989)

Crow, Benn, *Third World Atlas* (Open University Press, 1983)

Dockrill, Michael, *The Cold War 1945–1963* (Macmillan, 1988)

Freedman, Lawrence, *Atlas of Global Strategy: War and Peace in the Nuclear Age* (Macmillan, 1985)

Gilbert, Martin, *American History Atlas* (Weidenfeld & Nicolson, 1968)

Iriye, Akira, *The Origins of the Second World War in Asia and the Pacific* (Longman, 1987)

Keegan, John, *The Second World War: An Illustrated History* (Hutchinson, 1989)

   ed., *The Times History Atlas of the Second World War* (Times Books, 1989)

Kidron, Michael, *The War Atlas: Arms Conflict, Armed Peace* (Pan, 1983)

Kidron, Michael and Segal, Ronald, *The State of the World Atlas* (Heinemann, 1981)

Kinder, Hermann and Hilgemann, Werner, *The Penguin Atlas of World History Vol. II* (Penguin, 1978)

Mercer, Derrik, ed., *Chronicle of the 20th Century* (Legrand/Longman, 1988)

Natkiel, R., Sommerville, D. and Westwood, J. N., *Atlas of 20th Century History* (Hamlyn-Bison, 1982)

Palmer, Alan, *The Penguin Dictionary of Twentieth Century History 1900–1988* (Penguin, 1990)

Pitt, B. and Pitt, F., *The Chronological Atlas of World War II* (Macmillan, 1989)

Taylor, A.J.P., *The First World War: An Illustrated History* (Penguin, 1978)

   The Second World War: An Illustrated History (Penguin, 1976)

Tindall, George Brown, *America: A Narrative History (Illustrated)* (W. W. Norton, 1988)

Index

Page numbers in **bold** print refer to map entries; those in *italics* refer to captions and illustrations.

B

Duvalier, François 132, 134

E

East Germany **86**, 119, **130-1**, 132, 134, 136
see also Germany; West Germany
East Indies 70, **74**, 75, 91, 93, 143, 151
East Prussia **52**, **53**, **60**, **80**, **86**, 87
economies, world *see under* world
Ecuador 88, **113**, 136
Edward VIII, King 68
EEC (European Community) 132, 139, **142**, 143, 154
EFTA (European Free Trade Association) 132, **142**, 143
Egypt 13, **14**, 18, 21, 67, 89, 91, *92*, **100-1**, 102, **126**, 133, 135, 137
Suez Canal 39, 93, **98**, 99, **105**, **108**, 109, 132
Second World War 73, **73**
conflict with Israel **108-9**, 109, 135, 137
Eichmann, Adolf 79
Eisenhower, Dwight D. 90, 132
El Alamein, Battle of 81, **81**
El Salvador 18, **112**, 136
Elizabeth II, Queen 132
emigration *see under* population
Equatorial Guinea **100**
Eritrea **84**, **98**, **101**
Essen *11*, 48
Estonia **30**, 31, 34, **46**, **72-3**, **80**, 88
refugees **56-7**, **84**
Gorbachev era **128**, 129, 131, **131**
Ethiopia 67, 69, **84**, 89, **101**, 117, **117**, 135, *139*
see also Abyssinia
Europe *chronologies* 18, 20, 34, 66, 68, 88, 90, 132, 134, 136
dominance 8-11, **12-13**
Austro-Hungarian Empire 15, **15**
First World War **24-5**, 25, **26-7**, **30**, 31, **32-3**, 33
Western relations with Soviets **48**, 49
population movements **56-7**, 57, **84**, 85
exports **57**
monarchies and regimes **60**
Second World War **64-5**, 65, **72-3**, 73, **78-9**, 79, **80-1**, 81
Communist East **86-7**, 87, **130-1**, 140
US influences 105, **105**
United Nations **121**
Council of Europe 132
economic recovery 132, 139, **142**, 143
European Parliament 136
see also names of individual states
extermination camps **78**, 79

F

Faisal, King, of Iraq 133
Falange 45, **62**, 63
Falkland Is. 34, 136
famine 21, 49, *139*, 149, 154
Faroe Is. 88
Farouk, King, of Egypt 133
fascism 44-5, 49, 66, 68, 154
Nazism *38*, 39, **52-3**, 53, 54-5, *55*, **56**, 61, 68, 155
Finland **24**, **30**, 31, 41, **60**, 68, **72-3**, **80**, 88, 90
Fiume **30**, 31
FLN (National Liberation Front, Algeria) 97
FNLA (Angola) 117
food supplies **148-9**, 149
forests *139*, **151**
France 9, 10, 18, 68, 132, 133, 134, 136, *139*

social reform 11
French Empire **12-13**, 13, 19, 21, 37-8, 69, 92, 93, *93*, **96-7**, 97, **104**
population 17
First World War 25, **25**, **26-7**, 27, 29, 31, **32**, 33, 34
future of Germany 36, 66
League of Nations 41
Third Republic 45, **60**, 61, **61**
Soviet Union 47, 49
Depression 55
Spanish Civil War 63, **63**
Second World War 65, 70, *71*, **72**, 73, **78**, **80**, 81, 85, **85**, 88, 89, 90, 91
Middle East 99, 109
African decolonization **100-1**, 101, 133, 135
Caribbean **113**
NATO 118, 123
Brussels Treaty 123, 132
nuclear policies 134, **126**
space programme 141
EEC 143
immigrants 147
Francis Joseph, Emperor 15, 25
Franco, Francisco **62**, 63, 68, 136
French Guyana **113**

G

Gabon **100**
Gaddafi, Moamer 135
Galicia **15**, **28**, 29
Gallipoli 27, **28**, 29
Gambia **100**
Gandhi, Indira 135, 137
Gandhi, Mahatma 21, 39, *54*, 69, 89
Gdansk (Danzig) 41, 65, 68, **72**, **78**, **80**, **84**
Gemayel, Bashir 137
Geneva 41, 97, 111, 134, 127
Georgia (USSR) **128**, 129
Germany 8, *8*, 10, *11*, 18, 19, 20, **60**, 66, 136
German Empire **12-13**, 13, 15, 19, 29, **30**, **31**
immigration 17
First World War **24**, 25, 27, **28**, 29, **30**, 31, **32**, 33, 34, 39, 66, 89
post-war ('14-'18) status 36, *38*, 44-5
Nazism *38*, 39, **52-3**, 53, 54-5, *55*, **56**, 61, 155
elections 1928/1932 **52-3**, 68
refugees from Nazism **56**
Second World War **64-5**, 65, 70-1, *71*, **72-3**, 73, **76**, 77, **78-9**, 79, **80-1**, 81, 88
population movements 1945-52 **84**
occupation zones 85, **85**, 47, 49, 65
Spanish Civil War 63, **63**
Second World War 89, 90, 91
see also East Germany; West Germany
Ghana **100**, 101, 133
Gilbert Is. **83**
glasnost 129
Golan Heights 109, **109**, 135
Gold Coast (Ghana) 19, **100**, 133
Gorbachev, Mikhail 119, 127, 129, 136, 140
Great Depression 54, 55, **58-9**, 59
'Great Leap Forward, The' (China) 125
Greece **14**, 15, 20, **24**, 34, **60**, 134, 147
and Turkey 39, 66, 67
refugees **56-7**, **84**
Second World War 70, **72**, 73, **78**, 88
enosis 99
US aid 105, **105**
EEC 134, **142**, 143
Greenland 88

Grenada 113, **113**, 136
Guadalcanal **74**, 75
Guam 13, **74**, **82**, 91
Guangzhou (Canton) **42**, 43, **43**
Guatemala 18, 93, **104**, **112**, 113, **113**, 132
Guernica **62**, 68
Guevara, 'Che' 134
Guinea Bissau **100**, 101
Gulf War **114-5**
Guomindang 43, **43**, 67, 125, **125**
Guyana **113**, 134

H

Haile Selassie 67, 69, 89, 117, 135
Hainan 69
Haiti 20, 34, **113**, 132, 134, 136
Han ethnic group (China) **124**, 125
Hankou **42**, 43, **43**
Havel, Vaclav 119
Hawaii 13, 89
health, world *see under* world
Heath, Edward 134
hijacking of airliners 103
Hindenburg, President 53, 55
Hirohito, Emperor 67, 83
Hiroshima **82**, 83, 91
Hitler, Adolf 39, 45, 53, 54, 55, *55*, 65, 66, 68, 79, 81, 90
Ho Chi Minh 91, 93, *96*, 97
Ho Chi Minh Trail 110
Holland *see* Netherlands
Honduras 18, 66, **112**, 113, **113**, 136
Honecker, Erich 136
Hong Kong **74**, 75, 89, 93, **124**, 147
Hoover, Herbert 66
Hungary **30**, 31, 34, **48**, **60**, 61, 66, 132, 136
Austria-Hungary *see under* Austria
Communist government 44, **86**
refugees **56**, **84**
Second World War **72**, **78**, **80**, 88, 90
democracy 119, **130**, 131
Hussein, Saddam 115

I

Ibañez, Carlos 66
Iceland 88, 105, 123, 132, 134
ILO (International Labour Organization) 121
Inchon landing **106**, 107
India *8*, 19, 39, *54*, 67, 69, 89, 91, **127**, 135, 137, 155
independence 39, 92, **94**, 95, 133
non-aligned 102, 123
border dispute with China 125, 135
Indian Ocean **13**
Indo-China *see under* Asia
Indonesia 39, 93, 143, 151
industrialization, world 8, 9, 10, 141, **144-5**, 145
INF (Intermediate Range Nuclear Force) 127
Inter-Continental Ballistic Missiles (ICBMs) 127
International Brigades (Spanish Civil War) **62-3**, 63
International Monetary Fund (IMF) 121
Iran **86**, 87, 89, **98-9**, **114**, 137, **126**
revolution 103, 104, 115
war with Iraq 115, 137
see also Persia
Iraq 29, **31**, 39, 67, **98-9**, 109, **114-5**, **126**, 133, 135
Second World War **73**, **81**
Gulf War **114-5**
war with Iran 115, 137
Ireland 18, 20, 34, *37*, 38, **60**, 66, 132, 134, 136, 143, 155
Iron Guard (Romania) 45
Islam 39, 103, 136,

137, 156
Israel **98**, 99, **99**, 102, **126**, 133, 135, 137
conflicts with Arabs **108-9**, 109, 115, 132, 133, 135, 137
arms supplies 143
see also Jews
Istanbul *see* Constantinople
Italian Somaliland 89
Italy 18, 20, 45, **60**, 66, 132
Italian colonies **13**, 21, 37-8, 69, 89, **101**, 133
First World War **24**, 29, **30**, 31, **32**, 33, 34
fascism 45
refugees **56**, **84**
Spanish Civil War 63, **63**
Second World War 70, **78**, **80**, 81, 88, 89, 90, 91
terrorism 103
NATO 123
economy 139
Ivory Coast **100**
Iwo Jima I. **82**, 83, 91

J

Jamaica 20, **112**
Japan 10, 18, 19, 21, 36, 37, 137
Korea 21, 107
First World War 29, 31, **31**, 38, 39, 47
and China 38, **42**, 43, **43**, 65, 67, 69
invasion of Manchuria 41, 69
Depression 54
Second World War 70, 71, **74-5**, 75, 77, **77**, **82-3**, 83, 87, 88, 89, 90, 91, 92
US influence **104**, 105
economy 138, *140*
space programme 141
Java 91
Jews 18, 22, 44, 68
homeland 39
Nazi Germany 53, 55, 68
Second World War **78-9**, 79
Zionism 99, 156
Soviet Union 132
see also Israel
Jiang Jieshi (Chiang Kai-shek) 43, 67, 125, 133
Jiangxi **42**, 43
Jinnah, Muhammed Ali **94**, 95, 133
John Paul II, Pope 136
Johnson, Lyndon B. 111, 134
Jordan **98**, 99, **99**, **108**, 109, 133
Juan Carlos I, King of Spain 136

K

Kaliningrad (Königsberg) **46**, **86**, 87
Kampuchea *see* Cambodia
Karamanlis, Constantine 134
Kars **86**, 87
Kashmir **94**, 95, 133, 135, **124**
Katanga **100**, 101
Kaunda, Kenneth 135
Kemal Ataturk 39, 67
Kennedy, John F. 111, 134
Kennedy, Robert 134
Kenya 19, 101, **101**
Kenyatta, Jomo 101
Kerensky, A.F. 23
Khmer Rouge **110**, 111, **111**, 155
Khomeini, Ayatollah 115, 137, 156
Khrushchev, Nikita 102, *102*, 113, 132, 134
Kim Il Sung 107
King, Martin Luther 132, 134
Kissinger, Henry 109, 119
Kohl, Helmut 136
Kolchak, Admiral A.V. **46**, 47
Korea 19, 21
War 102, 105, **106-7**, 107, 123, 133, **124**, 125, **126**
South Korean economy 138
Kornilov, L.G. 23